War in Space

I Mam a Mamgu

War in Space

Strategy, Spacepower, Geopolitics

Bleddyn E. Bowen

EDINBURGH
University Press

Edinburgh University Press is one of the leading university presses in the UK. We publish academic books and journals in our selected subject areas across the humanities and social sciences, combining cutting-edge scholarship with high editorial and production values to produce academic works of lasting importance. For more information visit our website: edinburghuniversitypress.com

Edinburgh University Press Ltd
The Tun – Holyrood Road
12(2f) Jackson's Entry
Edinburgh EH8 8PJ

Typeset in 11/13 Adobe Sabon by
IDSUK (Dataconnection) Ltd, and
printed and bound in Great Britain.

A CIP record for this book is available from the British Library

ISBN 978 1 4744 5048 5 (hardback)
ISBN 978 1 4744 5050 8 (webready PDF)
ISBN 978 1 4744 5051 5 (epub)

Contents

Acknowledgements

This book is the result of many years of work and the help and contributions of many people. It began as an Economic and Social Research Council-funded PhD research project in 2012. After a successful examination in 2016, I have been able to revise and expand on the arguments in the thesis to produce this book. During these years I have incurred many debts from many friends, colleagues and institutions. The first institution is my alma mater, the Department of International Politics in Aberystwyth University (known to us as 'Interpol'). When I set out on the PhD at Interpol I did not have any inkling as to how the project would eventually turn out. Dr Alistair Shepherd was instrumental as my primary supervisor in guiding me through the trials of designing, researching and writing a PhD project and I would not have performed as well in the process without his exacting and consistent feedback and support on my work and career. Thanks are due as well to my secondary supervisor, Dr Kristan Stoddart, who furnished my work with many practical and Cold War historical insights on strategic weapons systems as I grappled with theoretical questions. Professor Hidemi Suganami and Dr Jim Vaughan, who respectively chaired and discussed my presentation at the Interpol Research Seminar in my PhD's third year, provided excellent feedback. Thanks are also due to my fellow travellers during my PhD years at Aberystwyth on the ground floor of the Interpol building. You helped make the PhD process anything but an isolated and lonely one.

As a student of Interpol from my undergraduate days through to my PhD, during which time Professor Martin Alexander properly exposed me to Clausewitz and Sun Tzu for the first time, I hope that this work stands as a decent representation of the tradition of strategic studies and classical military thought at Interpol in Aberystwyth. I also hope that this demonstrates the value of Welsh-medium education in higher education. I was able to learn, discuss and write about strategy and international politics through the medium of Welsh, and Interpol has been at the forefront of progressive attitudes towards Welsh-medium higher education. I am certain that part of my success in research is owed to being able to spend a good part of my most formative years as a young student engaging with international relations and strategy in my native tongue. *Diolch yn fawr a daliwch ati. Deuparth gwaith ei ddechrau: cefais dechrau da arni.*

The Space Policy Institute at the George Washington University kindly hosted me as a Visiting Scholar for a few months in 2014. I am very grateful for the welcome, support and insight their staff and students provided, particularly to Professors Scott Pace, Peter Hays and Henry Hertzfeld. Dr Michael 'Coyote' Smith kindly invited me to visit and present at the US Air Force's School of Advanced Air and Space Studies in Montgomery, Alabama. Thanks are also due to Professor Everett Dolman who provided extensive and detailed feedback. As for British support, I am very grateful to Dr John Sheldon and Ralph 'Dinz' Dinsley for their advice during the doctoral research, and continuing advice and engagement today in all matters astropolitical. Thanks as well to Professor Michael Sheehan of Swansea University and Professor Alastair Finlan at the Försvarshögskolan (Swedish Defence University) who examined the PhD thesis and provided excellent critique and engagement. I am also grateful to James Chisem and Mia Brown who reviewed the PhD thesis.

In the years since, I have been fortunate enough to be able to present the arguments and research of the book, and I am grateful to the Space Policy Institute, the Security Research Group at Aberystwyth University, the Defence Studies Department at King's College London where I lectured prior to taking up a position at the University of Leicester, the Centre for Science and Security Studies at King's College London, and the European Space Agency's lunchtime lectures programme for allowing me to test out and sharpen my arguments over the last few years.

Special thanks are due to my colleagues at the School of History, Politics and International Relations (HyPIR) at the University of Leicester, which I joined in early 2018, who provided extremely valuable insight on newer arguments and research as I developed the thesis into the book – Drs Andrew Futter, Steve Cooke and Josh Baker. Thanks as well to Professors Mark Phythian and George Lewis at HyPIR for allocating the resources necessary to ensure I had the time to complete this manuscript during a busy teaching year. I hope that this book makes a good humanities contribution to the University of Leicester's already prestigious position in the world of space research. I am extremely grateful to Meilyr Gwynn for creating such striking artwork for this book. Drs David Morgan-Owen, Cameron Hunter and Quincy Cloet also deserve my thanks as ideas and arguments about the book, seapower theory and space policy have been a constant topic of conversation for years and they have been reliable touchstones for developing and improving my research, writing and argumentation.

I also wish to express my gratitude to Professor Peter Hays again for providing numerous corrections and exacting comments as a reviewer of the draft manuscript, and the staff at Edinburgh University Press for making the process of publishing my first book a hassle-free and pleasurable one. Any errors or shortcomings in this book are purely my own.

Mae fy niolchiadau olaf i yn mynd i'r teulu. Diolch am y gefnogaeth a'r amynedd dros gyfnod fy astudiaethau ac am ddeall fy absenoldeb ers croesi'r ffin i Loegr. Hir yw bob aros.

Abbreviations

A2/AD – anti-access/area denial

ASAT – anti-satellite

ASBM – anti-ship ballistic missile

C4ISR – command, control, communications, computers, intelligence, surveillance and reconnaissance

CCS – Counter Communications System

CSpOC – Combined Space Operations Center (US)

DSP – Defense Support Program

ELINT – electronic intelligence

EO – electro-optical

GEO – geostationary or geosynchronous orbit

GNSS – global navigation satellite system

GPS – Global Positioning System

HEO – highly elliptical orbit

IAF – Indian Air Force

IGY – International Geophysical Year

IR – international relations

ISR – intelligence, surveillance and reconnaissance

LEO – low-Earth orbit

MEO – medium-Earth orbit

MILAMOS – Manual on International Law Applicable to Military Uses of Outer Space

MOL – Manned Orbital Laboratory (US)

NASA – National Aeronautics and Space Administration
NATO – North Atlantic Treaty Organization
NOSS – Naval Ocean Surveillance System
NRO – National Reconnaissance Office
OODA – Observation, Orientation, Decision, Action
PGM – precision-guided munition
PLA – People's Liberation Army
PRC – People's Republic of China
RF – radiofrequency
RMA – Revolution in Military Affairs
ROC – Republic of China
SAM – surface-to-air missile
SAR – synthetic aperture radar
SBIRS – Space-based Infrared System
SIGINT – signals intelligence
SPOT – *Satellite Pour l'Observation de la Terre*
SRBM – short-range ballistic missile
SSA – space situational awareness
SSF – Strategic Support Force (China)
SSN – space surveillance network
UAV – uncrewed aerial vehicle
USAF – United States Air Force
USSPACECOM – United States Space Command
USSTRATCOM – United States Strategic Command
WGS – Wideband Global SATCOM

Introduction

In 1996 Colin Gray asked 'where is the theory of space power? Where is the Mahan for the final frontier?'[1] This book answers that question by presenting propositions of spacepower and a strategic analogy of Earth orbit as a cosmic coastline. This book's spacepower theory shows how to think more constructively and critically about the use of space systems in warfare – satellites, their infrastructure, methods of attacking them, and their influence on modern warfare and strategy. Spacepower theory helps to answer questions like 'will a war begin or be decided in space?', 'how do satellites change the way war is conducted on Earth?' and 'what difference can space warfare make on Earth?' Engaging with these questions has never been so important, as the use and deployment of satellites and space infrastructure – or spacepower – have become essential for modern military and economic power. It underpins and shapes a global web of connectivity and information-based economies. It provides new methods of political–economic development and control for continent-sized states. Space warfare is a realistic prospect because space technologies are at the heart of military weapon systems, intelligence, logistics and economics, and the tools for harassing or disabling satellites are spreading. In short, spacepower and the spectre of space warfare cannot be ignored in international relations (IR) and modern strategy. Spacepower represents a logical extension of the concept of power – however defined – in IR and it 'consists of capabilities designed to control, deny, exploit, and regulate the use of space'.[2] An increasingly important infrastructure exists in Earth orbit which provides services for terrestrial states and non-state actors that cannot be ignored or done without; IR and strategy cannot continue to marginalise their vision of geography as restricted to the seas, air and the land. Earth orbit is now a major strategic arena in the conduct of international politics for all political actors on Earth itself. Spacepower's time has come.

Many scholars and authors tend to think about space based on terrestrial analogies. Viewing space as a 'new ocean' is one of the most prevalent analogies in contemporary literature and features eponymously in one of the landmark works on American space history.[3] Contrary to that analogy, an alternative is presented here to explain the nature of spacepower's influence upon modern warfare. Unlike interplanetary space, Earth orbit is more like part of a proximate, crowded and contestable coastline and a littoral environment, rather than a vast, remote, distant and expansive ocean. This new analogy and spacepower theory challenges some of the assumptions made by other spacepower theorists and debates in military space strategy, and provides new insights based on the experiences of seapower in continental rather than maritime wars. Contrary to much popular commentary, wars may not begin in space, or be decided by what happens in orbit alone, and space technology will not provide simple solutions to strategic problems. Spacepower theory is a type of strategic theory, it creates conceptual anchors to investigate the challenges of conducting, understanding and scrutinising strategy and warfare, an activity that defies excessive prescription and linear war planning. The seven propositions of spacepower theory presented in this book provide useful starting points for analysis and space strategy-making and the self-education of the reader. This theory eschews the concoction of superficial axioms for victory in war. Any reader seeking a war-winning strategy or prophecy of future war from this book will be disappointed but better equipped to find their own answers to their own unique strategic problems or curiosities. This book not only explains the qualities and characteristics of spacepower in Earth orbit, but also advocates a way of thinking about the use of spacepower in contemporary strategy that adheres to the timeless insights of classical military philosophers who strove to educate their readers and students about the practice, study and scrutiny of war. Space warfare still exists in the socio-political universe of war, and millennia of wisdom and experience in studying war should not be jettisoned just because war may happen in the relatively novel environment of Earth orbit. Just as the geographies of the seas and air have been subordinated to political and strategic interrogation, space – Earth orbit and beyond – should be as well. In that sense, space warfare is the continuation of Terran politics by other means; what happens in Earth orbit will reflect the politics of the international system on Earth. 'Terran', derived from the Latin word for Earth, is used interchangeably with Earth and terrestrial in this book. However, Terran is a more consistently specific term than 'terrestrial', which can sometimes include any rocky planetary body (such as Mercury, Venus, Mars as terrestrial worlds) and not just Earth. By the end of this book readers will hopefully have a more accurate and balanced comprehension of the possibilities and limits of spacepower in strategy and IR, and a clearer idea of what may happen in space should a war on Earth break out.

This book is also an attempt to place spacepower theory and the material implications of spacepower's influence on modern strategy into the mainstream of IR and strategic studies. Gray's plea for a Mahan for the final frontier remains unsatisfactorily addressed, despite some notable efforts at spacepower theory-making. This book is a new step in the collective effort of spacepower theory-making. Monographs on any aspect of astropolitics are rare, let alone on the conceptual aspects of space warfare as opposed to space arms control and the space-based elements of missile defence.[4] Scholarly research on the military aspects of space tend to be restricted to short pieces in scholarly journals, or books on space warfare are short, their theories intermingled with the policy issues of the day, and often from an American-centric perspective.[5] This book should be seen as part of a collective endeavour of theory-making about war, politics, strategy and space, and is intended to advance the theory, and not serve as another introduction to space policy issues.[6] 'Space powers' which are based on Earth are like continental or land powers using seapower. For Earth-based polities outer space is a secondary, littoral and contestable realm like coastal waters and oceans have been for continental powers. This is a contrast to bluewater and oceanic approaches to seapower based on the experiences of island powers who must engage with the seas to project their own power and deflect that of others. This bluewater vision of spacepower is a useful and necessary, yet conceptually limited, staple of much spacepower theory to date. Rather than an expansive ocean, Earth orbit is like a coastal zone: what flies in orbit is within reach of Earth-based countermeasures and adaptations, much like coastal defences against naval forces and intrusions. Earth orbit is not far away – it nominally begins at around 100 km altitude. 'Space' begins much closer to home than visions of open oceans tend to allow. This is different to island sea powers projecting power over oceans with the sea seen as a primary theatre and geographic medium. There is no space-based civilisation yet, and humanity remains a single planetary species. Earth remains the spatial beginning and end of politics and strategy. This continental and geocentric approach and the new vision of spacepower as operating within Earth's celestial coastline theorises many aspects of spacepower and space warfare for the first time, including the role of decisive space battles, logistics, third parties and neutrals, strategic manoeuvres, military astroculture and the dispersing influence of space technology on the modern battlefield.

This spacepower theory picks apart the prevalent astrodeterminist views of the nature and impact of spacepower on international relations and strategy that go back to origins of the Space Age. Astrodeterminism claims that events on Earth are primarily dominated by events in space. In October 1960, presidential candidate John F. Kennedy in a statement to the magazine *Missiles and Rockets* said that 'if the Soviets control space they can control earth, as in past centuries the nation that controlled the seas has dominated the continents'.[7] Though such rhetoric was used in the context of an election campaign, those sentiments about spacepower and the decisiveness of using outer space in warfare are prevalent in newspaper editorials, the blogosphere and some academic scholarship today. These misconceptions reflect the conceptual immaturity of spacepower and often simplistic interpretations of maritime and naval history. Controlling space is not a guaranteed way to control Earth, just as naval powers did not always dominate the fates of continents. In other words, the influence of spacepower upon modern warfare is more subtle and varied than most people assume, and the analogies people draw from the history of seapower to understand outer space today is often a selective reading of seapower based on bluewater or island-based naval powers whilst ignoring histories of continental navies and land-based seapower. When spacepower was far more of a niche subject twenty years ago, authors may have had to aggressively 'sell' the importance of spacepower for otherwise excessively geocentric audiences who did not grasp the importance of the development of Earth orbit as essential military and critical infrastructure. That may have led to some excessive astrodeterminism in theories, which are critiqued in the interests of moving the theory on as spacepower has become a more intuitive concept and mainstream talking point in defence and security policies, especially in the last ten years.

This book's primary aim is to advance the development of spacepower theory by identifying useful ideas that chart the influence of spacepower, which does not determine events on Earth but still has important inputs for them. Like seapower and airpower before it, spacepower needs theories that help individuals grapple with the 'grey areas' of how they influence the conduct of strategy. Such theory takes the form of seven headline propositions that encapsulate the many moving parts of spacepower in modern strategy. The seven propositions are:

I. Space warfare is waged for the command of space
II. Spacepower is uniquely infrastructural and connected to Earth
III. The command of space does not equate to the command of Earth
IV. The command of space manipulates celestial lines of communication
V. Earth orbit is a cosmic coastline suited for strategic manoeuvres
VI. Spacepower exists within a geocentric mindset
VII. Spacepower is dispersed and imposes dispersion on Earth

Proposition I's command of space refers to who can control or deny space infrastructure in a time of war to varying degrees, and acts of space warfare are meant to influence who can use or not use such satellite constellations. Any tactical action must contribute to something on the strategic level to meet political goals on Earth, otherwise it is a mindless act of wanton violence and destruction. The command of space is subordinated ultimately to the objectives of grand strategy. Space warfare is the continuation of Terran politics by other means; acts of space warfare do not suspend political intercourse or change the conduct of politics into something entirely different.[8] Proposition II argues that despite the initial conceptual resonance between seapower and spacepower regarding commanding a transitory medium, space is a unique geography in its use as supporting infrastructure – rather than centred upon combat platforms – meaning that it requires specialised knowledge to exploit it. Despite space being unique, Proposition II also cautions against viewing outer space as isolated from Earth as is sometimes done in spacepower literature. Proposition III examines the two principles of decisive battle and the decisiveness of dominating a medium in war. Victorious battles and dominant command should not be viewed as inherently decisive. This questions many assumptions or beliefs of outer space as the 'ultimate high ground' and the uncritical transposition of 'decisive' naval battles to anti-satellite operations. Proposition IV details how command in space works by visualising celestial lines of communication and applying the principles of chokepoints, blockades and desirable positions in orbit. These four propositions show the bluewater contributions to spacepower theory as an essential starting point for further theory that features across Propositions V and VI which draw heavily on continental seapower theory, and Proposition VII which brings in additional insights from airpower and modern warfare.

Proposition V breaks new ground in spacepower theory by theorising the bulk of activities that defines spacepower as we know it – the deployment, use and management of satellites and their services and data. Proposition V geographically contextualises the first four propositions into a coastal, rather than bluewater–oceanic, analogy to Earth orbit, and draws heavily upon continental analogies from seapower. Theorists such as Castex, Gorshkov, Menon and also Mahan provide the view of seapower from the land, which is highly instructive for modern strategists as Earth-bound states look up to outer space and satellites for support or prepare for threats to their terrestrial operations from the 'orbital flank', the cosmic coastline. This geocentric approach to spacepower highlights that spacepower and operations in Earth orbit must be seen as primarily a supporting force or capability, not a direct war-winning capability or a scene dominated by spectacular battles. Earth orbit is a realm for conducting strategic manoeuvres to assist the war effort on Earth, and provides a kind of strategic depth to those who can exploit it. Proposition VI considers the role of strategic and military culture as it applies to space, and again insights are provided by continental navies in land-based strategic cultures. As space is perceived as a secondary theatre, and not as essential or pressing as terrestrial ones, advocates of spacepower within states may struggle to fight for their corner in bureaucratic politics and resource allocation. Naval cultures suffer such problems in states like France, Russia and India, and in terms of spacepower every space-faring state is Earth-based, and therefore geocentric. Space is a useful ancillary, and not an essential medium for security and power projection as island powers see the oceans. The cultural aspects of spacepower – or astroculture – are explored in depth as a constructivist or ideational corrective to the otherwise materialist approach the theory favours. Proposition VII ends the theory with a conceptualisation of the influence of spacepower, and the conclusions of the other six propositions, on strategy, operations and tactics in modern warfare. Drawing heavily upon the work of John Sheldon, the dispersing influence of spacepower is theorised and its impact on concentrating forces and achieving mass effect from coordinated firepower is considered. This important influence of spacepower on modern warfare raises the importance of commanding space in the first place, bringing the reader full circle back to Proposition I.

This theory is not a theory about the totality of international relations or global politics in outer space – or astropolitics. Non-military aspects such as commercial space activities and non-state actors are relevant but are subordinated to the requirements of supporting a war effort, and are discussed more explicitly in Proposition V. This theory structures thought about the use of violence and force in Earth orbit and how space technologies impact terrestrial military operations at a time of renewed great-power war planning. Whilst much is drawn from the perspective of states, the propositions of spacepower contain insights about space warfare for any actor conducting or involved in the prosecution of political aims through violence. The theory draws primarily from seapower theories and is rooted in a Clausewitzian approach to theorising war as an unpredictable, chaotic, emotional and political activity. Spacepower theory helps encourage a way of strategic thinking about warfare in the Space Age through the creation and application of propositions. The propositions themselves do not amount to a space strategy or a specific war plan. The critical application of spacepower theory's seven propositions assists the individual's self-education about space, warfare and strategy to help devise 'better' space strategies or war plans or better equip the individual to scrutinise and interpret the actions of others. Spacepower theory is about charting possibilities that educates the reader, and not providing policy prescriptions or war-winning strategies. This way of thinking is rooted in a perpetual struggle to connect meaningful abstract universal concepts with ever-changing particular realities so that wider conclusions may be drawn that have relevance across time and space. Such an approach is rooted in historical research and theoretical flexibility that is turned to the end of providing information or arguments to enhance personal learning and strategic judgment.[9] Education is the goal of this book – not policy advocacy or providing a winning space strategy. Readers may be practitioners, scholars or curious observers. The theory should be just as useful to those who wish to prosecute a strategy as those who wish to hold power to account by being able to comprehend the practice of war. Space warfare should not be left in the hands of the practitioners alone.

An intellectual grasp of the proliferation of spacepower in IR is severely lagging behind the practical development of it. Six decades after the birth of a 'Space Age', space capabilities have earned 'a permanent place at the table in matters of international conflict, peace, national and international development, and international law', yet 'public complacency toward the importance of space has become the rule, rather than the exception'.[10] To better hold power and states that may use violence in space to account, a wider education about the strategic realities and possibilities about space is desperately needed. Spacepower should be normalised in grand strategic discussion and analyses of power in IR, as it is one of the essential 'elements, both military and non-military, for the preservation and enhancement of the nation's (wartime and peacetime long term) interests'.[11] One step in bringing spacepower into the mainstream of IR is to theorise the possibilities and pitfalls of space warfare and the conduct of modern warfare in the contemporary Space Age in line with the precedents set by wars on Earth. Space warfare is still warfare – its technological and geographic uniqueness does not allow it to escape the 'gravity well' of human politics and the universal principles of war. Space warfare, and the use of spacepower in warfare and grand strategy, is therefore susceptible to analysis with the concepts we use to understand war, strategy and IR on Earth.

Today, over 2,000 active satellites are deployed in Earth orbit by over seventy states and commercial entities. The global space economy in 2018 was worth around US$360 billion.[12] The uses of satellites and the potential consequences of their denial in a time of war are generating strategic effects that strategists and scholars must account for. The infrastructural and support services derived from orbital satellite constellations remains an under-theorised and under-conceptualised techno-geographic phenomenon in IR and strategic studies. These satellites provide a range of functions for military, economic, civilian, intelligence and scientific needs. The diverse technical qualities of spacepower and space systems are encountered throughout the book, and will not be presented as a taxonomy here, particularly when accessible primers written by practitioners and technical experts already exist.[13] Satellite systems enhance the efficiencies and combat power of terrestrial military forces; enhance terrestrial infrastructure; enable global mobile communications; gather data about Earth's natural systems and humanity's impact on its ecology; and enable critical intelligence and nuclear monitoring capabilities. Spacepower has perpetuated the shrinkage of Earth's relative geographic size in techno-economic terms by increasing the geographic scale of conventional military operations and making terrestrial transport and communications speeds and capacities far more efficient. Space technology by its very nature is global and enables networked and mobile communications, freeing state infrastructures – particularly leapfrogging developing states – from some of the tyrannies of terrestrial infrastructure constraints. Satellites are a material consequence and producer of the geopolitical 'shrinking' of Earth. The exploitation of space technologies in the spheres of intelligence and military targeting, navigation and communication have underpinned much of the military dominance that the US has enjoyed since the late-1980s. The proliferation of those technologies outside the United States is eroding one of the main advantages Western militaries have enjoyed since the end of the Cold War, levelling somewhat the conventional military and economic balances of the 'great powers' with significant implications for global power relations in the twenty-first century. Earth's major powers are exploiting their own space infrastructure and pursuing space weapons technology which have undermined an oft-assumed American dominance of outer space, but it has not necessarily ended American power preponderance on Earth.

The use of Earth orbit is now institutionalised among the most developed states and many smaller and developing states following the Cold War and the nuclear revolution.[14] Yet a student of IR would not easily notice this given the curious absence of spacepower in IR and strategy literature since 1957.[15] Despite the ubiquity of the academic study and mantra of 'globalisation' since 1991, the physical artefacts, if not embodiment, of that globalisation continue to be treated as a flight of scholarly fancy. Relative to areas such as nuclear weapons, missile defence and computer network or 'cyber' issues, space is a relatively understudied and underpopulated specialisation.[16] Unlike ships, aircraft and computers, spacepower works silently beyond sight and mostly as a mundane infrastructure rather than tangible weapons systems. Popular images of space tend to gravitate around proposed innovations, futures never realised and the 'famous spectacular technologies' – for example the Apollo Programme, Reagan's Strategic Defense Initiative ('Star Wars') or the Space Transportation System

(Space Shuttle) – at the expense of the 'low and ubiquitous ones' and the everyday 'things in use and the uses of things'.[17]

Scholars, practitioners and publics at large must recognise that the machines flying around in Earth orbit, the use of spacepower, is a mundane yet critical part of our technological existence as they provide infrastructural services – and these technologies are often rather old and challenge the fetishisation of innovation in space policy circles. The American Global Positioning System (GPS) has been in use for over thirty years, the fundamental techniques and technologies of satellite-based signals intelligence (SIGINT) dates back to the 1960s, the innovations of America's KENNEN array of imagery satellites emerged in the 1970s, the Iridium Communications satellite phone company is now twenty years old, and China, India and Europe have had operational space launch vehicles and satellites for decades. Focusing our understanding of spacepower based on what is already in use rather than what may or may not be being developed encourages a technological view that moves from the 'new to the old' and the 'spectacular to the mundane'.[18] Unlike deep space probes and the International Space Station, thousands of machines in Earth orbit are now essential in the conduct of international affairs and not least its military, intelligence and security elements.

The book is divided into three parts, with two chapters in each. Part I sets the rationale, epistemology, methodology and limits of the theory as well as charts the first four propositions of spacepower. Chapter 1 defines and explains spacepower, and challenges the undervalued role of spacepower in contemporary IR analysis by outlining its significance to modern warfare and grand strategy. It then explores the role of thinking about hegemony and geopolitical thought in outer space, and makes the case for embracing material factors in the analysis of spacepower as much current literature in international relations turns away from material considerations. Chapter 1 ends with an explanation of how pedagogical theory and strategic analogies work, and how the propositions should be used. Chapter 2 explains the first four propositions of spacepower theory by building on and critiquing the existing Anglo-American strategic visions of space, often derived from imperial bluewater sources of seapower.

These propositions provide a solid foundation for the following propositions and chapters which provide more insights into the nature of spacepower.

Part II builds on Part I by drawing on lesser-known and often counter-imperial experiences and theories of continental seapower that more accurately resemble spacepower as we know it today. This draws out additional insights that theorise the defining feature of spacepower as a more subtle, secondary and supporting form of power. Chapter 3 outlines this new vision of spacepower in the celestial coastline of Earth orbit in Proposition V, and theorises the supporting functions of spacepower's satellite infrastructure for the first time, as well as their influence on terrestrial strategy. Chapter 4 continues with the continental insights and reintroduces the human and cultural element to spacepower in Proposition VI, and considers the dangers of ethnocentrism in spacepower analysis, as well as how cultural factors and the geocentrism of strategic cultures on Earth will influence spacepower.

Part III, The Influence of Spacepower upon Warfare, takes the theory towards battle on Earth through the final proposition in Chapter 5 and a space-centric analysis of a Taiwan war scenario in Chapter 6. Chapter 5 theorises the ubiquitous dispersing effects of spacepower upon Earth, which continues a longer-term trend in military capabilities. It is through exploiting and challenging the dispersing power from commanding this coastline that we can integrate the real consequences of spacepower into thinking on grand strategy and international security on Earth. Chapter 6's illustrative application of the theory demonstrates how the propositions are instructive when critically applied to a scenario. In this case, the theory demonstrates how spacepower can influence terrestrial considerations for battle, in particular with long-distance precision-strike warfare, or 'anti-access/area denial' (A2/AD) warfare in current military jargon. Two contrasting strategies are critiqued in the case study as equally valid possibilities – the all-out first strike Space Pearl Harbor strategy and Counterspace-in-Being strategy of keeping space strikes in reserve for a critical moment. Projecting support from celestial communications down to Earth from the cosmic coastline changes the calculations of concentration and dispersal for military forces on Earth, and understanding the thorny questions of how and when to strike against space systems is aided by an understanding of all seven propositions.

The book concludes with a reminder of the need for IR and all its sub-disciplines to take space seriously in its own right. It is a geographic realm where all facets of human politics play out, not least the 'hard power' aspects of military power and strategy. This book is not a definitive statement about space and IR; it is a theory and a vision of spacepower's use in warfare, portrays Earth orbit as a celestial coastline, and dispels many misconceptions about the possibilities of space warfare. It is imperative that continuing debate on the distribution of power in the international system takes the now-essential material elements of spacepower into account, and such a task begins with outlining how spacepower 'works' should the actors of the international system come to blows against each other in an era when the spacepower in the cosmic coastline directly influences the conduct of modern warfare.

Spacepower theory is needed now to improve the quality of strategic thinking and debate among analysts, observers, researchers and practitioners in a way and that is not centred upon the cyclical and strategically marginal debates over the deployment of space-based weapons, particularly when the primary form of space weapon (or anti-satellite) proliferation is occurring on Earth and not in space itself. Practitioners do not have the luxury of waiting until after a conflagration in orbit – whether using Earth-based or space-based weapons – occurs to have a set of ideas to guide their decisions. Steven Lambakis was correct to argue in 1995 that 'when an enemy can use the orbital highways overhead at will, or interfere with U.S. space missions critical to the course and outcome of a war, space [warfare] will no doubt receive the attention it deserves'.[19] That time is now; the tools to do that are proliferating within and among America's potential adversaries. Spacepower cannot be ignored in strategy and IR, and this book hopefully provides a robust theoretical foundation to consider its practical dynamics in the conduct of Terran wars and grand strategy.

Notes

1. Gray, 'The Influence', p. 307.
2. Pfaltzgraff, 'International Relations', p. 40.
3. Burrows, *This New Ocean*.
4. For example, see these as texts focusing on missile defence and arms control aspects of military space: Bulkeley and Spinardi, *Space Weapons*; Long et al., *Weapons in Space*; Jasani, *Space Weapons*; Stares, *Space*; Hitchens and Samson, 'Space-Based Interceptors'; Peoples, 'Assuming the Inevitable?'; Liemer and Chyba, 'A Verifiable Limited Test Ban'; Peoples, 'Securitization'; Lopez, 'Predicting'; Hebert, 'Regulation of Space'; Shimabukuro, 'No Deal in Space'; Chaterjee, 'Legality of Anti-Satellites'.
5. This list is not exhaustive, but provides examples of literature that contains elements of spacepower theory which are short if not intermingled with discussions of applied American space strategy and US policy critique or advocacy: Lupton, *On Space Warfare*; Oberg, *Space*; Lambakis, *On the Edge*; Dolman, *Astropolitik*; Lambeth, *Mastering the Ultimate Highground*; Mowthorpe, *Militarization*; O'Hanlon, *Neither Star Wars nor Sanctuary*; Klein, *Space Warfare*; Coletta and Pilch, *Space and Defense Policy*; Sadeh, *Space Strategy*; Johnson-Freese, *Space Warfare*; Moltz, *Crowded Orbits*; Gray, 'Clausewitz Rules, OK?'; Mueller, 'Totem and Taboo'; Klein, 'Space Warfare: A Maritime-Inspired Space Strategy'; Kleinberg, 'On War'; Krepon et al., 'China's Military Space Strategy'; Duvall and Havercroft, 'Taking Sovereignty'; Hitchens and Chen, 'Forging a Sino-US "Grand Bargain" in Space'; Havercroft and Duvall, 'Critical Astropolitics'; Rendleman, 'A Strategy for Space Assurance'; Burris, 'Astroimpolitic'; Armstrong, 'American National Security'; Shabbir, 'Counterspace Operations'.
6. On introductory texts, see: Sheehan, *International Politics*; Moltz, *Politics*; Johnson-Freese, *Space as a Strategic Asset*.
7. Logsdon, *John F. Kennedy*, p. 10.
8. Clausewitz, *On War*, pp. 280–1.
9. On Mahan's approach to education, see: Sumida, *Inventing Grand Strategy*, esp. pp. 99–117.
10. Harding, *Space Policy*, pp. 1, 3.
11. Kennedy, 'Grand Strategy', p. 5.
12. BryceTech, 'State of the Satellite Industry Report'.
13. For example, see: Al-Rodhan, *Meta-Geopolitics*; Air Command, *AU-18*; UK Ministry of Defence, *UK Military Space Primer*.

14. Burrows, *This New Ocean*, pp. 610–11.
15. Notable exceptions in recent years: Harding, *Space Policy*; Sheng-Chi Wang, *Transatlantic Space Politics*; Paikowsky, *The Power of the Space Club*.
16. On the problems with the term 'cyber', see: Futter, '"Cyber" Semantics'.
17. Edgerton, *The Shock*, p. 212.
18. Ibid. p. xiv.
19. Lambakis, 'Space Control', pp. 418, 427.

PART I

Imperial Traditions:
Space Dominance

1. Spacepower, Empire and Theory

Space systems have for decades influenced the strategic level of war by improving the information available for top decision makers, nuclear warning and targeting, and the command and control of fixed and mobile military forces across Earth. Today, that influence reaches the tactical and operational levels of war as space communications are available to the individual trooper and guide missiles and other munitions to their targets with unparalleled accuracy. Spacepower underwrites and enables modern military power on Earth. Space technologies, satellite systems, services and their terrestrial peripherals are described as 'force multipliers' in American military literature because they increase the efficiency of combat forces. Spacepower influences the conduct of tactics and operations, not only strategy. Satellites allow military units and weapons platforms to communicate with each other and identify targets across planetary-scale distances whilst on the move; and the violent and destructive potential of such weapons are restricted only by political will, laws of engagement, and the effective ranges and speeds of the weapon systems of deployed military forces. Anything hot enough, big enough, electronically 'noisy' enough or polluting enough will likely be detected. If long-range strike systems are within range, that target could be struck due to space infrastructure's ability to gather data, navigate autonomous guidance systems, and patch together a dispersed collection of analysts, computers, troopers and weapon systems at great distances. In short, what America can detect it can shoot at, and efficiently so. These efficiency gains provided to the US military made an impact in the 1991 Gulf War and their effects are familiar to us today. America's traditional superiority in high-intensity conventional combat relies on ubiquitous space technologies. What is more, these kinds of technologies are increasingly entrenched in the militaries of America's allies, as well as its potential adversaries. Increasingly, select technologies with tactical and operational military applications are proliferating to many other states, both large and small, that are not American allies nor likely adversaries.

IR cannot ignore the fact that Earth orbit is a vital geopolitical and geostrategic arena in the international system, and not only the concern of the United States. If high-technology platforms and the creation of large complicated networks and systems is an indicator of the challenge posed to a US 'command of the commons',[1] it is in space that a consistent manifestation of these efforts can be observed. Spacepower is essential for modern warfare – whether on the receiving end or prosecuting end of those technologies – which itself is a major fixation of IR theory and its practice. IR should not ignore the fact that almost a dozen states can independently launch and place into orbit useful machines for military, economic or other purposes, and many states can disrupt or negate the effects of useful machines placed in Earth orbit. The need for a Mahan for the final frontier to theorise the meaning of spacepower for strategy has never been more acute, and this book presents a significant advancement in spacepower theory by providing a new vision of the cosmic coastline, how spacepower remains inherently geocentric, and is explicitly pedagogical and Clausewitzian in its approach, in contrast to previous theories of spacepower. Gray's call for a spacepower theory remains unanswered despite it being approximately thirty years since space technology demonstrated its potential to influence the conduct of war in the first so-called 'Space War'.[2] In Operation Desert Shield in 1991, spacepower was a new operational and tactical feature in the effort to expel the Iraqi Army from Kuwait. In this war, the then-head of the US National Reconnaissance Office (NRO) attributed the coalition's stunning success in terms of speed and low casualties to spacepower's support to the battlefield.[3] Space has become an essential part of the American military machine, global finance and critical infrastructure. Any modern command, control, communications, computers, intelligence, surveillance and reconnaissance (C4ISR) architecture depends on space infrastructure. As these systems become central to enabling Terran military capabilities of modern states, strategic thinking must accompany them so that they are protected and exploited, and those of the enemy's undermined and assaulted. These C4ISR systems are now being deployed by states that may be hostile adversaries to the United States, meaning that the US has to contemplate being on the 'wrong side' of spacepower in warfare, rather than always benefiting from their own.

These material trends matter. Any serious war plan involving 'conventional' or 'non-nuclear' warfare must consider the possibilities of space warfare, as the satellite systems that underpin these systems could be threatened because of the difference they make on the modern battlefield and in coercive or deterrent relationships. No prudent actor contemplating the use of war – whether a hegemon, great power, small state or non-state actor – dares ignore the possibility that satellites may not remain immune to disruption or destruction, or to the effects space systems have battlefield capabilities and tactics. The need for the kind of theory and debate informed by this book is extremely pressing, particularly as there are so few monographs on the subject. Useful concepts to educate readers about the pitfalls and possibilities of warfare against, with and in spite of space systems and their influence upon terrestrial warfare are needed. These useful concepts are put forward throughout the seven propositions of this book which offers a rigorous and original theory to take spacepower theory forward in the discipline.

Before delving into the seven propositions of spacepower theory, spacepower itself must be defined, as well as the underlying methodology (the way the propositions were formed) and the epistemology (the claim to knowledge made and how the propositions should be used) of the theory. As spacepower is important in material terms, scholars and specialists need theory to communicate its significance to a wider generalist audience. Spacepower theory is one approach to outer space which focuses on the conduct and exercise of military force and space technology. But it is not the only theoretical or philosophical approach to studying humanity's interactions in and uses of outer space. Studying space through the diverse theoretical lenses we have is necessary because the image we have of the extra-terrestrial realm ought to be such a contested terrain, for what we perceive space to be shapes our views of how it should be exploited, and his has very real implications for political, economic, and environmental development on Earth.[4]

The chapter ends with a discussion of the Clausewitzian foundations, pedagogical intent and analogical method of the spacepower theory that follows in the remainder of the book.

Spacepower

Spacepower refers to a diverse collection of activities and technologies in space or to do with outer space; it is a concept defined by how any actor can use outer space and what it possesses or effectively calls upon to enable it to do so. The nascent field of astropolitics enjoys a general consensus that spacepower – a range of space technologies and activities in space – can be deployed and sought by states for the purposes of war, development and prestige.[5] Earth orbit, the satellite constellations deployed there, and their terrestrial supporting infrastructure and downstream applications provide an array of ubiquitous and varied services and data that states, non-state actors and individuals can use for benign and nefarious purposes. Earth orbit, from around 100 km altitude up to around 40,000 km is a geographic environment that is used by actors in the international system for a range of now-essential political, commercial, diplomatic, scientific and infrastructural needs. In that strategic sense it is no different to the utilisation of Earth's oceans and atmosphere. In that most fundamental sense spacepower is a conceptual equivalent to seapower and airpower. Spacepower is 'the use of outer space's military and economic advantages for strategic ends', and a 'space power' is an entity that uses outer space for its political objectives.[6] The astrostrategic realm of Earth orbit is important to the global economy and vital to major military powers and their strategies, and specific details of the orbital environment and technologies are covered in Proposition II in the next chapter.[7]

Space technology is now part of critical infrastructure for any modern state and economy; therefore it follows that 'spacepower' is an important facet of power in international relations. Lupton described spacepower as 'the ability of a nation to exploit the space environment in pursuit of national goals and purposes and includes the entire Astronautical capabilities of the nation. A nation with such capabilities is termed a space power.'[8] Lambakis defined a space power as

> any entity that has the capacity to utilize effectively the space medium for commercial or national security purposes . . . the baseline measure of space power will be a country's ability to integrate space capabilities with other national activities and manage the rapid and immense flow of information.[9]

Spacepower can be described as both the material capabilities to achieve goals in and from space, as well as the ability to 'use space to influence others, events, or the environment to achieve one's purposes or goals'.[10] Sheldon, Gray, Sheehan and Pfaltzgraff continue this blending of materialist ('bean-counting' capabilities) and relational (outcomes between actors) understandings of spacepower.[11] Al-Rodhan agrees by stating that spacepower is 'the ability of a state to use space to sustain and enhance its . . . capacities'.[12] Ziarnick calls spacepower 'the ability to do something in space' as it can be applied to other types of actors, and not just the state.[13] Spacepower is tied to state power Klein argues, and the most advanced states today cannot do without it to achieve security and compete both militarily and economically, and to retain some influence in the patterns of development in the international system.[14] This is not restricted to Western states. In China and India specifically, spacepower can be seen as postcolonial techno-nationalist projects, where the development of space technology is seen as a normative marker of state power and status.[15] Space is an environment where states and other actors deploy their power in, gain power from, and may seek to deny such advantages to others.

Transposing geostrategic thought into outer space is an intuitive continuation of IR and strategic studies to beyond the atmosphere and into an astrostrategic environment. A founder of the geopolitical study of outer space in modern scholarship, Everett

Dolman, crystallised the ramifications of the use of Earth orbit by declaring that

> since the efficient movement of goods and capital in the nineteenth century was a factor of sea capacity, the nation or nations that controlled the most modern navies and the world's critical chokepoints could dominate the lanes of commerce, and thus the economic lifelines of an increasingly interdependent globe.[16]

There are many useful grounds for analogy such as this which are discussed throughout this book. However, analogical thought about space has its critics, who call for non-analogical thought to reflect its apparently unique qualities.[17] Analogical thought about space is discussed further below as a necessary step in strategic education about Earth orbit and spacepower. Nevertheless, it is not disputed in modern astropolitical scholarship that spacepower, through the use of satellites and the services they enable, is a present factor in the conduct of international relations and in the distribution of capabilities remains neglected relative to seapower, airpower, cyber and information warfare, nuclear weapons, and ballistic missile defence systems. This neglect of spacepower in IR is all the more troubling given space technology's ubiquitous presence in all these areas of activity. The importance of Gray's call for a Mahan for the final frontier has only increased with the proliferation of spacepower both within states and among them.

Spacepower is the vanguard of material factors complicating power analyses and military balances in the twenty-first century. Despite this it is something of a missing link in terrestrial considerations of grand strategy, particularly for middle or second-rank powers which have developed world-leading niche strengths in space whilst retaining key dependencies on allies.[18] The economic and commercial aspects of space are involved and subordinated to a military focus in the theory, bearing in mind E. H. Carr's view of the close interrelationship of economic and military power.[19] Multiple spacepowers today are developing strategically vital space capabilities as well as attracting or developing commercial companies and economic capabilities in space. Spacepower influences the economy of a state, and vice versa, to the extent that an economy disproportionately reliant on celestial modes of commerce will be more vulnerable if it does not secure the dominant 'lanes of commerce' (where valuable satellites and information streams travel) in orbit.[20] Indeed, one cannot imagine the globalisation of economics, finance and communications in the past thirty years without the space infrastructure that has emerged to facilitate it.[21] Commercial launch capabilities reflect the ability of states, or their registered companies, to not only provide more varied options for accessing space, but also present their attempts to secure profits or balance costs by selling rides into space for the multitude of less capable space actors that do not have their own independent means of accessing space. These capabilities, which still number only nine states and their registered commercial companies, are among the most expensive to develop, and can indirectly show a high level of both public and private investment in the space economy and infrastructure. The value and grand strategic significance of outer space may be set to only increase, as some private analysis shows that the global space economy may triple in the next twenty years from US$350 billion to over US$1 trillion.[22]

Few things illustrate the nexus of military and economic spacepower better than satellite navigation infrastructure. The American GPS, which is controlled by the US military, is a military system but provides a free position, navigation and timing service across the globe that has become ubiquitous and essential in the global economy and civilian infrastructure. As it enables the precision military capability that has defined high-technology warfare since the 1991 Gulf War, as well as the modernisation of almost every sector of economic and security activity on Earth, it is a necessary indicator of the capacity of a space power because of its technological complexity, expense and the strategic freedom of action that it provides on Earth.[23] It also provides a symbol of capability and technical influence in international relations with allies, potential adversaries and third parties.[24] In the years since GPS's emergence, different space powers have been deploying their own global navigation satellite system (GNSS) and hope to reap similar economic and military rewards. A sovereign GNSS is a crucial infrastructure for any modern military power that wishes to act independently and compete on conventional military terms with the West.

In 2003 Barry Posen claimed that 'it will not be easy for others to produce a comparable system [to GPS], though the European Union intends to try'.[25] Less than twenty years since Posen committed those words to paper, there are four GNSS constellations in operation, with an additional number of non-American regional navigation systems and GPS augmentation systems in place. Whether or not China and Russia should be characterised as 'opponents', the reality is that counterspace or anti-satellite capabilities and space-based military modernisation have proliferated beyond America and its allies in the last twenty years. Beyond the Revolution in Military Affairs (RMA) literature from the 1990s and 2000s, which focused on precision-guided munitions (PGMs), only specific space capabilities are invoked in contemporary strategic studies literature as they are relevant to the discussion of A2/AD warfare which are designed to challenge American military primacy in the air and maritime environments with long-range precision-strike weapons, a literature which features strongly in Chapter 6.

In describing America's command of the commons in the early twenty-first century, Posen also believes that:

> the United States enjoys the same command of the sea that Britain once did, and it can also move large and heavy forces around the globe. But command of space allows the United States to see across the surface of the world's landmasses and to gather vast amounts of information. At least on the matter of medium-to-large-scale military developments, the United States can locate and identify military targets with considerable fidelity and communicate this information to offensive forces in a timely fashion . . . U.S. forces can even more easily do great damage to a state's transportation and communications networks as well as economic infrastructure.[26]

Other states have developed and are continuing to improve their ability to undermine or mitigate the effects of that American command of the commons, not least of all in space through the development of counterspace weapons and long-range strike weapons. This possibly constitutes a form of 'hard balancing' against the United States.

On 11 January 2007, a Chinese anti-satellite (ASAT) weapons test generated a renewed interest and debate in the role of ASAT technology in international security and Sino–US relations, as well as chaotic, heated and embarrassing diplomatic fallout.[27] The test destroyed a defunct Chinese weather satellite, and in the process created thousands of pieces of debris which threatened other satellites in low-Earth orbit. In the following year, an American satellite interception (Operation Burnt Frost), which was claimed by the US government to be an environmental protection measure to prevent the satellite from reaching the Earth intact, appeared to confirm an equivalent sea-based American capability. These events, alongside continued Chinese Earth-based anti-satellite weapons testing and the Russian satellite close-in manoeuvres and restarted anti-satellite weapons development,[28] demonstrate a desire among the three most capable space powers to maintain capabilities to destroy the satellite components of space infrastructure.

The Chinese ASAT test, and its successive programme of 'cleaner' tests, is a fruit of the a larger programme of military modernisation in the People's Liberation Army (PLA) and its supporting defence industrial base that stretches back to Plan 863, launched in 1986 under the guidance of Deng Xiaoping who followed advice from senior scientific advisers.[29] This effort was given a boost in the 1990s, and in particular after the stunning success of the United States in the 1991 Gulf War, through the emergence of the 'precision-strike revolution'.[30] Space-based technology became the enabling backbone of the cutting edge of precise, rapid, low-risk and networked military successes now that the 'First Space War' had taken place.[31] Today, the Sino-US military balance is posing new challenges for strategists because, for the first time, war between spacepower-enabled and enhanced militaries is possible and thinkable. Today, Chinese spacepower cannot be dismissed as a marginal concern for strategists, as numerous investigations show its maturing Earth observation, reconnaissance, early warning and long-range weapons capabilities that provide a credible threat to US power projection, as well as America's entrenched 'way of warfare' which is highly dependent upon spacepower.[32] In 2019 India joined China and the United States as states with the capability to hit a satellite in LEO with an interceptor missile, whilst Russia has restarted its Soviet-era anti-satellite weapon systems.[33] Two different mobile ground-launched kinetic anti-satellite weapons have been developed and deployed by China, with one geared towards striking targets in LEO and another to reach satellites in medium-Earth orbit (MEO) and geosynchronous orbit (GEO). Russia too has a suite of capabilities to disrupt or deny the use of satellite by adversaries, and like China has been testing orbital inspection systems – satellites that loiter close to target satellites which may be able to 'listen in' on its communications.[34] This would be equivalent to the American Geosynchronous Space Situational Awareness Program. Such close-proximity capabilities open themselves up to future potential development as platforms for physically destructive systems, rather than reconnaissance and spying alone. These major powers are developing these 'hard' physical satellite interceptor systems, alongside other 'soft' kill systems such as electronic warfare and signal spoofing. Scholars and practitioners of modern warfare, international security and IR must be able to make sense of what the spread of satellites and anti-satellite capabilities mean for power politics and the conduct of strategy. Spacepower theory provides the timeless concepts to do just that and recognises the importance of space to modern warfare on their own terms.

Physically destructive systems are accompanied by directed-energy anti-satellite weapons, radiofrequency (RF) jamming and cyber intrusion efforts. As well as demonstrating technical progress in space warfare capabilities, the PLA is also making conceptual inroads into orbit by discussing the roles and utility of space warfare in its strategic thought and war planning, with an increasingly large and robust C4ISR network in place with satellite constellations providing a backbone to such a network. Modern military capabilities and their distribution means that the potential for effective use of good enough technology to counter or frustrate American and allied military capabilities cannot be ignored, and space is an understudied part of this change. It is not for nothing that space is seen in more and more states as a realm where warfare could occur.

Accessing and exploiting an entire environment on an independent and sovereign basis is not a 'niche' or 'miscellaneous' capability. Anti-satellite weapons, no matter the type, should also not be considered as strategic weapons systems or only through the lens of nuclear deterrence and ballistic missile defence. Indeed, some analysts downplayed the significance of the Indian kinetic anti-satellite capability and saw its significance mainly in terms of missile interception instead.[35] Yet the truth remains that it provides an emergent kinetic anti-satellite capability that will have uses in countering space systems that may be used by potential adversaries of Indian armed forces. The ability to conduct space warfare is relevant for political crises, low-intensity conflicts and regional non-nuclear wars, as well as high-intensity wars of survival which may go nuclear. Spacepower's influence on terrestrial power is diverse and uneven and space technologies cannot be placed into a single conceptual black box. Spacepower is diverse, and therefore it cannot be argued across the board, as some do, that all satellites in space are 'sitting ducks', or that first strike instability would be the norm with space weapons, that it is an inherently strategically (un)stable environment, or that quick technological kill chains enabled by space systems make for hasty decision-making cycles.[36] Much depends on the redundancies in those systems, the tolerance for risks, and local conditions as explored in Chapter 6.

The landing of a human on the moon or the construction of a space station undoubtedly has prestige value, as well as some effects of high-technology and industrial stimuli. But it is a far cry from the more practical, ubiquitous and systemic impacts on political structures and orders from nuclear attack early warning satellites, spy and observation satellites, precision guidance systems and timing services. Those systems and very useful and lucrative global infrastructures are increasingly parsed out between five major blocs today – the USA, 'Europe' (broadly defined), China, Russia and India. The growth in precision weapons, which rely on space systems, outside the United States in now well-recognised within contemporary scholarship. However, it is not often seen as a key consequence and driver of the proliferation of spacepower.

Whilst statements from various quarters in Washington on desires to secure US space dominance may cause new refrains of alarm from scholars and pundits – whether in the Bush or Trump administrations[37] – such ideas of being able to dominate space in a time of war go back in official written form to US Air Force doctrine in the early 1980s. American desires to secure a dominant control of space for its own needs is usually done in reference to a time of war, and not a time of peace as interpreted by some.[38] Since the 1980s, official military thinking in the United States

> noted the key issues that would dominate all subsequent policy – the need to protect US capabilities from space-based threats, to prevent space being a sanctuary for aggression against the US, and the need to exploit space to enhance US military capability.[39]

But thinking in terms of assumed dominance is strategically reckless and increasingly untenable. The outcome of a struggle for the command of space – a core concept theorised in Proposition I in the next chapter – in a time of war is not a foregone conclusion, and interrogating the possibilities and risks of action in space in a time of war should caution all theorists from taking notions of space-enabled primacy too far in their practical understandings of power and capability in the international system. With a spread in conventional high-technology capabilities and a persisting multipolar nuclear and missile order, space infrastructure can be devastated by several major powers in the international system, and pick apart the space-based backbone of modern American military and economic power. Spacepower theory shows what principles are useful to understand how the outcomes of space warfare and the influence of spacepower in terrestrial warfare are not foregone conclusions and makes the reader consider in a creative way what options are open. IR must still take material factors such as geography and technology into account, and spacepower theory does that by conceptualising how space can be used, especially in order to resist any unilateral desire to control and dominate space. Material factors and the ignorance of Clausewitzian principles of war constrain and enable resistance against an 'easy win' regarding commanding outer space and the decisive effects (or lack of) such dominance of space can have on Earth. Active satellites, now numbering above 2,000, a handful of states with satellite launch capabilities and fewer still with space warfare equipment all matter in IR.

Space empire and resistance

Much of the space power literature critiques visions of American hegemony or seeks to maintain its power preponderance, derived from its entrenched position as a leader of space technology and space-enhanced military and economic powers, and proclaim a more imperial or dominating approach to astrostrategy and space-power. Chief among such theories and arguments is Dolman's 2002 *Astropolitik* thesis, an extension of geodeterminist thought to outer space on how space dominance can be achieved, coupled with a normative argument on why the United States should dominate the use of outer space as a benevolent hegemon.[40] Stephen Lambakis in 2001 argued that America should deliberately seek to 'resist all attempts by foreign powers to establish permanent, or even situational, control over any of Earth's orbits' and should remain the pre-eminent space power.[41] Klein's 2006 bluewater and British-American derived maritime strategies takes such thought further and envisions turning space into a barrier, which would allow one side to close off space to its adversary, creating a hegemony in space.[42] The Bush administration's engagement with space-based ballistic missile defence concepts and space-enabled conventional military dominance in the early twenty-first century triggered fears of the expansion of 'the frontier of American empire into low-earth orbit . . . [a] sovereign empire of the future'.[43] Duvall and Havercroft theorise that space-based weapons:

> reconstitutes and alters the social production of political society globally in three interlocked ways that are rooted respectively in the three forms of deploying technologies/cartographies of violence in orbital space identified in the previous section: missile defence; space control; and force application. The conjoint effect of those three technologically induced processes of reconstitution is to substitute the consolidation of an extra-territorial system of rule – which we refer to as empire of the future – for the competitive sovereignties of the modern states-system.[44]

Although they acknowledge the massive technological hurdles to getting space-based weapons technologies to work,[45] the fact that

America's inability 'to target any individual, anywhere on Earth, on very short notice' is ignored, which allows them to theorise that controlling Earth orbit would 'give the possessor . . . unprecedented power to discipline these individual's interests and identities so that their actions comply with the will of the imperial center', including during peacetime economic activity.[46] The argument is based on an ahistorical and atechnological understanding of spacepower and shows the risks of not studying spacepower and decades of military, intelligence, economic and political space history as a specialisation in its own right. Space is a place in its own right and often a realm where 'too often observers lose their minds: becoming infatuated with the twin dreams of instant total destruction achieved by means of a precise antiseptic depersonalized warfare'.[47] Sharing Handberg's frustrations with the state of debate on spacepower, a primary motivating force of this book is that space warfare and the spread of military space systems is not an unprecedented or unduly alarming phenomenon. Spacepower is not entirely new in an abstract and grand strategic sense. It is still about the creation and exploitation of power across a contested medium or geographic environment that cannot be easily held. Spacepower does not herald an era of certain doom and destruction from above and its expense and difficulty will not provide easy solutions to problems on Earth.

For many scholars, as explored in Proposition III in the next chapter, the command of space and dominating the high ground or centre of gravity of Earth orbit underpins and entrenches American hegemony in the minds of readers. Domination-based thinking – the ability of an actor to act with practical impunity in a medium at a time of its choosing – is at odds with the contested nature of a common environment and transitory medium, and is characterised by a constant and conscious struggle to exploit and contest the command of that medium. This theory's starting point is that the command of a medium is normally in dispute, that dominance is not assumed or assured like Corbett demands of seapower theory.[48] A hegemonic perception of outer space strips agency and history away from other space actors by portraying space as a place that has only been militarised by the United States. A cursory reading of international space history will demonstrate the international history of military space programmes through-out the second half of the twentieth century. American actions in space do not occur in a grand strategic vacuum. Another issue with such domination-based thinking is that it tends to view Earth orbit as an ocean and perpetuates traditional forms of the geopo-litical gaze;[49] of a medium that can and should be dominated at a distance by a hegemon, such as Britain at sea in the nineteenth century as sketched often in discussion of hegemonic orders.[50] However, it is evident that even a hegemon at sea, such as the British Empire, could not unilaterally determine the ultimate fate of land-based states.[51] Continental powers, being weaker naval powers, took steps to ensure the Royal Navy did not have free reign in their coastal waters in a time of war. Similarly, space pow-ers are facing a widespread proliferation of anti-satellite technolo-gies on Earth's surface that can make Earth orbit a hostile littoral zone for even the most capable space powers – coastal defence guns by analogy. As detailed later, the bluewater-derived theories tend to implicitly relate space to a realm that can be dominated by a single power through the use of the oceans as a great sepa-rating and separated medium, before industrialisation led to an apparently 'closed' political system on Earth 'where events in one part inevitably have their consequences in all other parts'.[52] The coastal analogy of Proposition V rejects a classical bluewater view of Earth orbit as a separated and distant medium, emphasising the enclosing and contestable nature of spacepower in Earth orbit.

The notion of 'conquering' and 'colonising' space is all too common in popular visions of outer space, whether in the notion of a 'frontier' or as a potential place for settler colonialism. Indeed, the terms of imperialism and its ideological legacies are rife in astrofuturist visions and are difficult to escape in everyday language, where space is seen as a realm of domination and the 'acceptable' creation and conquest of utopia, and not contesta-tion.[53] Correct as it is to critique a continuation of imperialist attitudes and policies which exacerbate predatory development practices into space, the critique of imperial geopolitical intel-lectual history perpetuates the marginalisation of the agency of weaker and non-Western actors, of those who have resisted or checked imperial powers through their own military power,

33

and disguises how modern spacepower as we know it in Earth orbit is a tool for political–military contestation which can be deployed as a check on unquestioned hegemony. This vision is often imposed on space through the bluewater seapower analogies whose concepts, though limiting, provide a useful foundation for spacepower through the connection of spacepower to political objectives, the role of battle and lines of communication. A fixation on imperialism as ideology also lessens the importance of material factors and the universality of war as a socio-political phenomenon in geopolitical analysis. Resistance to empire is intelligible according to the same Clausewitzian principles of passion, reason and chance, and the geopolitical ideas of commanding transitory environments are universal for the strong and the weak. Weaker powers, small states, non-imperial military actors and resistance to any dominant power can be understood and explained according to the same 'universal' logics of strategy, of controlling and denying the use of territory and lines of communication and waging organised violence for political purposes: from centuries of successful Welsh resistance against Anglo-Norman conquest and colonisation,[54] to the successive Indian Zamorin and Maratha efforts to blunt multiple European encroachments with coastal fleet operations,[55] and the decades of firearm-equipped Maori tribes' struggles first against each other and then against the British Army.[56] None of those campaigns was a fait accompli for the imperial power, and understanding successful resistance requires understanding war and strategy. The practice of warfare is universal and not the sole purview of a hegemon, states, conquerors or European empires. The practice of viewing the sea as a dominion is not unique to the European empires, as the Omani sea empire of the seventeenth to nineteenth centuries shows, and naval-based innovations and economic aggrandisement also historically include the Chinese, Japanese and Koreans, particularly in the early-modern and industrial eras.[57] Exerting military power into and from a supporting medium need not be for inherently imperial ambitions.[58] To do that would be an inverse critique of the geopolitical gaze, to implement Eurocentric critiques of military power on what is a universal and 'essential experience' of politics, war, and strategy.[59] Dominance was never a given nor was it inevitable; the eventual imperial victor had to fight and bargain for that eventual domination or political settlement, an activity composed of at least two political entities with a capacity to wage organised violence. Understanding this requires a recognition of material factors such as technology and geography, as well as Clausewitzian principles of war's universal nature. Strategic and IR theory must not ignore the agency of weaker, non-Western or small powers, and the same is true for spacepower theory. This theory is crafted to provide useful abstract insights for any user – or victim – of spacepower.

Spacepower theory emphasises the role of practical resistance, uncertainty and human elements alongside material factors that complicate the picture of American space hegemony which pervades much astropolitical literature. Techno-geographic knowledge is required in IR, and the deleterious effects of an overbearing emphasis on roles and identity, as opposed to techno-geographic conditions, has been noted in defence and security analyses.[60] Deudney notes that swift and significant changes are occurring in material terms in the areas of violence, the environment and information – what he calls 'turbo change'. Conceptualising these factors are a rebuke to

> the schools of theorizing that have grown most rapidly over the last several decades, most notably 'constructivism' and 'post-structuralism,' [which] have largely turned away from explicitly theorizing material contexts . . . The aim of IR theorists should not be to demonstrate that the material is more important than the social or ideational (or vice versa). Instead, IR theory should be asking which practices, identities, and authority structures, in which material contexts, serve to realize which fundamental interests.[61]

Whilst it is true significant change is happening, its speed is debatable, as many of the technologies of spacepower are rather old and are now deployed in their successive generations, and tried and tested technological systems and principles are now more accessible and in greater numbers to more would-be space powers, invoking Edgerton's arguments about the 'shock of the old'.

Regardless, change is afoot in material considerations in international relations and spacepower is a part of that change, both in terms of consequences and sources of change.

Rump material factors generate effects of their own which influence the possibilities and probabilities of outcomes, constrain and enable different activities, and identity-based or relational accounts of power cannot act as if nature did not matter.[62] Being able to shoot what one sees in a timely fashion creates threats and dynamics to battlefield operations that all actors must take into account or seek to deny. Capabilities generate possibilities, but those possibilities are constantly conditioned by geographic factors, regardless of intent. Before capabilities are used there is rarely certainty how any material capability will be used, so a prudent planner must prepare against several of the most likely and dangerous uses of adversarial capabilities, particularly when surprise and doing the unexpected is at a premium in warfare. This is why strategic theory deals in possibilities, not prescriptive action. This practical materialism is a necessary (but not superior) consideration to identity and roles in power analyses and grand strategy.

Studying and theorising practice matters because no war is a matter of simple arithmetic or an 'algebra of action'.[63] The weak or small do not always suffer what they must; military history is replete with examples of smaller powers winning wars or creating no small amount of problems for their apparently stronger adversaries. Passion, reason and chance intrude on any application of brute material power, but material power itself shapes the possibilities of what can be applied in the first place. To study strategy is to study numerous instances of military upsets, of 'certain' successes foiled, easy wins ruined and 'slam dunks' denied. Nuclear weapons certainly are an unavoidable example of material power in IR. Conventional military power is still not entirely meaningless, whether as a flexible crisis response tool or a method to coerce and defeat organised rebellions and non-nuclear regional powers. Spacepower is at the forefront of conventional military changes within Earth's largest and most capable military forces which are developing and adapting to the spread of long-range precision-strike capabilities. Spacepower theory, a geographically orientated form of strategic theory, is an effort to theorise the practical possibilities and relatively objective pressures of outer space as a geography, and the means humans have to exploit, resist and adapt to its capabilities, whilst taking the passion, reason and uncertainty of war into account. To do so, terrestrial experiences can provide useful precedents to understand the possibilities and consequences of spacepower in the celestial coastline. As a result, this theory can only be measured on how successful it is at its pedagogical aims, and in how useful it is in educating its readers and users on the ultimate meaning of spacepower for waging warfare and conducting grand strategy.

Pedagogy and analogy

Spacepower theory is meant to challenge the minds of those who attempt to apply the propositions to their strategies and empirical knowledge of space warfare. If necessary, the propositions should be critiqued, amended, refined or discarded if better alternatives come about through this application of theory to empirical reality. This is done with a methodology that has 'a transparent and resilient conceptual foundation – transparent so that its validity can be challenged and reaffirmed, resilient so as to endure as conditions change'.[64] The seven propositions of spacepower theory are meant to be this transparent and resilient conceptual foundation behind any given strategy about outer space that may be developed for particular actors and times. As a relatively new strategic environment, space warfare may remain 'the undiscovered country' in some empirical respects, but spacepower theory can structure thinking about it in familiar and useful terms.

The seven propositions should not be treated in isolation from Clausewitzian principles of war. Clausewitz's concept of the trinity – that war is a socio-political phenomenon composed of the elements of passion, reason and chance – is important because it anchors spacepower theory's philosophical foundations about war in the same conceptual universe as the canon of classical military theorists in strategic studies. Wars which extend into the celestial coastline of Earth orbit will be conceptually no different to Terran wars. The trinity is a conceptual structure that forms an understanding of war as a three-headed phenomenon, with each head representing a universal element that manifests in reality in wars in very different forms. All wars are emotional, political and chaotic. The trinity identifies the universal tendencies of war between which any theory of war (e.g. spacepower theory) should hold a balance. Identifying the universal aspects of war is essential to understand how any strategic theory can claim to have relevance beyond a particular set of circumstances to a different time and place. It allows us to anticipate broad recurring dilemmas in the conduct and analysis of warfare for practitioners and scholars. It might be that the abstract phenomenon of 'war never changes',[65] but only in conjunction with the understanding that warfare and its actual conduct in reality most certainly changes. This corresponds to Clausewitz's distinctions between an unchanging nature of war, and an ever-morphing character of war.[66] Space warfare is still war, and therefore susceptible to the same conceptualisation. Space technology does not undo war's political, chaotic and emotional nature – it merely changes the way those elements may manifest in the real world.

Alongside the likes of Thucydides and Mahan, Clausewitz shared 'the premise that strategy contains elements independent of contemporary material conditions and common therefore to every time and place'.[67] Chance, passion and reason all play their roles in influencing a war's course and those making decisions in it. These three elements of the trinity should train minds to consider passion, reason and chance as organising factors in all wars. Strands of military thought in the Enlightenment established the general notion that military history and experience could be distilled to reveal some universal principles that may be put to use in future wars.[68] However, Clausewitz retained inclinations towards historicism: that every historical event was unique, moderating ambitions of distilling some form of theoretical truth from experience that could be relevant beyond a particular event's place in time and space.[69] The trinity was Clausewitz's conceptual tool to construct a theory which recognises that war has a certain universal nature that is unchanging and present in every conflict, yet still accommodate constant change and unpredictability in how war happens in reality. Clausewitz would never provide a specific solution to a problem, but would equip his readers with the conceptual tools to come to that answer themselves.

Clausewitz's writings crystallised persistent and recurring command dilemmas in war.[70] Despite all the changes in history and how any war is actually fought and won or lost, hard decisions need to be made, and the forces that make those decisions hard can be generalised in the trinity. Spacepower theory frames difficult choices through the seven propositions, and it does not prescribe which decision may be the correct one in a specific circumstance. This is demonstrated fully in Chapter 6 which frames a Taiwan war from the spacepower perspective and according to the possibilities raised by the propositions of spacepower theory. Spacepower theory explains what strategic principles are at work when considering whether and when to launch a large counterspace offensive or debilitating first strike against enemy space assets like a 'Space Pearl Harbor', but it will not settle the debate as to whether China and America would be best served by striking first in space. Deciding to go to war in the Space Age still involves making hard decisions in a chaotic and political environment. Commanders will continue to suffer from the 'rational and emotional elements of command dilemma',[71] even in an era of orbiting machines, satellite data and precision weapons. Waldman captures the overarching purpose of the trinity and its value to spacepower theory by explaining that the trinity:

> encourages consideration of the essential dynamics that underlie any situation of organised violence waged for political ends. The value of this lies in the way that essentials are often lost in the welter of overpowering images and the inordinate confusion of the 'here and now'.[72]

This is also true of the seven propositions. Strategic theory allows the reader to improve their analysis by comprehending the theory as a tool to assist the analysis of specific scenarios and to organise what would otherwise be a mass of phenomena or superficial observations that could overwhelm analysts. The theory stresses that no matter the situation, good strategy requires asking questions like 'so what?', and whether particular acts alter the nature of command in a medium, or the availability of lines of communication, or the knock-on-effects victories or losses in one place can have in another.

Theory helps the individual to think about, analyse, learn from and apply war plans. Strategic theory should be used to improve the individual's intuitive and deliberate strategic thought about possible actions.[73] This pedagogical intent of strategic theory is common among the major seapower theorists.[74] Often, readers of strategic theory seek support from the theorists to support or justify their war-winning plan. That is a misuse of their intellectual contributions. Corbett and Mahan will not outline how to win a specific maritime war. Yet engaging with their work will assist the reader in coming to a war-winning plan by themselves or judge which course of action may be the better one. It can also help non-practitioners to conceive of decision-making processes in war whilst lacking any direct experience themselves. Similarly, spacepower theory will not by itself provide answers to questions such as how to win wars – but it can help to frame analyses that might provide specific answers to such questions. Clausewitz's work 'is an effort to spare readers the burden of recreating the universe of war . . . whenever they needed to learn about war through books'.[75] The propositions are organising concepts or principles for critical application, self-education, analysis and thought; they are not axioms for action. Spacepower theory's propositions are a conceptual shorthand for others to use rather than having to create them from scratch. In other words, spacepower theory outlines the principles of space strategy, in the same way that Corbett's *Principles of Maritime Strategy* is in effect a seapower theory, and not a maritime strategy.[76] It is up to the reader to create or critique space strategies which may be applicable to specific actors for specific situations. This book only provides the universal concepts to help do so, but those concepts should be useful no matter the scenario or actors involved in space warfare or the use of spacepower. Without such tools and self-education in these concepts, analysts risk falling foul of the many issues raised in observations and concepts of space warfare as discussed throughout the theory's propositions.

Mahan's approach to seapower theory was very much in line with Clausewitz's own, and only strengthens its value as a base to draw from for spacepower theory.[77] Sumida writes that: 'he did not reject contradiction, but rather embraced it, recognizing that its production was inherent to the intelligent consideration of what was a range of possibility'.[78] Such an epistemology – a view as to what kind of knowledge strategic theory is – can be found from Sun Tzu's ancient text to Colin Gray's latest offering on airpower theory.[79] This theory requires a willingness by the reader to engage in learning of a highly individual and self-critical nature. Readers of this book should always critically apply the propositions and their arguments as they relate to the cases they are interested in, and not dogmatically accept them.

This theory cannot be 'falsified' in a positivist sense. It can be replaced with something that is more useful at educating the reader about the violent application of spacepower in grand strategy. Educational theory about practice is different to an analytical framework which intends to describe the totality of a phenomenon or object. For example, pioneering research on the English School and International Society as it applies to space aims to apply the

> analytical concept of international space society . . . [which] can enrich the study of the international politics of space as well as our understanding of the behaviour of China and India as rising space-faring actors in terms of their interaction with international space society. This is an important consideration, not the least because most analyses on the international politics of space are largely descriptive and 'undertheorised'.[80]

Stroikos's approach asks different questions, makes different knowledge claims, and aims to engage in a more analytical and explanatory role of political, economic and security behaviour in space, which is more concerned with peaceful or at least non-violent relations between members of the 'international space society' and the causal factors for such behaviour. Such is the purview of IR theory of most kinds, which tends to ask causal, relational or taxonomic questions. Spacepower theory is a theory of a different kind with different knowledge claims, or epistemology. Harding argues that spacepower theory possesses 'some solid pillars [from terrestrial thought] but yet [is] still unsure of its own place in international relations theory'.[81]

Contrary to that view, this book's spacepower theory offers a clear positioning of spacepower theory within the larger context of IR. As violence, destruction and their threat is the heart of war and of strategic theory, spacepower theory as a derivative of how to think about applying military power is epistemologically separate yet ontologically related to IR theory. Strategic theory, and spacepower theory as a result, does not probe the meanings or causes of anarchy in the international system, why states may go to war, or why particular actors choose various paths of economic development or patronage, whether domestically or internationally. Rather, strategic theory engages in how to structure thought, analysis and scrutiny about the practice of killing and destruction for political ends, a practice which no actor or IR theory can ignore. Just as seapower or airpower theory has never aimed to categorise every single aspect in how a state may use the sea or the air, spacepower theory must itself not become involved in every aspect of space politics and development. Spacepower theory is about the instrumentalisation of violence with space technology; it is about war, not the entirety of relations between actors in space. To invoke spacepower theory and its canon of theorists and intellectual traditions of strategic studies when studying all of astropolitics – much of which is benign, infrastructural, everyday, transactional – is to betray and unduly sanitise the violent, combative and othering subject matter of strategic theory.

This pedagogical approach is at odds with those who wish to develop specific strategies for specific space powers, or those who wish to create prescriptive, descriptive, explanatory or taxonomic theories. Some scholars conflate a space strategy with a spacepower theory, with the former being a specific plan for action in a time and place for an actor, and the latter being universal principles to guide thinking about action in any time and for any actor.[82] For example, Ziarnick believes a general spacepower theory must be able to

> include all space activities and offers insight into which activities are most valuable for aspiring space powers . . . to explain actions

[including] coloniz[ing] the Moon ... how commercial, political, and military space power interact with each other ... [offer] specific advice on what space power must do to gain, develop, and keep space power ... [and] to bridge the gap between military realism and enthusiast futurism.[83]

This is not to critique other theories in terms of their intent, content and epistemology, merely to outline that they try to do or claim very different things at the same time which may place too heavy a burden on any single 'theory'. Ziarnick's work is taxonomical, multi-epistemological, American-centric and displays a strong geopolitical gaze by invoking 'conquest' and 'colonisation' in its assumptions, language and recommendations.[84] This is in contrast to the pedagogical and military- and strategy-oriented spacepower theory, analogising from established military thought in strategic studies.

Declaring that space warfare is the continuation of Terran politics by other means extends the universe of strategic studies to outer space. It gives space warfare its political rationale and clarifies its quality as a socio-political phenomenon. The methodological link between Clausewitzian theory and analogical reasoning which influences the seven propositions of spacepower emerges strongly here. There is a consistency to the complexity and diversity of strategic experience;[85] and analogical reasoning is necessary to bridge the gaps between the vast particulars of each case of strategic experience, to distil recurring dilemmas and form some useful observations to guide thinking about an uncertain future. Through this fundamental analogy of Clausewitzian military thought to outer space, we can ask how wars on Earth and their associated strategic theories can provide insight into warfare in orbit and the grand strategic consequences of space technology on Earth. This analogy is well founded in the traditions of strategic studies which is constantly taking strategic concepts from diverse sources and authors and applying them to yet more diverse situations, walking a fine line between the worlds of history and theory. A sufficient grasp of historical method and its limitations is required to understand the limitations of empirical study and analogical thinking. History should be embraced within strategic studies and IR, much like the 'classical tradition . . . perhaps most obvious in figures such as Niebuhr, Carr and Morgenthau, which intimately associated the craft of international theory with deep immersion in history'.[86] There are no 'fixed points of historical settlement' and it can be viewed as an 'undecideable infinity of possible truths'.[87] Strategic theory tends towards generalisations and nomothetic inquiry whilst maintaining a requirement for historicism and idiographic epistemology. Spacepower theory must be in constant interaction and reflection with reality – be it in historical terms or in use in the present world. Strategic analogies are a means of developing higher-level critical thinking skills that may be extended to the entirety of war studies and Clausewitzian theorising.[88]

Handel argued that 'the contradictions within each of [the works of inter alia Clausewitz, Sun Tzu, Jomini and Mao] are more interesting than the contradictions between them'.[89] In contemplating these apparent internal contradictions, rather than resolving them, he hoped that the individual achieves a better understanding of war. As the spacepower theory demonstrates, the canon of strategic theorists are notable for how they grapple with similar problems by themselves, and not in how they argue against each other. Such a view may fall victim to the 'mythology of doctrines', or 'reading us in them'.[90] This 'myth of doctrine', however, is not necessarily so insensitive to proponents of historicism. The theorists used in spacepower theory are all Clausewitzian in the sense that they aim to promote structured critical thinking assisted with useful rules of thumb based on the complexity, diversity and contingency of historical experience, historical knowledge and the perils of considering action in an uncertain present. The point of strategic theory 'is not necessarily to resolve or eliminate every anomaly, but rather to understand why wrestling with these questions can bring better insight into the nature of war'.[91] The Prussian elaborated that principles, rules and methods are there to be used 'as required, and it must always be left for judgment to decide whether they are suitable or not . . . the person acting is to use them merely as aids to judgment'.[92]

Clausewitz argued that war is just a branch of political activity, and not autonomous, adding that as all wars are of the same nature it provides the basis to compare and judge different wars.[93] War as a continuation of political activity is a strategic concept that Clausewitz uses to infer strategic analogies between different wars. All wars are conceived of as something political in nature, therefore we may be able to detect or anticipate the recurring dilemmas of chance, friction, uncertainty, reason, command talent (genius), and passion because they were dilemmas that could be abstractly observed or sought out in at least one known case of war. This can then direct inquiry and scrutiny to discover how the lesser-studied historical war, or one yet to occur based on the best information available, manifested these characteristics, but also to highlight the particular differences in each case. This would be a strategic analogy and its application; transposing strategic theory or concepts from one or many cases to another to attempt to discover something useful about a new or lesser-known topic.

All acts of strategic theorising through Clausewitzian concepts are instances of analogical reasoning to some degree. A strategic analogy is the transposition of a strategic theory or concept derived from any particular case of warfare or strategic dilemma to another. The strategic dilemmas may differ in almost any conceivable way but can be analysed with similar rules of thumb. All wars are the same thing: a contest to impose will between opponents by the threat or use of force; a continuation of politics with the addition of other means; an activity composed of passion, reason and chance. This is contrasted with historical analogies which transpose historical outcomes, causal claims, or conclusions to another episode. Strategic analogies transpose concepts to new conditions. Because all wars are things of the same inherently political, chaotic and passionate nature, useful comparisons and contrasts can be drawn between cases, with a contest of political wills being the standard against which different cases of war are held in order to identify recurring dilemmas and draw generalisable observations to provide an education for those who lack strategic experience. The idea that all wars are political in nature is a useful starting point to delve into the particulars of the case at hand and make such a case study useful to researchers and practitioners. This book analogises classic terrestrial concepts such as commanding a medium, lines of communication, friction, military culture, concentration, and dispersal into orbit and how those concepts may shift in practice on Earth in light of the proliferation of spacepower.

John Sheldon argues that 'strategic analogies may provide a "shortcut to rationality" in new and poorly understood strategic environments where there is no known strategic experience or established principles for effective operations'.[94] A strategic analogy can be used between two geographical environments but some political and strategic conceptual unity is believed to be common among them. This is what Colin Gray refers to as a unity in strategic experience irrespective of time and geography.[95] Both the sea and space (as well as land and air) are subject to strategic logic in a contest of wills where war is the continuation of politics, and is the foundational analogy that this spacepower theory relies upon. Analogies, like metaphors, are useful pedagogical tools but require care in their construction and use. Part of that care requires transparency and consciousness about the limitations of their use, a discussion all too rare in IR and punditry which is replete with poor historical analogies.[96] Responsible analogies begin with knowing their limits.[97] It is difficult to be able to approach a problem or issue of any kind with a clean conceptual slate. Few may be free from the logics of their own 'rational' assumptions.[98] Sheldon argues that

> history, like analogies, suffers from inherent limitations that automatically affect the quality and reliability of both strategic and historical analogies. Often, the history used in analogies is treated as self-evident, complete, and objective, when in fact nothing could be further from the truth.[99]

Strategic analogies, as products of the use of historical analogies, rely on historical studies – taking on board their subjective and often contested form of knowledge. Often the uses of historical analogies do not engage with historiography. History is not scripture, nor is it a database of empirical information or ready-made 'lessons' that can be transposed to new situations.[100] This book is not about history, therefore analogical sources must be challenged if a reading or interpretations of the specific arguments of inter alia Mahan, Corbett and Castex or their military histories are critiqued in terms of historiographic debate – but with a view as to how historical detail changes the concepts and theory, if at all. Whilst Mahan may have some historical details incorrect in light of modern historical scholarship, it may not undermine the general principles of seeking blockade and commerce warfare as indirect pressures on continental adversaries.

Analogical reasoning may not help to identify a crucial difference between the source (seapower theory) and target (spacepower theory), or the source may create the illusions of the workings of a principle in the target that may not actually apply.[101] An example is the false analogy that satellites are analogous to battleships and satellite constellations are like fleets, as some thinkers have written. Satellites transmit information, they do not directly execute violence, like battleships or coastal attack and patrol craft. The closest analogy would be space-based weapons, which are not deployed in a meaningful sense at present but embryonic systems which could be deployed as weapons do exist, and do so in the constrained littoral environment of Earth orbit. This false analogy can lead to problematic applications of concepts of 'fleet' manoeuvring, a fleet in being, and concentration and dispersal in orbit that are not that useful to explore the realities of operating satellite constellations. These are explored further in Propositions I, IV, V and VII. Furthermore, the resonance of some aspects of seapower theory for spacepower is not a blank cheque for others to claim the existence of other analogical resonances from seapower theory. Seapower concepts that are not used in this book should not be assumed to work. This is not a blanket application of seapower theory; this theory has deliberately attempted to avoid an uncritical or unreflective exercise in analogical reasoning. The spacepower theory blends seapower analogies into a simultaneous discussion of the propositions of spacepower. The intent of this book is to present a spacepower theory, and is not a comprehensive review everything the seapower theorists have to say about seapower and maritime histories, and not all of what the spacepower theorists have to say about spacepower. This spacepower theory presents 'what works' as a coherent whole, and critiques existing theories where necessary, mixing argumentation into the pedagogy. The promises and pitfalls of analogies cannot be ignored whilst reading the seven propositions, making them transparent and more amenable to constructive critique and hopefully better subsequent theorising by the reader.

Conclusion

The propositions should produce a net gain for strategic thought and education about space, and that 'even bad theory can be harnessed in the service of making good strategic theory, if only to act as a means of proving how spacepower does not work'.[102] Even if the propositions developed are deemed bad theory by some, their application or critique might yet yield some useful results if better observations and theories take their place, fulfilling their heuristic epistemology. Strategic analogies are a means to provide general propositions. These are then intended to be declarations that should trigger critical thinking in readers about space warfare as a continuation of Terran politics. The seven propositions form a spacepower theory which stresses the need to think about practice in space warfare in an IR landscape that has eschewed strategic theory and the empirical realities of spacepower. Considering the practical and material aspects of spacepower should caution against any simplistic notion of accepting an American hegemony in Earth orbit, or a fear of a space-enabled empire. Earth orbit is a highly contested environment that, due to the multipolar nature of nuclear and space technological diffusion and its proximity to the influence of Earth-based powers itself, cannot sustain an unquestioned hegemony in orbit or on Earth. Beyond the specific content of the propositions, this theory should show why IR and strategic studies needs to take space seriously as a geographic specialism in its own right on a par with land, naval and aerial warfare and the supporting influences they provide for a war effort and grand strategy. With this theory, the terms of debating spacepower in international relations should be advanced by providing concepts that allow analysts and scholars to understand spacepower on its own terms in a way that is intelligible to non-space specialists.

Before delving into the next chapter and the first four propositions of spacepower theory, it is useful to re-state the seven propositions as a whole:

I. Space warfare is waged for the command of space
II. Spacepower is uniquely infrastructural and connected to Earth
III. The command of space does not equate to the command of Earth
IV. The command of space manipulates celestial lines of communication
V. Earth orbit is a cosmic coastline suited for strategic manoeuvres
VI. Spacepower exists within a geocentric mindset
VII. Spacepower is dispersed and imposes dispersion on Earth

Propositions I–IV are outlined in the next chapter, and are the result of engagement and constructive critique of existing spacepower theories, of which most draw upon a bluewater seapower analogy where Earth orbit is seen as a vast ocean. Familiar concepts of controlling and denying geographic mediums and lines and communications are introduced, as well as the role of decisive battle and specialist requirements in a joint environment as they apply to outer space. Propositions V and VI build upon these first four propositions as the result of a new vision of spacepower in Earth orbit as a celestial coastline, a littoral zone and secondary theatre of operations that is highly proximate to the primary theatres of Earth itself. With spacepower acting predominantly as a supporting type of capability in grand strategy, its effects are often indirect and Earth orbit may be the scene of subtle manoeuvres to assist strategies on Earth, rather than a scene destined to witness major conflagrations. This also allows spacepower theory to break new ground by theorising the bulk of space activity in warfare for the first time – how services and data from space indirectly influence wars and the conduct of strategy, rather than fixating upon space weapons and anti-satellite operations at the expense of all else. In this way Earth orbit resembles the influence of seapower and coastal operations in continental wars, both in terms of the influence of spacepower in strategy and in the cultural attitudes of terrestrially bound states towards this secondary and relatively esoteric theatre of outer space, mimicking the fate of naval culture in continental strategic cultures. Proposition VII brings the larger strategic considerations of Propositions I–VI down to Earth – it theorises the pervasive influence of spacepower on the modern battlefield, and how it can be best conceptualised as a dispersing influence, continuing the trends of increasing the scale of the tactical battlefield on Earth and improving the ability of evermore dispersed forces to concentrate firepower with terrifying accuracy. Modern warfare will in part take shape according to the ability of terrestrial military forces to exploit and resist friendly and hostile pressures of dispersion, as well as the other indirect effects covered in Proposition V, imposed on them and their foes from the 'coastline' of Earth orbit, itself then driving the importance of commanding space upwards in the minds of military planners, bringing the theory full circle to where it began. The nature of commanding space, and what it entails in how we think about grand strategy and political objectives is where the theory begins in the next chapter.

Notes

1. Posen, 'Command of the Commons'.
2. Anson and Cummings, 'First Space War', p. 45.
3. Preston, *Plowshares*, p. 3.
4. Sheehan, *International Politics*, p. 5.
5. Core texts: Dolman, *Astropolitik*; Klein, *Space Warfare*; Lutes et al., *Toward a Theory of Spacepower*; Lupton, *On Space Warfare*.
6. Bowen, 'British Strategy', p. 323.
7. There are many grounds for space not fulfilling strict legal definitions of an international common. See: Hertzfeld et al., 'How simple terms mislead us'.
8. Lupton, *On Space Warfare*, p. 7.
9. Lambakis, *On the Edge*, p. 46.
10. Lutes et al., 'Introduction', p. xiv.
11. Sheldon and Gray, 'Theory Ascendant?', p. 2; Pfaltzgraff, 'International Relations', p. 40; Gray and Sheldon, 'Space Power', p. 36; Sheehan, *International Politics*, p. 20.

12. Al-Rodhan, *Meta-Geopolitics*, p. 25.
13. Ziarnick, *Developing National Power in Space*, p. 13.
14. Klein, *Space Warfare*, pp. 35–43.
15. Stroikos, *China, India in Space*, p. 256.
16. Dolman, *Astropolitik*, p. 37.
17. For example: Al-Rodhan, *Meta-Geopolitics*, pp. 22, 24–5; Mendenhall, 'Treating Outer Space'; Sheldon, *Reasoning*, pp. 22–6.
18. Bowen, 'British Strategy', pp. 324–8.
19. Carr, *The Twenty Years' Crisis*, pp. 108, 132.
20. Dolman, *Astropolitik*, pp. 70–5, 130–4.
21. Hays and Lutes, 'Toward a Theory', p. 208.
22. Sheetz, 'The space industry'.
23. Pace et al., *The Global Positioning System*, pp. 12–17.
24. Ibid. pp. 17–18.
25. Posen, 'Command of the Commons', p. 13.
26. Ibid. p. 9.
27. Hilborne, 'China's Rise', p. 124.
28. Weeden, 'Dancing in the dark'; Weeden, 'Through a Glass'; Weeden, 'Dancing in the dark redux'.
29. Cheng, 'China's Military Role in Space', p. 57.
30. Mahnken, 'Weapons', p. 48.
31. Anson and Cummings, 'First Space War', p. 45.
32. For example, see: US Department of Defense (DOD), 'Summary of the National Defense Strategy'; US DOD, 'Annual Report to Congress', pp. 36–7, 59–61; Easton and Stokes, 'China's Electronic Intelligence'; Erickson, 'Chinese Air- and Space-Based ISR'.
33. Weeden and Samson, *Global Counterspace Capabilities*.
34. US Defense Intelligence Agency, 'Challenges to Security in Space', pp. 20–2, 28–9; Weeden, 'Through a glass'.
35. For example: Oberhaus, 'India's anti-satellite test'.
36. Johnson-Freese, *Space Warfare*, pp. 58–63.
37. For example: Duvall and Havercroft, 'Taking Sovereignty', pp. 755–6; Hunter and Bowen, 'Donald Trump's Space Force'.
38. Johnson-Freese, *Space Warfare*, pp. 88, 181.
39. Sheehan, 'Counterspace Operations', p. 96.
40. Dolman, *Astropolitik*, see the final chapter in particular.
41. Lambakis, *On the Edge*, pp. 275–6.
42. Klein, *Space Warfare*, pp. 100–6.
43. Duvall and Havercroft, 'Taking Sovereignty', p. 757.
44. Ibid. p. 763.
45. Ibid. p. 762.

46. Havercroft and Duvall, 'Critical Astropolitics'; Duvall and Haver-croft, 'Taking Sovereignty', p. 766.
47. Handberg, *Seeking New World Vistas*, p. 1.
48. Corbett, *Principles of Maritime Strategy*, p. 87.
49. Ó Tuathail, *Critical Geopolitics*, p. 25; Ziarnick, *Developing National Power in Space*, pp. 11, 21–2.
50. Wohlforth, 'Hegemonic Decline', pp. 111–12, 122–9; Posen, *Restraint*, p. 138.
51. Nye, *The Future*, pp. 154–5; Mearsheimer, *The Tragedy*, pp. 81–2.
52. Ó Tuathail, *Critical Geopolitics*, p. 27.
53. Kilgore, *Astrofuturism*, p. 51.
54. Davies, *The Age of Conquest*.
55. Panikkar, *India*, esp. pp. 40–67.
56. Belich, *The New Zealand Wars*.
57. Till, *Seapower*, 3rd edition, pp. 15–16.
58. Ibid. p. 16.
59. Gray, *Modern Strategy*, pp. 1, 8.
60. Gaskarth, 'Strategizing Britain's Role', p. 561, taken from: Bowen, 'British Strategy', p. 326; Porter, 'Geography, Strategy, and the National Interest', pp. 4–6.
61. Deudney, 'Turbo Change', pp. 226–8.
62. Wendt, *Social Theory*, pp. 96, 110–11.
63. Clausewitz, *On War*, p. 266.
64. Kiesling, 'Introduction', p. xviii.
65. The verbal leitmotif of the post-apocalyptic videogame series *Fallout*.
66. Gray, *Strategy and History*, p. 82; and: Clausewitz, *On War*, pp. 277–8.
67. Kiesling, 'Introduction', p. xiii
68. For an overview of Enlightenment military thought and Clausewitz, see: Gat, *A History*, Book I.
69. Ibid. pp. 188–9.
70. Sumida, *Decoding Clausewitz*, p. 45.
71. Ibid. p. 45.
72. Waldman, *War*, p. 179.
73. Sumida, *Decoding Clausewitz*, pp. 127, 135.
74. For example, see: Sumida, *Inventing Grand Strategy*, pp. xv–xviii, 6–7, 44, 67, 69. On agreement here with Corbett and Castex, see: Corbett, *Principles of Maritime Strategy*, pp. 1–9; Castex, *Strategic Theories*, pp. 21–5.
75. Echevarria, *Clausewitz*, p. 26.

76. Bowen, 'From the Sea', p. 535.
77. Sumida, *Inventing Grand Strategy*, pp. 104–5, 109–14.
78. Ibid. p. 106.
79. Sun Tzu, *The Art of Warfare*, pp. 275–7; Gray, *Airpower for Strategic Effect*.
80. Stroikos, *China, India in Space*, p. 11.
81. Harding, *Space Policy*, p. 19.
82. As explored in more depth in: Bowen, 'From the Sea', pp. 534–7.
83. Ziarnick, *Developing National Power in Space*, pp. 10–11.
84. Ibid. see throughout, but especially pp. 1–7, 9–11, 19–22, 27–30, 45, 47–51, 54–61, 75–105.
85. Waldman, *War*, p. 179.
86. Lawson, 'The Eternal Divide?', p. 206.
87. Ibid. pp. 207–8.
88. Sheldon, *Reasoning*, p. 297.
89. Handel 2001.
90. Lawson, 'The Eternal Divide', p. 216.
91. Handel, *Masters of War*, p. 7.
92. Clausewitz, *On War*, p. 366.
93. Ibid. pp. 279–82, 933–4.
94. Sheldon, *Reasoning*, p. 19.
95. Gray, *Modern Strategy*, pp. 1, 8.
96. Notable exceptions: Macdonald, *Rolling the Iron Dice*; Yuen, *Analogies at War*.
97. Fischer, *Historians' Fallacies*, p. 258.
98. Ibid. pp. xvi, 4.
99. Sheldon, *Reasoning*, p. 24.
100. Lawson, 'The Eternal Divide', p. 205.
101. Sheldon, *Reasoning*, p. 22.
102. Ibid. p. 297.

2. Commanding Space: Bluewater Foundations

Viewing outer space as an ocean that strategic actors can exploit for advantages is a rather intuitive approach to spacepower. Like the sea, space is home to objects that transmit communications and data through volumes which cannot be held or conquered in themselves. The works of Alfred Thayer Mahan and Julian Corbett provide an essential foundation for strategic thinking about space because they provide universal concepts regarding the command of a transitory medium, the nature of battle, and the lines of communications within them. Most spacepower theories are derived at least in part and at most directly analogised from bluewater or oceanic approaches to seapower which draw upon maritime empires, great distances and island-based powers exercising a dominant command of the oceans. This view of spacepower is a necessary starting point, but does not adequately articulate the proximate and more contested qualities of spacepower in Earth orbit as done from Proposition V onwards. The first four propositions detail the nature of commanding space – of controlling and denying the use of space infrastructure – and its subordination towards terrestrial political objectives, on the unique yet connected nature of Earth orbit as a separate geography, on decisive battle and the strategic influence of commanding space, and the manifestation of lines of communication in Earth orbit. These concepts and their naval origins have informed the work of many spacepower theorists. The works of Klein, Smith, Dolman, Sheldon and Gray are crucial sources of such thought. Through a critical analysis of their work, and the bluewater seapower theorists they often draw upon, four spacepower theory propositions are formed. The propositions' headlines do not represent the totality of arguments of the spacepower theorists, rather they are the outcome of a critical engagement with their works. These first four propositions are:

I.   Space warfare is waged for the command of space
II. Spacepower is uniquely infrastructural and connected to Earth
III. The command of space does not equate to the command of Earth
IV. The command of space manipulates celestial lines of communication

Propositions I–IV are shorter as their concepts are more familiar and have already been analogised by others to space, meaning that less exposition is needed to explain them. These first four propositions also represent the foundations of the theory because they link political objectives and grand strategy to the specialism of spacepower in an era of joint warfare, how to think about controlling and denying the use of Earth orbit through the overarching idea of the command of space, on questioning the concepts of seeking battle in space and the centre of gravity, and to considering how lines of communication and blockading works with spacepower. Propositions V, VI and VII represent the bulk of new contributions to spacepower theory and require more exposition. The fact that I–IV are described more briefly does not reduce their importance – all seven propositions are required for a holistic comprehension of spacepower's influence in modern warfare.

Proposition I: Space warfare is waged for the command of space

Acts of space warfare must influence who commands space to what degree if such acts of warfare are to have strategic meaning in a war. The command of space itself only has bearing in how it affects grand strategic objectives on Earth. Spacepower becomes relevant to Terran warfare and grand strategy if that command of space enhances or frustrates the military, intelligence, commercial and infrastructural uses of outer space in a way that contributes to the ultimate objectives of a grand strategy. Whatever those objectives are is not the concern of spacepower theory beyond what actions they necessitate and legitimise for use in war, along with their possible consequences. The command of space is the starting point of spacepower theory because it connects space warfare and spacepower towards terrestrial grand strategy, which gives the command of space its ultimate objective. That command of space can be composed of controlling and denying space, or one or the other, as exploiting space for terrestrial wars is not the same as simply denying that to an enemy. Command is about influencing who gets to use Earth orbit to what degree, and how.

Spacepower must have relevant effects on Earth for commanding space to pay dividends for terrestrial states. Space infrastructure provides force enhancements which make terrestrial military forces more precise, rapid, mobile, coordinated, survivable and efficient. Targeting this infrastructure is therefore a necessary part of war planning; the development of anti-satellite or counterspace technologies is not an idle technological exercise. Spacepower, or its denial, is inherently supportive towards terrestrial requirements, but that support requires a sufficient command of that medium to be relevant to and dependable in a terrestrial war effort. Since war is a political and social activity, space warfare must affect what people care most about and where they live for it to create strategic effects. Spacepower is important for strategic theory and practice in what it allows your terrestrial forces to do. Corbett famously declared that:

> since men live upon the land and not upon the sea, great issues . . . have always been decided – except in the rarest of cases – either by what your army can do against your enemy's territory and national life, or else by the fear of what the fleet makes it possible for your army to do.[1]

In the same vein, Mahan theorised that:

> the service between the bases and the mobile force between the ports and fleets is mutual. In this respect the navy is essentially a light

corps; it keeps open the communications between its own ports, it obstructs those of the enemy; but it sweeps the sea for the service of the land, it controls the desert that man may live and thrive on the habitable globe.[2]

Mahan's view of seapower's supporting functions transposes well to contemporary spacepower and how modern force enhancement, economic development and environmental monitoring on our blue planet are provided by spacepower. Space infrastructure itself has become useful for 'national life' in the early twenty-first century and therefore can make for potentially attractive targets. The command of space influences Terran warfare, but terrestrial capabilities can influence the command of space as well. The interactions between the celestial and terrestrial environments, as well as the political objectives of a war, make for an indecisive and unpredictable relationship where effects in one environment have to be exploited to impose their influence and outcomes in other environments, and not assumed as a matter of course.

The command of space forms a two-way connection between spacepower and grand strategy, much in the same way that the command of the sea makes the student or practitioner of war think of the role of seapower in a wider war based on the control, denial and exploitation of the sea. Both the control and denial of space can be sought in order to secure or contest the command of space and exploit that command on Earth. Whether through controlling space infrastructure or denying its use, the command of space refers to the influence one can project upon the use and non-use of the medium and theatre of Earth orbit. The command of space must in turn be exploited for spacepower to have strategic effects on Earth. That is, without a degree of the command of space, you cannot shape or influence how you or others can use outer space to meet objectives on Earth. This proposition holds true regardless of the type of weapon, method or basing employed. Whether through a nuclear strike, a space blockade, a comprehensive jamming effort, or hijacking satellites through cyber or computer network infiltration, they must all be made for the objective of influencing one's own control and denying the enemy the use of space infrastructure. Through methods of space control and denial, the command of space is exerted in specific times and places to support the pursuit of the ultimate purposes of the conflict at hand. Waging space warfare and commanding space is meaningless without tying it to supreme political objectives on Earth – a strategic reality developed further as a geocentric condition of spacepower discussed in Proposition V.

The command of space and the sub-concepts of control and denial are universally relevant in space warfare. Whether a dominant spacepower has achieved a confident control of most orbits and desired satellites, or a weaker power has achieved a momentary denial of various parts of space to the enemy so that its ground forces can act more securely, they are both commanding space to a degree and seeking to exploit that command on Earth. Commanding space is not the same as controlling space infrastructure. Being in command of relevant parts or volumes of space is not synonymous with controlling relevant space infrastructure; indeed, denying the use of certain orbits means only that one is commanding the non-use of certain orbits. This means that a power without an elaborate space infrastructure, but with rudimentary Earth-based anti-satellite weapons, can try to contest the command of space through a space denial campaign. An influence can be exerted in Earth orbit without a large presence based in orbit itself, such as simply ruining sections of orbit with debris or radiation.

Space control, as a sub-concept of the command of space, distances the theory from how space control is used within the confines of the American doctrinal and policy-advocacy space weaponisation debates, where one school is labelled as 'space control'.[3] Space control is one form of commanding space with a mind to possessing and exploiting an elaborate space infrastructure (satellite constellations, extensive terrestrial down- and up-link communications hubs, launch complexes, etc.). Controlling space tends to denote an ability to use one's own most essential celestial lines of communication without major disruption. Visions of space control tend to gravitate towards a large, perhaps dominating space power that harnesses spacepower for terrestrial warfare and economics on Earth.[4] When it controls space, it can make the effects of its spacepower felt in wars on Earth with ease and confidence in the most vital occasions. This has comfortable parallels to seapower theory, which are explored below.

Denying the use of celestial lines of communication, discussed further in Proposition IV, is still attempting to command space, as it refers to the ability to project influence into space with regard to who can use it in which way. A power able to only deny celestial lines of communication still possesses a degree of the command of space, an influence it can exert in orbit to shape the behaviour of the adversary on Earth. A successful denial operation – like crippling a few select satellites at a crucial time – may enable successful military operations on Earth whilst an opposing spacepower's usual support networks are impaired. Denial tends to prevent an enemy exploitation of an elaborate space infrastructure, whilst control intends to enable the exploitation of space infrastructure. Whether a space strategy in a war rests upon ensuring space control or space denial, they are both concerned with influencing the command of space in their favour, and must exploit it for strategic effect on Earth. It is possible that both sides may choose to engage in such acts of space warfare as to render Earth orbit unusable for both sides, meaning both sides have engaged in space denial as a form of commanding space, whilst both sides have lost the ability to control space because of their lost space infrastructure. Control and denial are two necessary distinctions of commanding space because being able to use space is different to being able to deny it to the adversary.

To have any strategic meaning any action must help to control or deny that medium, to contribute to the overall command of space, which then allows for the exploitation of that medium to create effects for the war on Earth. Such is the foundational theoretical truth espoused by spacepower theory, as derived from seapower and airpower theories. This concept is the foundation from which further strategic concepts for spacepower theory are developed. It also acts as a hedge against any discussion or theories of spacepower becoming bogged down in tactical or technological weeds – most notably on the merits or lack thereof of space-based weaponry. Whatever the merits of a system or the ways of war are, all must credibly influence the command of space in a time of war so that such acts have strategic effects and grand strategic utility. The command of space means that the strategic object of space warfare is always to secure and/or deny the use of celestial lines of communication where objects and information travel in, from, towards and through space.[5]

As spacepower is now so ubiquitous and proliferated the command of space can generate effects on all levels, from the tactical to the grand strategic, and in the political, economic and societal realms. The command of space highlights the common purpose of space control and denial, especially as space-based systems can be used to better target the enemy's ability to control its own space systems. Control and denial signify different activities, yet they often impact each other. No strict categorisation should be made in practice, as control and denial can be employed and mixed by both large and small spacepowers to varying degrees. Whether an action fits more into a denial or control framing could depend on its context and particular effects, rather than on the means used. This is especially important given the use of 'control', denial', 'offensive' and 'defensive space control' terms in space doctrine language.[6] This corresponds to Clausewitz's practical approach to terms that drive at the heart of concepts but are blurred at their edges.[7]

The concept of the command of space exposes the possibility of space denial being the primary objective of a space strategy and therefore what an actor's command of space may look like, as opposed to commanding space in order to control space infrastructure. If a state has only counterspace capabilities, it need not necessarily be the case that it has satellite constellations of its own or space-enabled and enhanced terrestrial forces, such as North Korea. Space denial operations alone improves the odds of success for terrestrial operations by levelling the terrestrial battlefield somewhat by denying a degree of the adversary's spacepower support to its terrestrial forces for a specific engagement. Denying space control to another does not inherently result in an ability to exploit space systems for oneself. Exerting a command of space is therefore open to all actors with the necessary technological capability. Depending how far one wishes to control or deny the use of space infrastructure, different levels of commanding space are required. This shows the value of distinguishing between space control and space denial, yet subordinating them to terrestrial political strategy through the overarching concept of commanding space, as both control and denial space strategies aim to influence and exploit a possession of a commanding influence in orbit.

The command of space encourages a space-centric and single-environment mode of thought without undermining the 'joint' realities of modern warfare. Whether a high-altitude nuclear strike from North Korea disables American and allied spacepower, or the United States isolates Iraq from space communications in a space blockade, or China disrupts America's space infrastructure in a Taiwan war, all such campaigns are conceptually alike in how they engage in space warfare to dispute or exploit the command of space for advantages on Earth's varied environments, using a mix of control and denial methods. To illustrate the workings of command, seapower's influence in spacepower theory can be drawn upon. With a strong and intuitive conceptual resonance from the sea to space, many spacepower theorists have analogised accordingly from bluewater seapower theory. Gray claims that 'controlling space is the idea that most usefully directs attention to the emerging status of the space environment as a (global) combat "theatre."'[8] Furthermore, the basic idea of commanding the sea as analogous to commanding space 'accommodates the minor qualifications . . . that our space/sea forces will suffer some harassment and losses in space/at sea, and that the enemy will be able to secure erratic and minor-scale access to some orbits/put to sea in a small way'.[9] Dolman's *Astropolitik* advocates dominating the medium through geopolitically derived chokepoints in accessing orbit and various transfer routes and lanes of commerce into other regions of the cosmos.[10] Klein's work made an important contribution by analogising Corbett's core seapower theory and stressed the usefulness of celestial lines of communication for the instruments of state power.[11] The notion of commanding the sea translates well enough into orbit, so much so that merely changing key naval terms to refer to outer space does the concept justice in Corbett's own words and following Klein's lead:

By winning [the] command of [space] we . . . [place] ourselves in position to exert direct military pressure on the national life of our enemy [on Earth], whilst at the same time we solidify [a barrier] against him and prevent his exerting direct military pressure on ourselves . . . [The] command of [space], therefore, means nothing but the control of [celestial] communications, whether for commercial or military purposes. The object of [space] warfare is the control of communications, and not, as in land warfare, the conquest of territory.[12]

This strategic analogy is an essential foundation to spacepower theory. However, analogising from bluewater seapower theory that is restricted to experiences of imperial ocean-spanning conflicts sometimes distorts spacepower theory by analogising satellites in orbit as battleships in relatively isolated seas, and implies that an opposing space power must also have ocean-going assets or vehicles in orbit to be taken seriously as a threat. Such views of seapower are based upon armed ships at sea with seapowers' interests separated by large distances, and that only sea lines of communication connect them. Using only a bluewater vision of seapower creates an illusion of the need for space-based cruisers to protect and strangle space-based commerce, and obscures the actual threats of the proliferation of Earth-based space denial weapon systems.[13] Earth-based denial weapons can already produce hostile effects whilst space-based weapons system remain embryonic or have not proceeded beyond initial blueprints and flight tests. Orbital-based weapons platforms will suffer the same vulnerabilities as the satellites they target, and in lower orbits will be vulnerable to a degree that is not comparable to ships on open oceans, but very comparable to ships in fortified and defended coastal zones. The full theoretical consequences of Earth-based anti-satellite weapons are explored in Proposition V through the analogy of the 'hostile coast'. Whilst presence in orbit is important, continental powers have upset bluewater navies by projecting power from the land. Analogically, the same is possible with counterspace capabilities with Earth-based powers. This is not to ascribe who would 'win' a war, rather, it is wrong to assume dominance or security gained via presence in the medium or environment of outer space. This is one consequence of viewing Earth orbit in bluewater terms, rather than as a coastline, as seen in analogising from Corbett's work alone.[14]

Some previous seapower analogies to outer space have not adequately acknowledged the unity among the seapower theorists regarding the permeability and qualified nature of the command of the sea.[15] Both Mahan and Corbett noted the permeable and variable nature of the command of the sea; it does not have an absolute quality even after a decisive engagement.[16] The command of the sea is sometimes mistakenly interpreted as an ability to command all of the sea at all times, rather than controlling or denying select areas for specific time spans.[17] Mahan is in general agreement with Corbett when it comes to the command of the sea's nuanced and permeable traits.[18] Like Corbett, Mahan was interested in the interactions of politics, economics, history and the practice of seapower, and not just the actions of battle fleets.[19] This is explored further in propositions V and VI.

The command of space is therefore useful for both small and large space powers. Spacepower theory makes no prescriptive or positive claims as to how easy or difficult it is to secure varying levels of command in any given case. Any condition of the command of space must take into account any relevant party's ability to control and deny outer space, no matter how transient. Commanding space is not synonymous with unquestioningly dominating it, as is sometimes inferred through bluewater interpretations of the command of the sea.[20] The permeable and relative nature of the command of sea is also transferred to outer space, meaning that a 'good enough' degree of command in time and place is the objective, rather than absolute dominance. Mahan called this a 'reasonably secure communication'.[21] The command of the sea, and of space, is therefore not an archaic concept relevant only to large powers.

This was analogised to explain the command of the air as well. The pioneering mid-twentieth-century Italian airpower theorist Giulio Douhet commented that it was:

axiomatic . . . that coastlines are defended from naval attacks, not by dispersing ships and guns along their whole extent, but by conquering the command of the seas; that is, by preventing the enemy from navigating. The surface of the earth is the coastline of the air. The conditions pertaining to both elements, the air and the sea, are analogous; so that the surface of the earth, both solid and liquid, should be defended from aerial attack, not by scattering guns and planes over its whole extent, but by preventing the enemy from flying. In other words, by 'conquering the command of the air'.[22]

The core strategic concepts of seapower and airpower theory are complementary when thinking about the command of space. Given this crucial resonance from the sea to the air, seapower theory is a fruitful source of strategic analogies for outer space based on influencing the communications of a geographic medium. Douhet's understanding of both command of the sea and of the air implies the need to prioritise access to and the use of that medium, and not merely scattering weapons systems like a blanket. The remaining propositions of spacepower theory detail the principles that should guide strategic thought and priority-setting of how to command and exploit space.

The command of space is a common idea among spacepower theorists, with Klein and Fox making the explicit transpositions from Corbett.[23] Space control is Gray's first point on the significance of spacepower in future warfare,[24] and he defined 'space control' as a 'condition wherein friendly forces can use the space environment on a reliable basis, but enemy forces cannot'.[25] Sheldon defined space control as possessing access to space, freedom to conduct operations in space, and the ability to deny the same to others.[26] Gray, like Klein, stressed the importance of the interdependence of spacepower with those of the other media and theatres of war.[27] Few analysts and practitioners now deviate from the notion that seapower only retains its relevance insofar as it affects landward events,[28] but this has not prevented some in the field of spacepower theory to believe otherwise and attach too much potency or decisiveness in conflict to possessing the command of space as seen below in Proposition III. Smith and Oberg are American-centric and assertive over the importance and decisiveness of a command of space, and share a dominant imperial vision of commanding the sea. Smith argues that 'space control' is not optional: 'If you fail to achieve a healthy measure of space control in the larger of the possible wars of the twenty-first century, you will lose.'[29] Oberg describes space control as 'the linchpin upon which a nation's space power depends'.[30] Dolman's *Astropolitik* theory rests upon the notion that the control of Earth orbit by one dominant state will confer dominance over Earth through the use of the solar system's resources and securing access to them – in other words commanding space between Earth orbit and solar resources.[31]

There is little doubt that American military forces could suffer heavily if their spacepower is aggressively denied. It may make achieving victory far more costly than otherwise anticipated. Yet the issue of decisive strikes in space for wars on Earth can be over-sold, particularly in the cut-throat environment of policy advocacy and inter-service or even intra-service budgetary battles and the historically ignored role of space technology in modern warfare as a distinct specialism. Reconciliation is needed on how strategically 'decisive' the command of space can be for theory, which is the subject of Proposition III. The command of space will not be as decisive in every circumstance, but it cannot be dis- missed as merely a useful adjunct in warfare given the dependency of modern military forces on celestial lines of communication, as detailed in Proposition IV. The theories proposed by Smith, Oberg and Dolman, though logically extreme, are useful to encourage critical strategic thought and vigorous debate about American space strategy and policy.[32] Yet as this book is creating a univer- sal spacepower theory and not a space strategy for the American military, the theory must allow for conditions where the com- mand of space may not be the most decisive strategic objective in a grand strategy. The ultimate aim of the war will always obtrude itself in space warfare through the actual use that is made of the command of Earth orbit.[33] Sometimes the destruction of enemy satellites or a 'space blockade' may be necessary, but sometimes not. Sometimes a terrestrial force could do without space support for a time, or attacks may have little effect due to resilience and a successful 'denial' approach to deterring attacks on space systems. The command of space makes all such tactical and operational military options subordinate to the political objectives and mate- rial conditions of the war in order to provide conceptual disci- pline for the reader when presented with the overwhelming chaos and immediacy of war.

The command of space has constituent elements and consequences beyond the purely military, as Mahan and Corbett noted about the command of the sea. The consequences of a dispute over command could be systemic if a conflagration involves the largest space powers, particularly if successive kinetic weapons are used and the debris population proliferates. Determining the most relevant parts of space infrastructure and where and when the command of space needs to be prioritised towards a terrestrial war requires space-centric thought and specialisation in a time of joint or multi-domain military operations. Despite 'jointness' and the need for generalists at the top levels of decision-making bodies, the role of the specialist cannot be ignored. Different powers may have varying degrees of control and varying successes in denial in certain orbits and certain times with certain space systems according to their needs and strategies. Command can be orbit-specific and it is the role of specialists to furnish the general abstractions with practical and contingent details.

Proposition II: Spacepower is uniquely infrastructural and connected to Earth

Proposition II makes the case for treating spacepower as a distinct specialism in its own right, yet cautions against detaching it from the need to communicate to generalists and recognise its ties to terrestrial environments and political inputs. Spacepower as we know it is largely defined by its quality as supporting infrastructure and how it enhances activities on Earth. Space technology today is used as part of critical infrastructure, and should feature more strongly in spacepower theory than done so previously. Building on Proposition I, space warfare should not happen for its own sake. It is about who gets to extract what kind of support from orbital infrastructures to meet their political objectives.

Materialism must be studied and accounted for in theoretical constructs; ideas are not a tyrant despite resonant conceptual analogies between Earth and space. Despite the resonant analogy between commanding the sea with commanding space, Earth orbit must still be considered a unique place that places specific demands on any knowledge base and technical skills of any actor. The objective of commanding space is a universal strategic truth and part of the unchanging nature of space warfare, but the way this can be achieved and manifested will vary in each war in part based on material factors – technology and geography. This proposition also acts as a very brief and basic introduction to the most salient and unique geographical and strategic realities influencing spacepower in Earth orbit, which begins to add detail to abstract notions of commanding space. Space systems and the infrastructures they provide are not homogenous, and outer space is not a barren waste nor a uniform geographic expanse. Understanding these different regions and uses of outer space is essential for any strategist because they will change in relevance and effects in every war. Indeed, the strategic consequences that spacepower is mostly concerned with infrastructural and support services characterises much of Propositions V and VI.

Strategic analogies with other operating environments, whilst useful, sometimes disguise important and unique tactical and operational distinctions between space and the source environment of the analogy in question.[34] Proposition II is the corrective to that; satellites do different things at different altitudes and inclinations, and the defensibility and vulnerability of satellites will vary with each as well. The devil is in the detail and any application of spacepower theory requires a good grasp of material realities. The diverse astrography of Earth orbit influences what kind of satellites go where in terms of altitudes and inclinations of orbit, how much time it takes for weapons platforms or effects to reach them, and how easy they are to detect and strike. Dolman articulated that

> what appears at first a featureless void is in fact a rich vista of gravitational mountains and valleys, oceans and rivers of resources and energy alternately dispersed and concentrated, broadly strewn danger zones of deadly radiation, and precisely placed peculiarities of astrodynamics.[35]

The view of space as an ocean from bluewater seapower theory, far away from a coastline, does not describe Earth orbit as well as it could, because technologies and events on Earth's surface directly affect what happens in orbit in a way that land-based weapon systems or coastal craft could not impact the open oceans and fleets operating beyond the coast. Space is a distinct medium and requires a level of astrophysical understanding in top decision makers and leaders, and not an application of narrow terrestrial techno-geographic doctrinal thinking to outer space operations.[36] Some unique aspects of strategy in space concern economics and dispersion, which are covered in greater depth in Propositions V and VII, respectively. The dual-use nature of space technology, and the close integration of commercial actors in space infrastructure makes distinguishing commercial and military targets in space more difficult than in other geographic environments. Spacepower is defined today by its character as infrastructure that supports terrestrial requirements, not least modern warfare, and theories and strategies should not be unduly fixated on weapons platforms as is more easily justifiable in bluewater seapower theories.

'Outer space' itself can mean anything beyond the Kármán Line – Earth/Terran space, Lunar space, solar space and the entire universe beyond.[37] 'Space' is a distinct volume separate from the surfaces and atmospheres of celestial bodies (e.g. planets other than Earth, moons and asteroids), a distinction expressed in Article IV of the 1967 Outer Space Treaty. Only the placing of weapons of mass destruction (usually referring to nuclear, chemical and biological weapons, but not explicitly defined as such) is banned in orbit, and not other weapons (such as lasers, particle beam weapons, radiofrequency weapons and kinetic-kill vehicles). Yet all 'weapons' are banned on celestial bodies. This spacepower theory is primarily concerned with Earth, and Earth space – from its surface up towards geosynchronous orbit and the Molniya-type orbits whose highest points reach towards the 40,000 km mark over the northern hemisphere, as it is only these regions that are of direct relevance and use to military power today and for the foreseeable future. All else is futurism at this point. Regions beyond Earth orbit, including the Lagrange points, are of less practical value for contemporary astrostrategists than building a spacepower theory that focuses on its contemporary use in Earth orbit and Earth itself.[38]

Space may be geographically distinctive and possess unique conditions and effects, 'but then so is the land, the sea, the air, and even cyberspace';[39] geography is inescapable.[40] The uniqueness of every environment does not necessitate the jettisoning of all strategic wisdom from the classic theorists used in these propositions on the higher levels of strategy, as opposed to operational and tactical concepts. In this sense, space is not isolated from terrestrial experience and strategic wisdom. Although the command of the medium may conceptually resonate at sea, in the air and in outer space, the way such command is exerted differs in each due to techno-geographic conditions and offers unique manifestations of general strategic concepts such as concentration, mass, communications, proximity and chokepoints. The critical application of such concepts demonstrates how the command of space can be disputed and exploited, and this requires a general grasp of physical realities in orbit.

Over time, satellites need to be able to correct their orbits due to environmental disturbances and peculiarities in order to remain useful. Human commands or new automated systems governed by a synthetic intelligence are necessary to issue corrections, and space weather forecasting and environmental surveillance of space are necessary for a properly functioning space system. Friction – both in the Newtonian and Clausewitzian senses – is still a phenomenon that occurs in orbit. Satellites cannot be launched and forgotten – they rely on celestial lines of communication to maintain and extend their useful lives, as explained in Proposition IV. Even should autonomous satellites emerge, they would need to rely on elaborate information networks and degrees of human oversight to accurately gauge the course corrections needed. This also makes it harder to track satellites and build a reliable space situational awareness (SSA) picture, even with increasingly capable space radars, particularly in lower orbits given the higher number of satellites and their more variable orbital characteristics.

The properties of orbital motion affect the capabilities of satellites and the composition of traffic in orbit. Satellites in LEO can take detailed views of small patches of Earth, but are in constant forward motion relative to Earth's surface. Satellites in the geosynchronous belt (GEO), however, appear stationary over a point on Earth's surface but are actually travelling at a faster velocity at greater altitudes. Higher altitudes are reached by increasing pro-grade orbital velocity – to accelerate more in the forward direction of travel, rather than 'up' away from Earth.[41] There are four general classifications of orbit: low-Earth orbit (LEO), medium-Earth orbit (MEO), geostationary-Earth orbit (GEO) and highly elliptical orbit (HEO). LEO ranges between 150 km altitude to 1,600 km, with orbital periods of ninety minutes.[42] Satellites in LEO typically perform remote sensing, Earth observation (which includes optical and signal spy satellites), weather and scientific missions. There are some communications satellite constellations at this altitude as well, such as Iridium, with its constellation of over sixty satellites. Moving up to orbits of approximately 20,000 km (within MEO), this is where GNSSs are usually found. China's GNSS, *Beidou*, is made up of satellites that are based mostly in MEO but some are based in GEO for additional services. The boundaries between LEO and MEO are ill defined. Most GNSS satellites are generally placed into 19,000–24,000 km altitudes. Up at 35,786 km are geostationary and geosynchronous (GEO) satellites. Their orbital periods are approximately twenty-four hours long, and geostationary satellites appear to remain or loiter above the same point of the Earth's surface, and generally orbit directly above the equator. Geosynchronous orbit refers to a sat-ellite with a twenty-four-hour period, regardless of inclination.[43]

In GEO, satellites tend to perform communications roles, space observation, nuclear detection and ballistic missile early warning, and some weather observation functions. These are highly prized but also congested areas of orbit, and as a consequence physically destructive acts here risk high rates of collateral damage. These conditions may create a degree of existential deterrence given the high level of risk for all users of GEO should debris run amok after kinetic or explosive counterspace weapons fire. HEO are orbits that can be designed to loiter above a hemisphere of the Earth for a longer time, whilst passing over the opposite hemisphere very quickly. An example is the Soviet Union's Molniya satellites which reach an apogee (highest orbital altitude) of around 40,000 km above the northern hemisphere to detect missile launches from the United States, and fly quickly (relative to the surface) over the southern hemisphere with a perigee (lowest orbital altitude) of around 400 km to return to the northern hemisphere as quickly as possible.[44] This stresses the importance of deciding which parts of space one wishes to command as the ability to do so will only affect certain regions of space at certain times, impacting different support services and data.

Earth orbit, as a proximate coastline, is always intimately influenced by what can be achieved on Earth as well as in space. Launch sites closer to the equator have an efficiency advantage for most kinds of orbital launches that travel from the west to the east, especially for GEO. For most west-to-east LEO, MEO and GEO orbits, it is advantageous in economic terms to launch as close to the equator as possible in order to benefit from the increased effect of the Earth's rotation at equatorial surface. The spaceport at Kourou, Le Centre Spatial Guyanais, French Guyana, has 17 per cent greater fuel efficiency at 5 degrees north of the equator than the American Cape Canaveral spaceport at 28.5 degrees north.[45] China's launch centre on Hainan Island has a greater west–east launch potential due to its tropical location and seaborne access routes, compared to spaceports in its mainland interior. The Wenchang spaceport will reduce China's railroad-based logistics restrictions on its space programme due to it being the first Chinese site to have a seaboard. The attraction of equatorial launch sites can provide potential for chokepoints, which are discussed further in Proposition IV. Terrestrial infrastructure matters, and so do the quality and quantity of launch sites and vehicles. Satellites can fly from east to west – in a retrograde orbit – but at great costs to fuel efficiency and lift capacity. Other orbits, such as north-to-south polar orbits (named so because they will fly near Earth's northern and southern poles) derive less of a benefit from the equatorial gravitational boost and therefore higher-latitude launch sites are as efficient as equatorial ones.

An important feature of Earth orbit is that there are two bands of highly intense radiation and charged particles that produce a very hazardous realm for the electronic systems of unshielded satellites, called Van Allen belts (at 5,000 km and 16,000–20,000 km).[46] There are other bodies of potential future strategic interest in the cosmos – asteroids, planets, comets and moons each having their own unique atmo- and magnetospheres (or lack of them) – as well as areas of gravitational oddities – such as the Lagrange libration points between any two orbiting bodies. In the future, the L_4 and L_5 points could be highly advantageous positions in military and economic terms due to the energy efficiency of loitering there and moving from there to other parts of the solar system.[47]

As well as physical constraints, political geography matters too. Israel's spacepower, for example, has been shaped by them both. Israel has developed an east–west retrograde launch capability over the Mediterranean Sea for its reconnaissance satellites, so that they do not launch over neighbouring states and risk accidents and the loss of sensitive equipment to other powers. This imposes costs on the launching mass of Israeli satellites and rockets because it goes against Earth's spin, but it provides Israel with a safer launch capability. Israel developed its Ofek series of reconnaissance satellites, and their own means of launching them, as a result of America's unwillingness to share timely intelligence on Egyptian and Syrian military activities in the 1970s.[48] This demonstrates a manifestation of spacepower as a product of politics, geography and economics.

Political upheaval can change astrostrategic considerations overnight. With the breakup of the Soviet Union, Russia had to negotiate over the Baikonur spaceport in Kazakhstan and cooperate on its future development. However, Russia will be increasingly self-reliant on its own spaceports, such as the northern Plesetsk Cosmodrome and the planned Vostochny space centre in Russia's Far East. Since Russia's Crimean annexation and the war in eastern Ukraine in 2014, Russia's hold on Ukraine's space sector has loosened considerably. Both Ukrainian and Russian space sectors had to adapt rapidly to new terrestrial political realities, especially with the former's space companies suffering an estimated drop of 80 per cent in revenue.[49] Now that Russian–Ukrainian space industry integration has broken up, Ukrainian rocket technology has seen an influx of investment and opening up to Western capital in the form of small satellite launch companies such as Firefly and Skyrora.

Spacepower theory will not state in advance which specific orbits and space systems are the most important to the war at hand. Understanding the character of one's own and an adversary's space infrastructure and weapons capabilities is a task requiring good intelligence capabilities, sensory equipment and analytical judgment. Anyone wishing to control or deny certain space systems, especially if the space segment is the target, also cannot expect there to be a simple kill-switch for a major spacepower's entire space infrastructure in orbit. However, some specific systems may have greater susceptibility to single points of failure than others, depending on their redundancy planning. For example the GPS constellation is designed to operate with no less than twenty-one satellites in orbit; three below that figure may be lost before significant service degradation would occur, and there are a number of redundant GPS satellites already placed in orbit, ready to replace any losses through accident, mechanical failure or hostile actions.[50] Small satellite constellations made up of hundreds of satellites would provide a far more redundant constellation that could weather larger attacks, but small satellites are more restricted in capability. This complicates thinking about spacepower as a centre of gravity as taken up in Proposition III.

Redundancy is not only a feature of the space segment: disabling key nodes in ground segments such as Schriever Air Force Base in the US would take out a major control node of the GPS constellation. Severe disruption can also come from the cyber intrusion of control mechanisms and from simple software or programming errors. A small input error which lasted six seconds on one GPS satellite's timing service caused 110 of 800 cellular phone sites in the eastern US to crash for a few hours in March 1997.[51] There is a high premium on space specialists to be integrated into wider military structures.[52] Against a small and self-reliant spacepower, targeted assassinations of these experts may be a feasible option, like a small state's nuclear, biological or chemical weapons expert communities. As space is a distinct operational medium, it requires a space-specific professional class, like land, sea, air and cyber realms. Yet good strategy-making and its execution cannot be dominated by the needs of specialist technology and operational requirements alone.[53] The skills and talents of humans, least of all in multi-environment strategic thought, should not be ignored, even in such a high-technology dominated realm as outer space. The issue of people and culture in space-power is returned to in Proposition VI.

Space is different in that it is dominated by technologies that provide ubiquitous and sometimes acutely important infrastructural services across critical areas of state activity, and certain areas of space are crowded and the vulnerability of satellites to debris generation may impose some level of existential deterrence on debris-generating counterspace activities. In addition, Earth orbit is not a uniform geography: different physical characteristics and satellite types characterise different altitudes and orbital paths. These material realities and the limitations they pose on human agency must be mastered in detail when applying spacepower theory. Despite this uniqueness, space is not a panacea for terrestrial warfare and politics. The continuing human element of spacepower ties together the uniqueness of the demands of using spacepower to a common unifying 'logic' of strategy.[54] The uniqueness of orbital geography must 'find expression in unique technology, operations, and tactics. That unique geography does not, however, point the way to some unique logic of strategy.'[55] Single-environment analyses should not be taken too far because they are still subject to war's universal nature of passion, reason and chance.

For all its physical uniqueness, there may be a problem in 'the inability or unwillingness of people to approach space as just another geographical environment for conflict'.[56] However, this may be changing. Although the US Air Force has spoken this language since the 1980s and the UK has done so for many years as well, the creation of a US Space Force, along with declaring space as a warfighting domain, has brought such language into the mainstream and outside the doctrine manuals.[57] Although Earth orbit and outer space have unique and astrographic features and technical specialisms, it is still subject to the parameters of human socio-political activity as understood through Clausewitz's trinity of passion, reason and chance. Even if the command of space is won and exploited prudently taking full account of Propositions I and II, Proposition III stands ready to apply friction, because, unlike some bluewater caricatures of seapower theory, decisive battles are often a chimera, and commanding a medium is not inherently decisive by itself.

Proposition III: The command of space does not equate to the command of Earth

Dominating space through presence in orbit or in destroying enemy satellites does not necessarily lead to the domination of Earth. The command of space is not inherently decisive in a terrestrial war. Should a dominant command of space be achieved it alone will not necessarily win a war. Proposition III addresses frequent claims to the contrary in the spacepower literature and moderates them to theorise the grey area of the indecisive yet indispensable quality of commanding space in modern warfare. Dolman's *Astropolitik* theory coined the astropolitical dicta 'he who controls low-Earth orbit controls near-Earth space. Who controls near-Earth space dominates Terra. Who dominates Terra determines the destiny of humankind.'[58] *Astropolitik* takes readers to an indeterminate future where humans are harvesting strategic resources from beyond Earth and intentionally pushes realpolitik logic to its extreme to develop theory and astropolitical thinking. *Astropolitik* takes the view that 'the resource potential of space, like Mackinder's heartland, is so vast that, should any one state gain effective control of it, that state could dictate the political, military, and economic fates of all terrestrial governments'.[59] As bold and crystallising as such an assumption is, as well as a useful thought exercise, it requires many qualifications when discussing spacepower and grand strategy which are restricted to Earth and its orbital regions. Gray and Sheldon are sympathetic to such long-term thinking, when they claim that in 'the long run . . . the security of the human race most likely will depend upon its space power'.[60] As space activity 'is not a major economic force, but . . . a potent economic enabler'[61] for the foreseeable future, grandiose visions akin to Dolman's remain theoretical testing grounds and engaging thought exercises.[62] Spacepower theory must remain practically useful to practitioners and scholars of contemporary war and strategy. As long as human life clings to the landmasses of Earth and the resources that feed civilisation come from Earth, spacepower by itself may struggle to be decisive, no matter the level of preponderance or hegemony in space by any state or entity in Earth orbit. This is a recurring feature of Propositions V and VI, which embraces the secondary importance of space in terrestrially orientated grand strategy because it analogises from continental seapowers.

The primacy of battle and seeking decisive battle may be something of a fetish in strategic studies,[63] and the role of large clashes in space warfare must be more nuanced than how it appears in some existing spacepower theories. Astrodeterminist approaches view space as the ultimate high ground or where the political fate of Earth may be sealed. In other words, the view that events in outer space determine outcomes on Earth. There are two primary challenges to such astrostrategic thought. The first is that winning a command of space may not always be easy. Second, exploiting the dominance of one strategic geography only provides indeterminate strategic effects that must be consciously exploited afterwards and coordinated to have a significant impact on the overall course of a war – not simply assumed in theory. The impact of dominance in one environment on another is rarely linear, proportionate and automatic. Understanding the decisiveness of the command of space on Terran wars – or the influence of spacepower upon Earth – cannot be done without engaging with the classical strategic concepts of decisive battle or the 'high ground' and the centre of gravity.

Determining the decisiveness of the command of space requires applying the principle of the centre of gravity to an adversary in order to identify ways of engaging in decisive battles against space infrastructure and weapons systems to the point from which the foe may never be able to recover. The bluewater-derived seapower analogy to space provides many insights into the role of battle and the potential influence of the dominance of outer space. The history of seapower is rife with strategically indecisive naval battles. Even should a battle be spectacular, there is no inherent value on its decisiveness, as Mahan observed on Franco-British maritime warfare during the American Revolutionary War.[64] Seeking battle in space or against terrestrial targets from space are subject to similar qualifications as Mahan and Corbett saw through the role of battle in settling the command of the sea. Although preferable in principle, being able to comprehensively destroy enemy forces are rare opportunities in practice and should not fool commanders into believing that battle is always worth pursuing at all costs.[65] It is in applying the principle of seeking out and destroying enemy forces that critical thought and command judgments are needed the most. Some analogies from bluewater seapower offer a misleading vision of seeking 'battle' in space warfare as taking place between 'space fleets'.[66] Contrary to popular interpretations, Mahan did not argue that seeking battle was always the correct decision in naval command. Corbett used Mahan's own arguments to criticise the US Navy's misguided decision to axiomatically pursue a decisive battle against the Spanish in the Spanish–American War, which neglected the more strategically decisive and vulnerable American amphibious operations on Cuba that the Spanish fleet could threaten whilst giving the US Navy battle fleet the slip.[67] The Spanish had correctly surmised that the main objective in this theatre was to threaten American transports to Cuba, rather than facing the US Navy in battle.

Decisive engagements with space systems in orbit or against terrestrial space infrastructure (such as control stations and spaceports) could lead to a more efficient command of space. Space warfare may entail Earth-to-space, space-to-space and space-to-Earth operations that can involve physical destruction (hard kill) and electromagnetic or cyber disruption (soft kill). A space warfare campaign can include comprehensive strikes on an enemy's launch capabilities and facilities, space-capable missile batteries, major airfields, 'missile defence' ships, SSA nodes in space and on Earth, and the neutralisation of key enemy satellites and ground stations. The exact manifestation of decisively crippling an enemy's space warfare capabilities and the sources of its spacepower may change dramatically as technological, political and economic conditions vary across time as well as among the belligerents involved. Whether or not battle involves Earth-based anti-satellite weapons or terrestrial strikes on ground-based space infrastructure, the role of engagements in spacepower will still be subject to the same theoretical truths of seapower theory with regard to decisive battles. Decisive battle is a theoretical ideal to structure thinking for securing a command of space – but it may be difficult to bring about and its results may well be strategically indecisive.

This logic of strategy is not always noticed within Mahan's work, which is sometimes wrongly accused as only focusing on decisive battles and the offensive actions of primary battle fleets.[68] Klein's Corbettian analogy of a fleet in being (where forces afloat are kept in reserve or for opportune guerrilla-style attacks only) for combat satellites in orbit – a force in being – may not be particularly feasible given the potential vulnerabilities and the challenges of efficient manoeuvring of space-based assets in the coastline of Earth orbit, when compared to ships on the open ocean.[69] This is an outcome of transposing concepts of weapons platforms and the centrality of battle at the expense of the other aspects of spacepower.

Criticisms of Mahan's apparent fixation on battle belies his recognition of wars where 'navies were of great direct military value, though they fought no battles'.[70] This is highly analogous to outer space today, where space-to-space combat is only an emergent concern given the prevalent spread of Earth-to-space weapons, and spacepower's primary utility is its support services on Earth. Earth-based anti-satellite weapons systems are only now maturing, if still lacking in quantity, and space-based weapons are an exotic and embryonic technology.[71] As Proposition V explains, if violence is to occur in orbit, it will be analogous to coastal guns or specialised coastal attack craft firing at ships in a littoral zone rather than fleet-on-fleet battles in isolated and vast expanses of ocean. Whether on the high seas or upon a coast, the limits of decisive battles are still present. Space-based weapons systems should not disproportionately dominate strategic thinking about outer space. They are important, but are not the totality of spacepower and space warfare. Space warfare can happen even without space-based weapon systems. Earth-based systems – including many so-called missile defences – can intercept satellites providing services to terrestrial militaries and economies. Regardless of basing, attempting to destroy specific satellites is no guarantee of securing the command of space and then winning the war, if precedents set by seapower theory are borne out in orbit.

If losing a decisive battle in orbit is a major risk, then the weaker side may seek to undermine efforts to allow that decisive battle to happen, or enact alternatives to mitigate the strategic effects of such a battle. Corbett argued that 'the [thorniest] questions [British commanders] had to decide . . . was not how to defeat the enemy, but how to bring him to action'.[72] Corbett was not averse to seeking battle. But it was his willingness to say that it was sometimes unhelpful to seek battle at all times that gained him some notoriety among his peers and the Admiralty.[73] The 'rough generalization that the command depends upon the battle fleet' is a constructive one, if only to help discern when an enemy fleet needs action to be taken against it, and when not.[74] This action–reaction dynamic of seeking and denying battle continuously alter the odds and feasibility of imposing battle, and that strategic logic applies to the cat-and-mouse, if not paradoxical, relationship between satellites and counterspace weapons where expectations of likely courses of action are undermined by the fact they are known to be likely in the first place.[75] The more decisive and therefore riskier an engagement may be, the more likely that one side may prevent that battle from taking place. The threat of engagement and battle have an effect, even if they do not actually take place, because of their expected outcomes should they happen. The same is true of threatened counterspace actions on spacepower postures and strategies.

Corbett commented that

what the maxim [of seeking decisive battle] really means is that we should endeavor from the first to secure contact in the best position for bringing about a complete decision in our favor, and as soon as the other parts of our war plan . . . will permit.[76]

Here Corbett is exercising in effect both Propositions I and II. Command is important, but it cannot operate in isolation from the concerns of other theatres, in this case, the land. If the primary theatre of operations is on land, then efforts to secure a decisive battle must be tempered by the needs of the land war.[77] This has parallels to spacepower being integrated into terrestrial support operations. Larger spacepowers will be caught between the dual horns of spending resources to secure a command of space, or spending resources to exploit such command for strategic effects on Earth. The needs of terrestrial wars should temper any desire to dominate outer space for its own sake, or seeking decisive battle in space above all else, rather than attacking enemy support systems or exploiting one's own in joint warfare.[78]

Transposing Mahan and Corbett's views of (in)decisive battle into space would mean that significant, or the most threatening, enemy space forces and assets should be destroyed where and when such targets and opportunities exist. Such enemy space systems should be put out of action through destructive or non-destructive methods for at least the expected duration of hostilities to ensure the greatest degree of probability in maintaining a general command of space to enable space systems to support operations on Earth and deny them to the foe. If this action is feasible and judged appropriate to the scenario at hand, it should be pursued. But this does not mean blindly chasing what may be an illusory grand battle or a 'decisive' counterspace strike against enemy space systems. It creates the risk of manipulation and deception by a foe that is happy to bait the enemy with the promise of an illusory, distracting or decisive but strategically futile clash. Destroying a large swath of enemy satellites at the outset, a 'Space Pearl Harbor' attack, may not always be the correct course of action. This is particularly true if the adversary is counting on it happening. This dynamic is demonstrated in Chapter 6.

The nuance and qualifications within Mahan's and Corbett's views on seeking battle derive from the pedagogical nature of their works. Successfully commanding the sea relied on good judgment in applying the principle of seeking battle or avoiding it, to reflect upon the many imponderable variables that confront commanders at every turn in every war where no two particular circumstances are ever the same. If the self-reflective and pedagogical aspect of the principles of strategy and spacepower theory are not embraced then propositions risk becoming dogmatic axioms or sources of prescriptive directions. In this case, seeking battle is good if it can be done without sacrificing a command of space where it matters and if it will make a meaningful change to one's fortunes in the overall war. Otherwise, if the enemy can too easily avoid such battle or make its consequences irrelevant, seeking battle at all costs is ill-advised. The correct course of action cannot be prescribed in advance, but possibilities can be identified by the consideration of theoretical ideals.

To help in deciding whether a decisive battle is desirable, the concept of the centre of gravity has been used to identify a single point of failure or strength in the adversary, which, if struck, would result in a loss that the foe could not recover from. A space strategy for the United States today may have many reasonable grounds for describing American space infrastructure as a military centre of gravity. This should be contrasted with the more persuasive case that space is not an economic centre of gravity for the United States today.[79] Even though the commercial space industry keeps growing it remains rather volatile and must always be compared to the value and utility of other economic sectors, notably seaborne trade, of which the 'space economy' is an important part. This theme is revisited in Propositions IV and V. The US military would undoubtedly be severely disrupted should its military communications and navigation satellites be denied. In that vein, spacepower theorists have often referred to spacepower as an American centre of gravity.[80] For Clausewitz the centre of gravity was 'the hub of all power and movement, on which everything depends. That is the point against which all our energies should be directed.' The competent strategist must try to identify what the enemy's centre of gravity is, and strike it if possible. On many occasions, this tended to be the primary military force or city of the enemy, and required a 'decisive battle' or siege to subdue it. However, a centre of gravity does not always have to be enemy forces or a capital city. It could also mean destroying something intangible that supports the enemy's will and capacity to fight.[81] The idea of the centre of gravity is useful because seeking a vulnerable decisive point in the enemy is, in general, good practice. Even if a vulnerable centre of gravity is not found, the process of thinking about its applicability trains strategic judgment and encourages more thought on the opponent's strengths and weaknesses, be they many or few. It is understandable, and useful for practitioners, to think of American spacepower as a possible centre of gravity – but it is an act of subjective judgment to do so. As discussed in Proposition VII and Chapter 6, narrowing down American spacepower to a single centre of gravity is a difficult task as the 'devil is in the detail'.

In light of Proposition II's call to deal with space on its own material terms, it is unclear how directly the concept of the centre of gravity may apply to space infrastructure as a whole. Different satellite constellations and orbits provide different concentrations of assets and degrees of essential or redundant functions. The highly dispersed and redundant nature of some satellite constellations – such as Iridium's sixty-six communications satellites or PlanetLab's dozens of Earth observation small satellites – make for a target-rich environment but also provide systems capable of plugging gaps, providing replacements and absorbing attacks. Reliance upon a handful of communications satellites in GEO may provide several points of failure for crucial government and military communications (as in the case of the UK's Skynet constellation) and may be more feasibly struck and interpreted as a centre of gravity. Yet the UK will have access to commercial and allied communications systems which provides dozens if not hundreds of potential alternatives should the entire Skynet network be silenced. The United States may have far more options for distributing its celestial lines of communication should its usual space infrastructure be compromised, owing to its high integration with allies and its commercial sector – providing the US with more spacepower and deterrence by denial than Russia and China.[82]

A communications bottleneck in the ground segment – such as through a centralised satellite control or information distribution headquarters – may provide a vulnerable centre of gravity or merely one chokepoint among several. These complex and contingent considerations show how, even though the centre of gravity may be a chimera in outer space, its illustrative use here is developing strategic thought regarding potentially vulnerable points, backup systems and adaptive countermeasures. Strategy is an iterative process as much as a plan of action. Any declaration that space is a centre of gravity must engage with Proposition II and detail which space systems in which scenarios may create single points of failure in a network-centric military force, because to say that space is a centre of gravity is a gross simplification of an increasingly diverse and dispersed suite of capabilities and assets. Declarations that spacepower is a centre of gravity for the United States, and that spacepower enhances an ability to target enemy centres of gravity are problematic for a universal spacepower theory that must provide propositions that are useful for almost any feasible scenario and for any space powers.[83]

Proposition III counters the extreme – or astrodeterminist – application of the centre of gravity. Astrodeterminism forecasts that 'space dominance heavily shifts the balance of forces tactically, operationally, and strategically' in favour of space capabilities.[84] Whilst exploiting spacepower and countering it are very important factors in success in terrestrial warfare, spacepower theory and astrostrategists must not be swayed by the false promises of astrodeterminism or a reductionist view of space as a centre of gravity. They should embrace the grey area of a supporting yet indispensable tool and supporting infrastructure of grand strategy, as Propositions V and VI dwell upon further. Spacepower is a team player in joint warfare with ubiquitous yet indirect effects.[85] This may make 'flying the flag' more difficult in budgetary battles as it argues against sweeping arguments, but that is not a problem for spacepower theory to solve. Theoretical truth, not spacepower advocacy, is the aim of spacepower theory. Spacepower theory must still allow for the possibility of decisive action on Earth following a 'decisive battle' in orbit, but it must also accommodate the possibility that dominating space may also not automatically generate strategic success on Earth, regardless of one's command of space even when it is won or lost after a decisive engagement.

Theorising the decisiveness of spacepower's influence may be similar to those featured in the debate over airpower's potential as an independent war-winner, and is reflected in some extant spacepower theories and picked up again in Propositions V and VII. The risk with such determinist views is that it undermines the multilateral and non-linear strategic interactions between different geographies. Sheldon warned that 'if anyone were to claim for space power an ability to independently win wars and to do so quickly they would do much to hamper its strategic value and evolution by making promises that it could not possibly keep'.[86] Smith advocates a combined arms approach to space warfare, as well as insisting on the coercive and compelling elements of spacepower.[87] By placing this thinking within the framework of

83

the seven propositions, this indeterminate and muddled grey area of theory is outlined between spacepower's solitary indecisiveness and its indispensability in joint warfare; of the potential of space as a vulnerable centre of gravity and the risk of fashioning a silver bullet. Key to understanding Proposition III is how military power and an actor's influence moves from one environment to another. This is another area where bluewater seapower theory provides useful insights.

Mahan stressed that a command of the sea needs to be consciously exploited for strategic effect. He examined the failure of the French Navy to exploit their decisive victory against the English at Beachy Head in the Nine Years' War (1688–97) by not acting to cut off English communications to Ireland based on the command of the sea they had won. Although England was defeated at sea, Anglo-Dutch land forces went on to win the more important Battle of the Boyne in Ireland due to the French failure to blockade Ireland. The same theoretical truth applies to spacepower. This does not mean that the army should dictate everything a navy does, or that terrestrial forces must rigidly control 'space forces'. But a supporting tool of grand strategy must be intelligently used to contribute objectives to where humans live and its ultimate political objectives. Echoing Proposition II, the needs, requirements and elevated importance of terrestrial environments (whether accurate or misguided) places restrictions on space-centric strategic thought. Placing weapons in outer space, for example, would be a waste of resources for the United States if the enemy can adapt to a loss of space infrastructure, sufficiently target American space-based weapons and valuable unarmed satellites with ground-based weapons systems, or retaliate with escalatory measures such as nuclear weapons. A dominant command of space can be strategically useful, but only to a point. The interactions between terrestrial forms of power and spacepower are never fixed in their character, and it is a common theme among spacepower theorists. Gray argues that 'military behaviour, no matter what its tactical form, ultimately can have strategic meaning only for the course of events on land. It follows that seapower, airpower, and now spacepower function strategically as enabling factors.'[88]

The dominance of space did not automatically lead to American grand strategic success on Earth in dealing with its wars and post-conflict occupations in Afghanistan and Iraq, despite ensuring military preponderance in space. Superiority as a spacepower was not sufficient for strategic 'victory', but it may have been necessary for the US as a part of a larger causal chain to 'victory' that has since been closed off through the tenacity of Taliban resistance and failure in the occupation and state-building of Iraq.[89] A dominant command of space does not provide omniscience nor omnipotence. Spacepower must complement an appropriate grand strategy on Earth to the peace that would follow war, to occupy territory, influence daily life, and threaten actions that coerce or deter the adversary or would-be vassal in a desirable way. Assuming success from space dominance hides the necessity of continuous exploitation of any dominant position in any medium.

The enabling and paralysing effects of controlling or denying lines of communication are exemplified by Mahan's narrative of British forces in the American Revolutionary War. The French Navy had secured the command of the seas between the British strongholds in New York and Chesapeake long enough to help force a capitulation of British forces. Although the Royal Navy was not annihilated in a decisive battle, France was able to exercise its local and persistent command of the sea in the North American theatre for long enough against the British for the French and colonial rebels to exploit a British inability to use their sea lines of communication to logistically augment their North American forces.[90] For spacepower, this can mean that even though a power's space capabilities may not be decisively put out of action, a good enough command of a particular area of space, or celestial lines of communication for long enough against certain deployed forces could have great strategic effect, if consciously exploited at the right time.

Without access to celestial lines of communication, space-supported armed forces are less efficient, more vulnerable to surprise attack, and possibly cut off from external support such as fire support from distant over-the-horizon weapons platforms. The logistical aspects of spacepower are explored further in Proposition V, and the consequences of spacepower (and its loss) on the battlefield is the heart of Proposition VII. However, for now, it is pertinent to end this proposition on decisiveness and preponderance with Mahan.[91] On the Spanish War of Succession (1701–14), Mahan narrated that:

> once only did great fleets meet, and then with results that were indecisive; after which the French gave up the struggle at sea, confining themselves wholly to a commerce-destroying warfare. This feature . . . characterizes nearly the whole of the eighteenth century, with the exception of the American Revolutionary struggle. The noiseless, steady, exhausting pressure with which sea power acts, cutting off the resources of the enemy while maintaining its own, supporting war in scenes where it does not appear itself, or appears only in the background, and striking open blows at rare intervals, though lost to most, is emphasized.[92]

The potentially significant effects of the exploitation of sea lines of communication can be analogised to space, and are taken further across the next two propositions. A general and persistent command of space will not automatically translate into a command of Earth, but it helps. Conversely, even relatively modest abilities can contribute greatly to a war, in keeping with the non-linear and disproportionate nature of war. Decisive engagements in space, should they happen, will not by themselves decide a war; the consequences of space warfare on the command of space and the celestial lines of communication must be exploited for strategic effect. Judging the decisiveness of space warfare and the command of space should be done through characterising the unique characteristics of the space environment and infrastructure via the relevant celestial lines of communication, their composition, locations, users and effects on terrestrial activities. The strategic concepts of Propositions I and III are complemented by Propositions II and IV which provide the operational and tactical details

Proposition IV: The command of space manipulates celestial lines of communication

Celestial lines of communication visualise the command of space and how it connects space infrastructure with users and facilities on Earth. Proposition IV structures how to think about Proposition III and the possible centres of gravity by identifying converging celestial lines of communication. With the largest of space powers, Proposition II should remind the reader that the highly distributed nature of some space infrastructures, plus some terrestrial back-ups, may make such a task insurmountable. The lines of communication between Earth orbit and Earth, spaceports and satellites, and their communication streams between users and controllers, must be denied or controlled as Proposition I stressed to project a degree of the command of space. Space communications refer to the things that are transported, such as trade goods, materiel, space-craft, electromagnetic transmissions, data and military effects, and the means of doing so. Celestial lines of communication refer to the routes and points between which the various kinds of space communications travel.[93] Although useful to define and categorise celestial lines of communication, bluewater seapower theory tends to assume that sea lines of communication connect two distant regions together, which makes blockading and isolating an enemy with an ocean-going navy a feasible option for navies. This is not analogous to warfare in Earth orbit, which has no distant regions in the twenty-first century in either the physical or the electromagnetic realms. Before that distinction is drawn within Propositions IV and V, the base bluewater-derived concepts of lines of communication and blockading must be applied to space. Celestial lines of communication contain two types. First, the routes that physical objects, like satellites, must travel according to Newtonian–Keplerian physics and logistical constraints. Second, it refers to lines of communications along which useful particles and energy can travel, such as wireless communications, particle effects and lasers.

The terrestrial element of celestial lines of communication cannot be overlooked. The fixed nature of many satellite control and receiving stations form concentrations of celestial lines of communication between Earth and space. This would provide a concentration on Earth that may be useful to deny in some form of local 'space communications blockade'. But the users may be able to disperse and conceal themselves from enemy strikes, develop mobile command terminals or provide a high degree of redundancy to make a total neutralisation difficult if not time-consuming. For example, a

Chinese sensor net to warn of incoming US warships and aircraft in a Taiwan scenario may include a fleet of seemingly innocuous civilian fishing vessels which possess satellite phones connected to Chinese satellite networks and the military's maritime early warning system.[94] But the PLA's surveillance system may have centralised receiving, processing and dissemination centres which may provide other methods of neutralising such a sensor system. Mapping these celestial lines of communication help to determine congregations of space communications, if they occur, and may help to identify more lucrative targets for attacks.

The electromagnetic spectrum is as diverse as the physical realm of orbital mechanics as introduced in Proposition II. Different frequencies are used for different purposes. For example, Very High Frequency bands are used for generic satellite uplinks, where satellite communication of higher importance and sensitivity climb up the frequency bands, ending with the most survivable military satellites using Extremely High Frequency, with ground transmitters able to provide microwave data links and 'active denial systems' including narrow beam communications pointed at specific cooperating receivers, as opposed to wide-area omnidirectional broadcasts like conventional radio.[95] Narrow beam communications are harder to intercept because they broadcast along a tight and acute arc. With geosynchronous satellites and fixed ground terminals, narrow beams provide a reliable and secure method of radiofrequency communication, but their fixed locations make them vulnerable against direct physical action because it would make terrestrial communications more predictable and easier to counter or disrupt. Wide beam broadcasts can involve dispersed and mobile senders and receivers, but their signals are easier to intercept and to jam. Powerful signals can drown out weaker ones. Two signals on the same frequency being broadcast near each other can make it difficult for a receiver to pick out the correct one. Unintentional radiofrequency interference can also occur if an antenna is pointed at the wrong satellite.[96] These capabilities have already become established. The 4th Space Control Squadron, of the 21st Space Wing of the United States Air Force (USAF), is assigned to operating the Counter Communications System (CCS) deploying in-theatre for space superiority operations, and evaluating new counterspace technologies. If satellites are deemed to be vulnerable to jamming, space-based weapons will share such vulnerabilities as well.

Lines of communication, both Newtonian–Keplerian and electromagnetic, can converge to form chokepoints. Advantageous locations in orbit can form high-value positions and their economic, strategic or gravitational attraction to users also form chokepoints. High-value positions are the most economical and effective locations and trajectories to achieve what is needed with the relevant satellites. For example, in Operation Desert Shield in 1991, navigation, communication and early warning satellites were moved to the high(er) value position of a GEO slot closer to the Middle East theatre to provide additional communications bandwidth.[97] Any satellite constellation benefits from using them through utilising their optimal orbital altitudes and inclinations.[98] However, congregations of satellites or communications pathways converge to produce attractive chokepoints for adversaries. John Klein makes a distinction between physical and non-physical chokepoints. Non-physical chokepoints are locations where there is a significant concentration of communications emanating from or going through them.[99] Physical chokepoints are locations such as specifically predictable orbits through which recently launched satellites must pass and could be intercepted, such as the antipodal point from a launch centre. Fewer and more important chokepoints could lead to more reasoned thinking of centres of gravity in space, as discussed in Proposition III. Some regions of space can themselves be seen as a chokepoint, such as GEO, which are fixed and predictable valuable strategic positions.[100] However, adding to this complexity, chokepoints are not the same as 'high-value positions' which denote wider areas of space that have become useful for important satellites that do not form concentrated chokepoints.[101]

Systems such as satellite navigation constellations form a high-value position based on the services they provide from MEO. But their dispersed nature and the large void that is MEO prevents its labelling as a chokepoint, which refers to a more geographically focused point. A chokepoint can be the poles at LEO, because most polar orbit satellites pass over similar points above the north and south poles and form a dense region of traffic. A high-value position, by contrast, can be a large geographic realm, depending on

89

the specific belligerent involved. It is the specific use made of an area by a certain belligerent, and not the general value of the geographic position itself, that gives it its high strategic value. Controlling MEO in its entirety may not be feasible because it is too large a volume of space, unlike trying to control a definable chokepoint in radiofrequency traffic or efficient rocket launch vectors from spaceports. Contrary to MEO, polar states with Earth-based anti-satellite weapons may have a strong hold on the orbital chokepoint of polar orbits in LEO altitudes, given the high density of traffic therein. Countries at extreme latitudes may have greater potential for holding polar chokepoints at risk in LEO as celestial lines of communication converge at their respective poles.

The Van Allen radiation belts are high-value defensive positions or regions for shielded satellites that may be able to evade stalking satellites or homing warheads that may not be able to survive the enhanced radiation within the belts. If a satellite without proper shielding is forced into these regions or orbit, they are then negative value positions. A belligerent may be forced to use positions of 'negative' value if another can reliably command chokepoints and high-value positions. Negative value areas are where a relative disadvantage is realised.[102] In other words, it is a bad or undesirable orbit. The Van Allen belts are not chokepoints, but they can present advantages or threats as potential positions of value for various satellites. Geographic value in space changes with the technological capabilities available.

If a belligerent has a general and persistent command of space, it could be exercised through 'blocking' and establishing space as a 'barrier', as Klein argues. Blocking refers to the specific practice of 'disrupting, degrading, or denying an adversary's ability to use his celestial lines of communication, thus minimizing the movement of spacecraft, equipment, materiel, supplies, personnel, military effects, data, or information'.[103] However, blocking does not assume the enemy is totally helpless; disputing a blocking campaign is always a possibility as Proposition I reminds us. Celestial lines of communication may move or change their composition, so an analogy of a stationary fleet at sea conducting a close blockade may not be particularly apt, but the principles of denying an adversary most of the use and access of a medium through passages of frequent and desirable travel via a distant blockade are conceptually similar. To the powerful actor that has imposed a general and persistent command of space, using space as a barrier enables it to 'take as much or as little space warfare as [it wants]', enabling a conflict to be limited to a particular theatre and helping to prevent any space-transiting or spaceborne retaliation from the enemy which may have its effects in the blockading power's core territory.[104] This represents a bluewater approach to blockading in space which mimics the use of ocean-going armed fleets across relatively vast and isolated distances.

Throttling chokepoints and imposing blockades are possible outcomes when vital transit points are used to prioritise space warfare or counterspace efforts.[105] In space warfare, one could blockade certain areas or chokepoints in orbit through space denial without necessarily controlling their own space infrastructure. Space can be commanded, and therefore blockaded, in this way through denial because of Earth-based weapons and countermeasures. However, orbital assets to monitor and act within orbit will be useful if available. This reinforces the importance of seeing space control and space denial as two equal sub-concepts of the command of space in Proposition I.

The quasi-predictable Hohmann transfer orbits, where spacecraft must accelerate to efficiently change their orbital altitude, become akin to the 'strategic narrows' of Earth orbit.[106] In examining Newtonian space warfare, Dolman believes that assets deployed at the top of Earth's gravity well, or in stable Lagrange libration points, will enjoy great defensive advantages (in time and energy) from incoming hostile forces that are still climbing up the gravity well because they must expend energy to climb it.[107] Expending energy, and propulsion in particular, makes movements and behaviour easier to observe and predict. A deployed weapons system in orbit may have some combat advantages over kinetic weapons or projectiles being launched from Earth, should a state of hostilities already exist. If kinetic, jamming or laser equipment is placed in the correct orbits and their targets are in the appropriate orbits for the weapons range and flyby schedules, orbital weapons can reduce the time needed for Earth-based weapons to hit them. The advantages of Earth-based weapons systems do not trounce space-based weapons systems across the board, but they are often overlooked. Whether space-based weapons are needed to control Earth orbit's chokepoints and narrows, as opposed to cislunar or the solar system's chokepoints, remains doubtful because the distance from Earth to the desired orbit is relatively short from Earth's surface given the velocities and inertial restrictions involved with kinetic, energy or particle-based anti-satellite weapons. Indeed, kinetic orbital weapons systems will suffer logistical and range problems in ensuring reliable coverage of Earth for various orbital intercept missions, especially for midcourse missile defence and the orbital interception of satellites.[108]

Nevertheless, the expense of space activities puts a premium on efficient routes to and in Earth orbit. Taking inspiration from the policy-advocacy side of Mahan, Dolman analogised that:

> the nation or nations that controlled the most modern navies and the world's critical chokepoints could dominate the lanes of commerce . . . In space there are specific orbits and transit routes that because of their advantages in fuel efficiency create natural corridors of movement and commerce.[109]

Weapons based on Earth that may have fields of view and lines of sight across converging points of communication in Earth orbit, or the valuable lines of communication of adversaries, are undoubtedly advantageous, but the degree to which that is useful will vary with each particular war. Proposition IV stresses that commanding space – whether through control, denial or both – must be done efficiently and by configuring campaigns to protect and attack the relevant lines of communication for the war at hand.

Despite the strong resonance of naval blockading concepts to space, the strategic analogy of blockading based on bluewater analogies can be taken too far. Blockading visions often rest on space-based weapons platforms performing the duties of armed vessels at sea, consequently ignoring the realities of space capabilities today where satellites tend to perform passive support roles and where space weapons systems are based on Earth for the most part, and not in space. Blockading in Earth orbit would be like attempting a close naval blockade of a fortified and hostile coastal zone within coastal weapons range, thanks to the proliferation of Earth-based anti-satellite capabilities. Orbital weapons would increase the problems and create the difficulties faced by navies in imposing 'close' (as opposed to distant 'open') blockades, meaning the blockading vessels are more vulnerable to resistance. This flawed basis of a bluewater seapower analogy to space undermines attempts at closely transposing Corbettian concepts of blockade, dispersal and concentration into space warfare. But the higher concept of 'space blockade' in terms of efficiently controlling and denying lines of communication at points of convergence or highly valuable celestial lines of communications is still useful for the astrostrategist. The economic consequences and exploitation of blockade and commerce warfare in space – or astroeconomic warfare – are explored further in Proposition V.

Spacepower theory must consider the long- and short-term consequences of a disruption to celestial lines of communication, as well as their potential discrimination. Exercising or disputing the command of space is valuable in that it can enhance relative combat capabilities on Earth and the chances of success of combat operations at sea, on land and in the air. Conversely, losing a large degree of the command of space could degrade combat performance if a significant amount of capabilities are dependent on satellite services and if terrestrial militaries do not have easy and timely workarounds. As well as the more tactical and operational concerns of the preservation or loss of satellite services on over-the-horizon targeting munitions,[110] spacepower theory must also accommodate subtle, delayed or long-term consequences of space warfare. A state may lose vital satellite intelligence, Earth observation, missile launch detection and space situational awareness capabilities. Some high-end military and intelligence satellites may take years to be replaced. A state which benefits from the taxation of space-related commerce may be targeted with a blockade or *guerre de course* (commerce destroying) strategy to inflict punitive economic costs on the adversary, as explored in the next proposition.[111]

With the general themes of blockade and how to enforce one, the roles of concepts such as concentration and dispersal of assets and effects come to mind, and these are explored further in Proposition VII. On the highest strategic level, seapower, airpower and spacepower theories is about attempting to drive out the enemy from an entire medium as far as is practically feasible and relevant to the conflict at hand. Mahan argued that:

> it is not the taking of individual ships or convoys . . . that strikes down the money power of a nation; it is the possession of that over-bearing power on the sea which drives the enemy's flag from it, or allows it to appear only as a fugitive . . . This overbearing power can only be exercised by great navies.[112]

An overbearing power on the sea – 'driv[ing] the enemy's flag from it' – means preventing the use of sea lines of communication for the enemy, and being able to enjoy it for oneself. Economic and combat efficiency costs can be exacted upon an enemy by denying its celestial lines of communication and exploiting one's own. This notion of the power of great navies shows the inevi-table break in a bluewater seapower analogy to outer space. Great 'space navies' or orbital battle systems are not necessarily needed to drive an enemy's trade from space, or significantly inhibit celestial lines of communication, because of the relative distances involved when considering spacepower in Earth orbit. Earth orbit is more like a coastline, which allows power projection from Earth into space, making a close blockade in Earth orbit a potentially costly proposition against a state with anti-satellite capabilities. Bluewater seapower analogies to space cannot accommodate how land powers can challenge the command of the littoral or coastal environments, and by analogy how Earth-based weapons project power and capability into Earth orbit. As Earth orbit is a proxi-mate coastline, and not a distant region, thinking of chokepoints and blockading needs to occur within the confines of a littoral and contested environment, which is the basis for Proposition V.

Another problematic aspect of analogising from seapower theory is that celestial communications carry different communications to sea lines. As satellites and the communications that travel between them and terminals on Earth are part of the global political-econ-omy, it is not unreasonable to think of them as lanes of commerce. Yet the economic importance of space commerce in its current state cannot be compared to Corbettian and Mahanian notions of sea commerce in their bluewater theories.[113] It is true that fundamental energy and foodstuffs would still be transported across the sea if relevant celestial lines of communication for their support were threatened, albeit at a reduced efficiency because modern ports and shipping rely on space communications and navigation services. Yet it is possible to see abstract similarities between space commerce and maritime commerce in terms of their strategic utility – it is the particular consequences of a breakdown in the use of the respective lines of communication that vary between maritime economic warfare and astroeconomic warfare. Targets in space and at sea can be directly militarily relevant (e.g. military communications satellites or warships), or they may not be built for battle but carry out economic functions (e.g. commercial satellite networks and merchant fleets). Hertzfeld argues that 'space commerce' is inherently strategically valuable when commenting that:

> government policy and security aspects of space do not treat commercial space as they treat automobiles, soap, or furniture. Because of the strategic value of space as well as the huge dependence of almost every industry on the space infrastructure, space commands special importance and has become a critical national resource.[114]

Celestial lines of communication do differ from sea lines of communication in terms of their economic functions and composition, but the degree of that importance to the biggest economies in the international system is debatable. The consequences of blockading lines of communication are difficult to predict when no material goods travel through them, while the information they convey is often of very high importance in both civilian and military worlds. Furthermore, the political object of the war changes the significance of losing lines of communication. As the political intensity or desire of a war's object changes, so does the tolerance of pain from losing lines of communication, wealth and infrastructure.

These lines of communication and the consequences of actions in Earth orbit may be shared among participants and third parties; the consequences of extensive space warfare may be felt across the terrestrial economy. However, it is important not to assign space commerce the same degree of importance as sea-based trade. Sheldon criticises seapower analogies to outer space because too many theories possess 'an implicit assumption that space power is able to exercise the same leverage as sea power. All of these assumptions are far from definitive, and often ignore crucial differences between sea and space power.'[115] True, bluewater theories about sea commerce can be taken too far so that some may believe that the aggregate effects of spacepower, including economic effects, may be 'incalculable' and therefore insufferable if lost.[116] Yet Corbettian and Mahanian theories are not the entirety of seapower thinking on commerce, as demonstrated in Proposition V in the next chapter. Continental thought adds to bluewater interpretations of the subject, and has made economic warfare and maritime commerce relevant to continental states that always have alternatives to seapower and sea lines of communication. Analogously, space powers are based on Earth: they are Terran in nature, culture, perspective and priority, and can invest in alternatives to space-based infrastructure for many tasks and lines of communication. These are different to the bluewater empires that relied on sea commerce for their economic vitality. Although concepts of blockade and advantageous positions are relevant to warfare in the cosmic coastline, blockading may not be feasible to achieve or even that important to certain foes because typical visions of blockade assume that sea lines of communications are the only routes between oneself and the enemy. That is not true of spacepower and the strategic context of space warfare because contemporary space powers exist on the same planet, and often share borders and live as terrestrial neighbours.

Summary: Command and communication

This chapter's four propositions critiqued and synthesised bluewater-derived spacepower theory and have offered insights regarding the command and communication of a strategic geography and medium. Proposition I connected space warfare to grand strategy and political objectives, and explained how space control and space denial are equal sub-concepts of commanding space. Proposition II reminds us that despite the conceptual similarities between the sea and space in Proposition I, space is its own unique environment, requires single-environment specialists, and is best seen as supporting infrastructure. Proposition III then claimed that even if a dominant command of space was achieved, it does not guarantee dominance on Earth. Commanding space is not decisive by itself, should not be seen as an inherent centre of gravity, and seeking decisive battles should not become dogmatic axiom. Proposition IV substantiated the vision of space communications, and stressed that the command of space is ultimately about the use or denial of celestial lines of communication in the physical and electromagnetic worlds. The extent to which ideas of blockade can be realised in ignorance of the challenges posed by terrestrial counterspace forces and combined arms (Proposition III) as well as terrestrial alternatives (Proposition II) serves as a reminder that analogies break at some point. Still, these bluewater analogies have created a useful discussion of the early efforts, and spacepower theorising and constructive propositions for the rest of the theory to build upon.

Bluewater seapower theory can provide a useful ideal to structure strategic thinking about space through the quest for decisive battles, yet one must remember that seeking battle for its own sake will create intellectual as well as material problems. Decisive naval battles were quite rare, and even large battles were strategically indecisive without a conscious exploitation of the effective command of the sea that was won as a result. Celestial lines of communication were drawn directly from bluewater seapower to illustrate space communications and chokepoints, but the notions of blockade based on oceanic expanses do not describe contemporary spacepower in Earth orbit, which is not that far away and not the only route through which strategic effects can travel in modern warfare. Although much of Mahan's Influence series was focused on French experiences as a continental sea power, much of the maritime struggles involved colonial warfare. The narratives were of clashes between Britain and France over possessions separated by great expanses of water, of distant regions far from home connected only by the sea where blockading caused significant economic and military effects. However, as shown in the next chapter, Mahan also wrote extensively about the use of seapower in continental European wars, but such insights have not been applied by spacepower theorists until now. As well as drawing on the continental insights of Mahan, the next chapter brings the work of Raoul Castex to the fore, an early to mid-twentieth-century French strategist compelled to think of seapower from a continental perspective. Continental thinking about seapower is extremely useful because they are not fixated upon distant regions separated by oceans, and builds upon the foundations provided by bluewater thought. Continental thought projects a littoral or coastal vision and mindset towards Earth orbit, and reflects the strategic dynamics of proximate land powers using seapower. Seapower theory is more relevant in modern strategy because it theorises the dynamics between neighbouring Terran powers with proximate and shared orbital coastlines. A continental school of seapower congeals the insights of continental seapower into a new vision of Earth orbit as a cosmic coastline.

Notes

1. Corbett, *Principles of Maritime Strategy*, p. 14.
2. Mahan, *The Influence of Sea Power upon History*, p. 329.
3. Klein, *Space Warfare*, pp. 60, 175, note 1. On the control school doctrine, see: Lupton, *On Space Warfare*, pp. 60–9.
4. Klein, *Space Warfare*, p. 60; Smith, *Ten Propositions*, p. 74; Oberg, *Space*, p. 130; Dolman, *Astropolitik*, pp. 8, 70–5, 130–4.
5. Brown, 'Space', p. 237.
6. UK Ministry of Defence, 'UK Air and Space Doctrine', pp. 7-7-7-14; US Joint Chiefs of Staff, *Joint Publication 3–14*.
7. Clausewitz, *On War*, pp. 786–7.
8. Gray, *Another Bloody Century*, p. 308.
9. Gray, *The Navy*, pp. 156–7.
10. Dolman, *Astropolitik*, pp. 8, 70–5, 130–4.
11. Klein, *Space Warfare*, pp. 24–8, 51–60. See also: Fox, 'Some Principles of Space Strategy', pp. 7–11.
12. Corbett, *Principles of Maritime Strategy*, p. 87.
13. Klein, *Space Warfare*, pp. 111–13; Worden, 'Space Control', p. 233.
14. Klein, *Space Warfare*, pp. 61–2.
15. Bowen, 'From the Sea', pp. 545–51.
16. Mahan, *The Influence of Sea Power upon History*, p. 14.
17. Till, *Seapower*, 3rd edition, p. 145.

18. Mahan, *The Influence of Sea Power upon History*, p. 14.
19. Ibid. pp. 53–5, 225–6, 514; Mahan, *The Influence of Sea Power upon the French Revolution*, p. 386; on a dismissal of Mahan in spacepower theory, see: Klein, *Space Warfare*, p. 20.
20. Hill, *Maritime Strategy*, p. 35.
21. Mahan, *The Influence of Sea Power upon History*, p. 514.
22. Douhet, *The Command of the Air*, pp. 18–19.
23. Klein, *Space Warfare*, p. 60; Fox, 'Some Principles of Space Strategy', pp. 7–11.
24. Gray, *Another Bloody Century*, p. 308.
25. Gray, *The Navy*, p. 147.
26. Sheldon, *Reasoning*, p. 106.
27. Gray, *The Navy*, pp. 157–8.
28. Smith and Uttley, 'The Changing Face of Maritime Power', p. 186.
29. Smith, *Ten Propositions*, p. 74.
30. Oberg, *Space*, p. 130.
31. Dolman, *Astropolitik*, esp. pp. 8, 70–5, 130–4.
32. For example, see: Burris, 'Astroimpolitic', esp. pp. 109–10. For a critique of logical absolutism among the space arms control proponents, see: Lopez, 'Predicting'.
33. Corbett, *Principles of Maritime Strategy*, p. 209.
34. Sheldon, *Reasoning*, esp. Chapter 1, and p. 22.
35. Dolman, *Astropolitik*, p. 61.
36. Oberg, *Space*, p. 126.
37. Dolman, *Astropolitik*, pp. 69–70.
38. For example: Straub, 'Application of a Maritime Framework', pp. 65–77.
39. Gray, *Modern Strategy*, p. 258.
40. Gray, 'Inescapable Geography', p. 162.
41. On orbit types, see: UK MoD, *UK Military Space Primer*, pp. 1-44–1-53; Air Command, *AU-18*, pp. 89–112.
42. Air Command, *AU-18*, p. 89. Note that the *UK Military Space Primer* says 100–1,200 km for LEO on p. 1–46.
43. Air Command, *AU-18*, p. 92.
44. On apogees, perigees and HEO, see: UK MoD, *UK Military Space Primer*, pp. 1-30–1-31, 1-36–1-37, 1-50–1-51
45. Klein, *Space Warfare*, p. 10.
46. Air Command, *AU-18*, p. 118; Watts, *The Military Uses of Space*, p. 9
47. Dolman, *Astropolitik*, p. 75.
48. Paikowsky, *The Power of the Space Club*, pp. 161–3.

49. Messier, 'IMF'.
50. Pace et al., *The Global Positioning System*, p. 48.
51. Worden, 'Space Control', p. 228.
52. Smith, *Ten Propositions*, p. 74; Oberg, *Space*, pp. 46, 128, 131.
53. Sheldon, *Reasoning*, pp. 310–15.
54. Gray, *The Navy*, pp. 99, 126.
55. Gray, *Modern Strategy*, p. 259.
56. Gray and Sheldon, 'Space Power', p. 27.
57. Bowen, 'The RAF', pp. 58–65.
58. Dolman, *Astropolitik*, p. 8.
59. Ibid. p. 68. For a similar view of the future of spacepower, see: France and Sellers, 'Real Constraints'.
60. Gray and Sheldon, 'Space Power', p. 25.
61. Fuller et al., 'The Commercial Space Industry'.
62. On the potential political-economy of the solar system, see: Dudley-Flores and Gangale, 'Forecasting'.
63. Heuser, *The Evolution*, p. 224.
64. Mahan, *The Influence of Sea Power upon History*, p. 469.
65. Ibid., pp. 338–9; Corbett, *Principles of Maritime Strategy*, pp. 99–100, 103–4, 113–18.
66. Brown, 'Space', p. 243.
67. Corbett, *Principles of Maritime Strategy*, pp. 170–1.
68. Klein, *Space Warfare*, p. 20; Sheldon, *Reasoning*, p. 150.
69. Klein, *Space Warfare*, p. 122.
70. Mahan, *The Influence of Sea Power upon History*, pp. 14, 53–5, 193, 225–6, 514.
71. Coats, 'Worldwide Threat Assessment', p. 13.
72. Corbett, *Principles of Maritime Strategy*, p. 167.
73. Till, *Seapower*, 2nd edition, p. 62.
74. Corbett, *Principles of Maritime Strategy*, p. 113.
75. On the paradoxical nature of war, see: Luttwak, *Strategy*.
76. Corbett, *Principles of Maritime Strategy*, p. 209.
77. Ibid. p. 209.
78. Smith, *Ten Propositions*, p. 74; Oberg, *Space*, p. 130; Sheldon and Gray, 'Theory Ascendant', pp. 14–15.
79. Hays, *United States Military Space*, pp. 8–14.
80. For example: Kleinberg, 'On War', pp. 9–10; Lambakis, *On the Edge*, p. 101; Berkowitz, 'National Space Policy', pp. 50–1; Lambeth, *Mastering the Ultimate Highground*, p. 99.
81. Clausewitz, *On War*, p. 921.
82. Moltz, 'The Changing Dynamics', p. 87.

83. Smith, *Ten Propositions*, pp. 64–9; Gray, *Another Bloody Century*, pp. 311–12.
84. Brown, 'Space', p. 239.
85. Gray, *Another Bloody Century*, p. 309; Sheldon, *Reasoning*, p. 303.
86. Sheldon, *Reasoning*, p. 261.
87. Smith, *Ten Propositions*, pp. 105–6.
88. Gray, *Modern Strategy*, p. 259.
89. However, unlike in Afghanistan, in 1991 Iraq had attempted to counter US space assets. See: Richelson, *America's Space Sentinels*, p. 172.
90. Sheldon, *Reasoning*, pp. 374–97.
91. An entire book written by Mahan on the riverine operations of the Union Navy makes such accusations incredulous: Mahan, *The Gulf*, esp. pp. 3–4, 11–12.
92. Mahan, *The Influence of Sea Power upon History*, p. 209.
93. Klein, *Space Warfare*, pp. 52, 56.
94. McVadon, 'China's Navy', p. 382.
95. Weeden, 'Radio Frequency Spectrum', p. 3.
96. Ibid. p. 3.
97. Spires, *Beyond Horizons*, p. 248.
98. Klein, *Space Warfare*, p. 80.
99. Ibid. p. 82.
100. Ibid. pp. 82–4.
101. Ibid. p. 84.
102. Ibid. p. 88.
103. Ibid. p. 92.
104. Ibid. pp. 93, 98, 103.
105. Gray, *Modern Strategy*, p. 258, footnote 119.
106. Dolman, *Astropolitik*, pp. 39, 73.
107. Dolman, *Astropolitik*, p. 75; Klein, *Space Warfare*, p. 157.
108. See: Center for Strategic and International Studies, 'Space-based missile defence'.
109. Dolman, *Astropolitik*, pp. 37–9.
110. On the maritime warfare aspect of the development of over-the-horizon weaponry, see: Friedman, *Seapower*.
111. Klein, *Space Warfare*, pp. 49, 91–9, 123.
112. Mahan, *The Influence of Sea Power upon History*, p. 138.
113. Sheldon, *Reasoning*, p. 195.
114. Hertzfeld, 'Commercial Space', p. 216.
115. Sheldon, *Reasoning*, p. 146.
116. Brown, 'Space', p. 239.

PART II

A New Vision of Spacepower:
The Celestial Coastline

3. Continental Insights and Strategic Manoeuvring

Spacepower cannot escape the reality that it exists on and close to Earth. It is in the proximate littoral environment of Earth orbit and used for objectives and needs on Earth. Civilisation has yet to leave this 'cradle of humanity' and is only dipping its toes into the cosmic shore.[1] The 'oceans' of interplanetary space and the solar system are a distant prospect in terms of strategic relevance for power politics on Earth. The vision of a cosmic coastline provides a firmer geographical footing for the first four bluewater-derived propositions. The Earth-centric, or geocentric, coastal analogy stresses that space can be commanded from Earth by Earth-based weapons systems. The reality that power can be projected from Earth into orbit is often lost in discussions focusing on space-based weapons or orbital operations. Platforms in space, weaponised or not, will be like coastal vessels in range of landward weapons and political–economic influence. Space-based weapons will share the same vulnerabilities as the satellites they target. The fact that many states can create problems in a coastal environment due to its proximity and relative ease of access challenges the emergence of any space-faring hegemon or empire wishing to dominate Earth. Any would-be celestial hegemon must also secure its hegemony on Earth itself, because commanding space alone does not command Earth (Proposition III), and taking terrestrial actions against other space-faring states may be more effective than attacking their space infrastructure. This demonstrates how space cannot be viewed in isolation as Earth orbit is merely Earth's coastline and not a vast, separate ocean (Proposition V).

Proposition V follows from Proposition II in that the conditions of the environment must be taken into account. Analogies from bluewater seapower disguise the littoral nature of Earth orbit. Seapower in continental wars bears a striking conceptual resemblance to spacepower as we know it, particularly as expressed by Mahan as the noiseless pressure working in the background and as infrastructure from Proposition II to support wars on Earth.[2] Whilst Corbett dwelled upon the interactions between the land and the sea in maritime strategy, it was still from the perspective of an island sea power.[3] A continental school of seapower refers to the insights drawn from several sources that draw from the naval experiences of continental powers, and specifically the works of Raoul Castex, an inter-war French admiral of the twentieth century, among others.[4] A continental school of seapower allows us to more explicitly theorise something that is in the grey area of being neither decisive nor merely a sideshow in war. The idea of strategic manoeuvre helps one to visualise the myriad forms that influence projects on Earth, much in the same way seapower influenced continental wars. Contrary to bluewater seapower theory's frequent focus on large fleets, massive oceans, great expanses and the question of battle at sea, continental seapower theory resembles aspects of spacepower that do not fixate upon battle or destruction in orbit, but are defined by their contributions to warfare on Earth and their proximate geographic condition. Mahan was not limited to thinking on the seapower of maritime empires with distant colonies. It is unfortunate that 'because many students are taught that battleships and colonies make up the heart of Mahan's writing, he is frequently discounted as being of little consequence to discussions of today's challenges'.[5] Through continental seapower theory, the subtler yet defining aspects of spacepower that can be brought to bear during a war are theorised for the first time, and Mahan somewhat rehabilitated through his continental seapower insights.

After sketching the strategic analogy between continental seapower theory and spacepower in Earth orbit, Castex's concept of strategic manoeuvre is used to bind together the five components of Proposition V to theorise how spacepower manifests in the littoral realm of Earth orbit to support terrestrial grand strategies. Strategic manoeuvres are constituted by making Earth orbit a hostile coast-line for enemy forces on Earth from orbit or towards enemy satel-lites in orbit by the placement of counterspace weapons on Earth. Manoeuvres with spacepower also involve astroeconomic warfare and commerce raiding, as well as neutral and third parties which must face the problems of armed and abused neutralities. Space logistics are also considered as the arbiter of opportunity for action in space and on Earth, and finally, strategic manoeuvres can cre-ate strategic depth for terrestrial strategy and the primary theatres of Earth. Each component of Proposition V describes the relatively subtle effects of spacepower that all constitute the strategic manoeu-vring space powers can conduct.

A continental seapower analogy: Commanding space from Earth

The foundation for the coastal analogy is that Earth orbit is within weapons range of Earth's surface, space powers can be neighbours on Earth, may also share a cosmic coastline without vast, isolating distances between them, and celestial lines of com-munications are not the only ones available for strategic actors to use in war. However, before Proposition V is introduced the caveats to this analogy must be recognised. Denying celestial lines of communication during a battle may have more influ-ence on tactical terrestrial military capability than denying sea lines of communication for land battles. Even though claims on its inherent quality of 'decisiveness' were critiqued in Proposition III, tactical and operational combat capability could be acutely diminished if a space-dependent terrestrial force lost its access to celestial lines of communication. This acuity is something that cannot be theorised in advance as it pertains to particular material conditions, though the general effects of spacepower integration with terrestrial forces is theorised in Proposition VII. Although this is a significant difference in terms of the degree and tactical effect of seapower support to land forces and spacepower support to terrestrial forces, it is not a complete break from the abstract concepts in seapower theory. Mutual support between the land

and the sea can still advance thinking about the mutual supports between terrestrial forces and space systems.

Another caveat to this analogy is that amphibious operations and sealift have no direct equivalents today. Moving troops and heavy materials to various points on Earth through ballistic 'space-lift' is beyond what is practical today. The coastal analogy can resonate in a possible future for terrestrial wars where significant numbers of troops and materiel may be transported via celestial lines of communication. Dropping troops from orbit could loosely correspond to coastal raids and amphibious assaults, though without an ability for raiding parties to exit the theatre of operations in the same way they arrived. It is not unreasonable to imagine the paralysing effect of the threat of amphibious assaults from sea as being resonant with the threat of orbital troop drops that could strike in many places. Orbital bombardment from space-based weapons could be like coastal shelling and gunboat diplomacy but with a much greater internal reach of its target, encroaching on the classic debates of airpower's 'strategic bombing' and close air support.[6] Orbital-based conventional and nuclear strike systems, with warheads which re-enter the atmosphere after loitering in orbit, whilst gaining some degree of mobility and range, will suffer many logistical penalties by being based in space, even though it is technically feasible. These shortcomings are addressed later in this chapter. As these space-to-Earth capabilities remain merely blueprints and are not being seriously pursued, operational, deployed and developing Earth-to-space and space-to-space weapons are favoured for analysis.[7] Should orbital logistics become far more affordable and the political, economic, logistical and normative constraints on placing bombardment systems in space be overcome, conceptual resonances and precedents are at hand through the use of the coastal analogy to Earth orbit. Strategic paralysis caused by the fear and overextension from anticipating a space-borne ground assault for the defender and the difficulty of sustainment from space for the aggressor may all find precedent in coastal warfare, with no promises of easy victories or helpless defenders.

Isolated instances of thinking of Earth orbit as a coast or a littoral environment have not gone unchallenged. Sheldon argued that 'near-Earth space is not bounded by landmasses like terrestrial littorals and issues such as shallowness or deepness are meaning-less in space . . . Thus the analogy is an imperfect fit.'[8] Criticisms of an imperfect analogical fit in terms of physical features are accurate but insubstantial, as the 'existence of mismatches . . . does not necessarily invalidate the analogy'.[9] It is the derived concepts from the matches that do exist that matter most for a strategic analogy. These analogies arise from the resonance of using a geographic medium to command lines of communication in it, as explored in the previous chapter, and the proximity of Earth orbit to all ter-restrial environments, relative to oceans, as just outlined. All geo-graphic media or physical environments are diverse, but the air, sea and space are all strategically analogical at a highly abstract level through commanding the medium and exploiting its lines of com-munications for effects elsewhere, as argued in Propositions I and II. The 'shallowness and deepness' of coastal regions are of little conceptual concern for spacepower theory, other than to note that the cosmic coastline itself is not a uniform 'astrography' and there are different characteristics to the different altitudes and regions of the cosmic coastline as detailed in Proposition II. The principle that the coast's adjacency and proximity to other strategic geogra-phies is useful.

Despite such limitations, the resonances of the analogy are use-ful to consider the nature of spacepower in Earth orbit. As Earth orbit is a cosmic coastline, weapons based on Earth produce strategic effects in orbit, undermining the need for space-based weaponry as their advantages in mobility and firing ranges are not significantly greater over the mass deployment of terrestrial coun-terspace assets. This is analogous to coastal waters in the presence of land-based anti-ship defences. The astrodeterminist theories espoused by Deudney and Dolman under-emphasise the ability of states to challenge an orbital hegemony with Earth-based coun-terspace weapons and nuclear weapons technology. They down-play the fact that space-based weapons are not needed to conduct effective forms of space warfare, and that space weaponisation would not necessarily herald a new era of international rela-tions.[10] Understanding Earth orbit as a cosmic coastline, rather than a vast expansive ocean, casts practical doubts on the theo-retical achievement of global hegemony through spacepower and in its place promotes a more realistic vision of spacepower that reflects its contested, proximate and multipolar nature. Even in altitudes where space-based weapons may be timelier than terrestrial equivalents if they are forward-deployed in the correct locations, such as in GEO for close-inspection, jamming and physical interception, their deployment may trigger adaptive responses. In line with Proposition III, this reduces their potential decisiveness, demonstrating the paradoxical nature of strategy. If assets are forward-deployed during peacetime, other parties will have time to develop countermeasures in space or on Earth. If the GEO weapons are not deployed when war begins, their advantages on timeliness and perhaps surprise are lost, as any launch may tip off the adversary, if other forms of intelligence gathering and analysis had not already revealed intentions. Deploying weapons in orbit is not necessarily a game-changer once the limitations of orbital technologies are taken into account alongside the reality that Earth orbit is a secondary, littoral and adjunct environment. The presence of adjacent environments dilute the strategic effects of activities and weapons in any single environment.

In continental wars, sea lines of communication are not the only route to reach an objective and sometimes there are no 'distant regions', as seen with island powers and maritime empires. Continental powers can circumvent sea lines of communication over land to put pressure on maritime empires.[11] Terrestrial capabilities, political objectives, and operations will dominate the space strategies of Terran powers in the same way as land priorities shape a continental power's maritime strategy. Mahan noted and studied conditions when seapower was 'used in the service of the land'.[12] Due to the lack of distant regions and the proximity – or adjacency – of other geographies, the possibilities and relative ease of commanding space from Earth to support terrestrial warfare and war aims on Earth is the epitome of a strategic analogy from continental seapower theory to spacepower theory.

What if there are no distant regions between continental sea powers? What if the bulk of resources committed are towards the land forces, the vast number of troops and civilians killed are on land, and strategic decisions made are always with the overbearing needs of the land war in mind? Where do navies and seapower fit into such calculations? Bluewater seapower theory does not examine these problems. Using continental seapower analogies allows one to consider these terrestrial precedents that match Terran space powers fighting each other on Earth. Modern 'space powers' are in fact Earth-based or Terran powers that use spacepower like continental land powers use seapower (e.g. Sparta, Carthage, Rome, Russia, India). Continental sea powers may share borders on land. Likewise, space powers may be close neighbours on Earth. A 'true' space power may be a space-based power that thrives on the resources of the solar system and depends on celestial lines of communication for everything it does, as opposed to that of Earth's. This would correlate with the seapower of an island or sea-dependent polity (e.g. Athens, Britain, the Netherlands). If some political-economies truly become dependent on space-based resources and habitation beyond Earth, they may claim more credibility as a 'true' space-based space power. A continental seapower approach therefore begs the following questions of spacepower: what if spacepowers are neighbours on Earth? What if space infrastructure is in reach of terrestrial space denial weapons on the other side of the globe because many powers are on a shared cosmic coastline? How should spacepower be strategised when major objectives, events and violence are on Earth, and not in space? So what if Earth orbit is 'merely' a flank in a secondary theatre and not the focus of grand strategy?

Any discussion of flanking – of attacking in a supposed weak point and not at the enemy's frontal strong points – must not lose sight of its cardinal principle that flanking is not an advantage in and of itself. Clausewitz argued that 'in itself, [flanking] is as yet nothing; but it will become something [either advantageous or disadvantageous] in connection with other things'.[13] Developing further from Proposition III, consciously exploiting and using the coastal flank in conjunction with other theatres and objectives matters more than securing that flank itself. Theory must embrace this and endeavour to theorise the exploitation of the celestial flank of Earth orbit in detail. Clausewitz argued that 'action against the lines of communication is directed against . . . all the means which the enemy requires to keep his army in a vigorous and healthy condition'.[14] This description is apt when considering actions to attack Proposition IV's celestial lines of communication that support the force enhancement of modern militaries.

Spacepower concerns the exploitation of a potential flank upon terrestrial powers that can develop systems that project effects from Earth into orbit, and hold celestial lines of communications and a command of space at risk. Continental seapower allows a greater scope to theorise and anticipate the possibilities of minor and handicapped sea or space powers, not merely the would-be hegemons of the sea, the cosmos or the international system. Continental sea powers could achieve various degrees of the command of the sea in coastal regions without using large ocean-going fleets. They could instead use their land power to complement their attempts to secure a degree of the command of the sea for their more immediate landward concerns, or develop specialised coastal attack craft and shoreline fortifications to frustrate any hope of an unchallenged amphibious landing or close blockade. Developing counterspace measures are easier and cheaper than developing space systems, including space-based weapon systems which must also be based in space and share their vulnerability to terrestrial fire as normal satellites do.[15] This of course is not the same as employing space for terrestrial force enhancement, however. This should caution against any view that space-based weapons are a silver bullet or transformative solution to strategic problems because of the threat of accessible terrestrial capabilities. This adjacent character of spacepower in Earth orbit is far more profound for spacepower theory than Corbett's view of the interaction of land and sea power allow. Corbett's theory was conditioned by the experiences of an island power that had to use the sea for every strategically meaningful action, unlike seapower between continental powers. Grand strategy in the Space Age must embrace the terrestrial origins and ends of spacepower, and not only space-based infrastructure and weapons systems. Only through grasping Earth orbit as a coastline for strategic manoeuvring does this become apparent and constructive for education, alongside the cultural and political consequences of this geocentrism discussed in Proposition VI.

The coastal area for outer space, for the purposes of spacepower theory, includes what Dolman calls Terran space, which extends from 100 km to around 36,000 km altitude, just beyond the GEO belt, and 40,000 km to include the apogees of the highly eccentric Molniya orbits. Beyond the GEO belt, going into cislunar (between Earth and the Moon) or interplanetary space, space may become more akin to the high seas where spacecraft may enjoy relative safety and obscurity away from the Earth, unlike spacecraft on Earth's cosmic coastline between 100 km and 36,000–40,000 km altitude. Just as a coastal region includes the land near the sea and the sea near the land, discussion of the cosmic coastline must not ignore Earth's surface which is near space and the parts of space which are near Earth. Oberg is correct to argue that 'space is nearby. Just a hundred kilometres above us.'[16] This re-emphasises Proposition II that space is so close by it cannot be isolated from terrestrial considerations. There are geographically bound forms of power (air, land, sea) that can influence spacepower capabilities in Earth orbit – therefore it is akin to a coastline and serves as a juncture for continental seapower theory to be brought in under the capstone of 'strategic manoeuvre'.

Proposition V: Earth orbit is a cosmic coastline suited for strategic manoeuvres

Strategic manoeuvre means moving one's forces, resources or capabilities to, between or within primary and secondary theatres that are more profitable for overall strategic results, usually by resorting to gaining some measure of success in secondary theatres that can be translated into support for the main theatre of the war. Conducting operations in the hostile coast with neutral and third parties, harnessing logistical realities and utilising strategic depth are all ways of manoeuvring in the secondary theatre of Earth orbit to support the primary theatre of Earth's surface. Raoul Castex argued that it is

> a *method* used by strategy to improve the conditions of the struggle, to multiply the return on her efforts, and to obtain the greatest results, whether in the duel between principal forces themselves or to the benefit of particularly important nonmaritime requirements.[17]

The sea can provide opportunities for strategic manoeuvre for two land powers with shared coastlines through coastal flanking and using it to impose changes in the disposition of land forces. In addition, goals in the environment can be important objectives for maritime forces, imposing the influence of land priorities on naval strategy.

Castex's strategic manoeuvre discusses the basics of being strategically flexible in order to: (a) disperse your own forces where possible; (b) concentrate them against whatever may be the enemy's 'vital points' in a Jominian sense; and (c) delineate priorities between primary and secondary theatres and distribute forces accordingly. The perceived necessity or opportunity of flanking via the sea assumes that a major land front has stabilised and does not need the totality of your resources and capabilities, comparable to the trenches of the Western Front in the First World War. An economy of force necessitates weakening some positions to strengthen others. A manoeuvre from A which may weaken itself in places, may cause B to unwisely disperse its forces in some areas to provide greater advantages in crucial areas to A, epitomising Luttwak's claim on the paradoxical nature of strategy.[18] However, there are always risks in strategic manoeuvring. Exposing a new vulnerability to an alert foe becomes a greater risk if the manoeuvre is more pronounced and entails more resources to the detriment of other fronts, theatres or objectives.[19] Given this targeted and instrumental view of continental seapower, one can appreciate Soviet Admiral Sergei Gorshkov's insistence that 'in a struggle even against a continental adversary an important role is played by the navy'.[20] Manoeuvres are conducted in the secondary theatre to support and influence the primary theatre. Those risks are magnified, however, if the enemy in practice has anticipated such moves, and the line of least expectation may paradoxically become the most 'frontal' approach.[21]

The cosmic coastline is a venue to make such strategic manoeuvres, and through the deployment of Earth-based anti-satellite weapons and the support satellites provided for terrestrial militaries, the cosmic coastline is already a potentially hostile and contested one fraught with risks for terrestrial powers. Statements about the sea as a secondary and supporting medium is at odds with the general visions of bluewater seapower that have shaped most analogies with spacepower from the sea in the literature. Viewing space as a secondary and supporting theatre to trigger movements by the enemy in other theatres, such as those on Earth, is a form of flanking. This is not an attempt to portray a war-winning 'indirect approach' for space strategy along the lines of Liddell-Hart in the twentieth century.[22] Instead, this continental seapower approach to spacepower allows for a structured theorisation of less spectacular, more mundane, and everyday space activities that contribute to the war effort and characterise the bulk of space-based activities today, and in the process putting space warfare activities, including space-based weapons, into a larger geostrategic understanding of spacepower and what it enables in war.

Hostile coasts

Terrestrial powers can threaten orbit, and conversely space systems in orbit can threaten terrestrial powers through the force enhancement of terrestrial military and intelligence capabilities. Hostile coasts refers to threats to space and threats from space. Treating space as a barrier that can separate adversaries, as mentioned in Proposition IV, does not anticipate conditions that are analogous to coastal warfare and continental wars. For a powerful actor that has established a general and persistent command of space, it can be a barrier that enables it to 'take as much or as little space warfare as [it wills]', enabling a conflict to be limited to a particular theatre and helping to prevent any retaliation in, to and from space which may have effects in the blockader's core territory.[23] A space blockade, by being able to intercept things that try to get into space or loiter there, is based upon a British–American and usually imperial notion of vast oceans and dominant battle fleets separating belligerents' core territories. This concept of a barrier falls short of being universally relevant because it does not account for the adjacency of Earth orbit, the diversity of space powers, and how viewing Earth orbit as a shared, proximate and hostile coastline puts 'domestic' space infrastructure at risk from weapons stationed on the other side of Earth's surface from a multitude of actors.

Raja Menon, a retired Indian Navy Rear Admiral, articulated this gap in bluewater views of seapower theory and asked what if there are no distant regions?[24] Menon also turned to Castex as he 'actually defined a scenario where two adjacent coastal powers engage in a major land war'.[25] Establishing space as a barrier does not quite work when two major powers may be neighbours on Earth, in a similar way to how two neighbouring land powers cannot isolate themselves from each other through seapower alone, unlike between bluewater maritime empires. A barrier in space may be an unworkable option for adjacent terrestrial adversaries, such as India and Pakistan. Even should India close off celestial lines of communication to Pakistan, turning orbital space into a 'barrier', the shared land, air and sea frontiers do not allow India to take as little or as much from the war as it wills. Pakistan can still resort to other strategic geographies for resistance and retaliation. The barrier concept overlooks the possibilities of 'coastal fire' from the Earth towards space, how hostile actions in the cosmic coastline may not be easily contained due to runaway debris or widespread jamming, and how celestial lines of communication are not the only lines of communication in a war. Continental thought about seapower often assumes the need to operate with or against the advantages enjoyed by a coastal defender. The advantages yielded to the defender in coastal warfare – such as the ability to harness internal landward communications for resupply, repair, maximum resource availability, and embedded, prepared and specialised firing equipment and positions – could make a coastal theatre very inhospitable to the coastal attacker.[26] Mahan saw value in such defences as well, where relatively fixed assets on land would complement mobile assets at sea to defend the coastline and project influence outwards.[27] As space-based weapons in Earth orbit can mimic coastal attack craft, it is important to remember the land-based coastal defences in the analogy in the form of Earth-based anti-satellite weapons. The latter are deployed today and constitute the primary and proven form of space warfare potential to turn Earth orbit into a hostile coast.

The possibilities in continental seapower and coastal warfare vary depending on the measure of resources given to protecting maritime flanks and engaging in sea-denial activities. Callwell concluded that an inferior continental naval power's coastal defences must 'compel the respect of the hostile fleets' or have its naval forces face certain destruction and its territory prepare for invasion.[28] With enough resources committed, a hostile coast can frustrate an enemy's maritime strategy that has not considered a land power's reach over the littoral waters, despite a preponderance earned on the high seas or the level of command of the sea enjoyed by the enemy. Till insists that 'sea denial may ... act as a complement to sea control' in coastal and continental warfare denial strategies and such capabilities should not be overlooked.[29] Examples of continental seapower struggles against bluewater seapower include Zamorin resistance against the Portuguese empire in the sixteenth century and the Maratha's coastal waters-based repulsion of the Dutch and British ocean-going fleets during the eighteenth century.[30] These materially inferior continental sea powers challenged bluewater sea powers by using the advantages provided by coastal waters and their proximity to land, much in the same way it is possible for powers without a great presence in orbit to challenge others who may have a significant presence and infrastructure there. Projecting power and influence from Earth into orbit with specialised capabilities can challenge a power that may be more dominant in general terms, and should check any fantastical vision of space becoming the domain of a single hegemon should there be a political will to resist it. Even bluewater-derived imperial dominance had its limits when it encountered the coasts of capable land-based defenders.

Parallels can be drawn between orbital combat spacecraft and the French *Jeune École* (Young School), which emphasised the use of torpedo boats in coastal waters to challenge the primacy of the Royal Navy in the late nineteenth century, as opposed to bluewater capital ships, cruisers and supporting fleets.[31] However, in the absence of a range of orbital combat spacecraft and deep space fleets that go beyond Earth orbit, it may be many generations before constructive analogies to space may be constructed from discussing the merits of specialised orbital combat spacecraft. The chief reason is that humanity's use of spacepower today has barely escaped the range of coastal Earth-based weapons fire in both the Newtonian and electromagnetic realms, where even orbital combat spacecraft may not be desirable to wage space warfare. In Earth orbit, there is no bluewater environment for materially superior powers to dominate with presence alone – only the cosmic coastline which is within reach of a multitude of anti-satellite weaponry and other Earth-based methods of countering the advantages of spacepower derived from the celestial coastline. The concepts and experiences of landward guns firing effectively at naval vessels, and turning other land-based assets against naval ones,[32] is analogous to Earth-based weapons system firing upon satellites, and can derive advantages that space-based weapons systems may not enjoy. In addition, terrestrial operations against the ground-based segments of space systems may be easier and 'cleaner' – relative to debris-generating weapons fire in orbit – such as storming a satellite ground station with Special Forces and capturing or killing its staff and destroying or commandeering the facility. The actual efficacy of these activities will vary with each case of counterspace operation and its targets, but the principle is valid due to the proximate condition of spacepower in the celestial coastline. It is worth remembering that space-based weapons will suffer similar vulnerabilities in the terrestrial command and control segments.

Terrestrial weapons systems can be specialised to take advantage of terrestrial logistics chains and physical security through direct and manual human operation to a greater extent than orbital combat spacecraft, and generate hostile coastal zones for satellites. Manoeuvres and weapons fire from Earth can be used to force enemy assets into less advantageous positions, as detailed Proposition IV, to hamper their normal celestial lines of communication for strategic effects elsewhere. Joint actions and the terrestrial capabilities can impact upon celestial lines of communication and the distribution of orbital assets and the terrestrial units that rely on them. As operations on land could influence the command of the sea, operations on Earth can influence the command of space. A Chinese educational text on space warfare operations encourages thought along these lines when it declares that:

> firepower strikes involve applying space strength and other service and branches' long-range precision strike capability against the enemy's aerospace bases in a sustained, ferocious firepower assault. The

goal is to destroy key points in the base, including aerospace instruments, space launch equipment, launch facilities, and various supporting facilities.[33]

Space infrastructure is not immune to destruction just because space has not been 'weaponised'. Earth orbit can be turned into a hostile littoral even when facing an opponent that may have little space-based space warfare capabilities of its own, especially when electronic warfare and cyber infiltration options are considered. Internal lines of communication, and raising the seapower profile of a land-based power if it manages to fortify its coastal zones, is applicable to spacepower in the way that a weaker or terrestrial 'space power' can still threaten the space systems of a major space power if they invest in 'coastal space weapons' such as Earth-based lasers, cyber and electronic warfare systems directed against satellite systems.

An illustration of a missed opportunity for 'counterspace coastal fire' is Iraqi anti-satellite capabilities in the Gulf War (1990–1). During the war, 'Iraqi electronic countermeasures were, in principle, logistically possible early in the conflict, but they very rapidly lost that capability during the air campaign as radar sites were neutralized.'[34] Perhaps not anticipating the American response to their invasion of Kuwait, the Iraqi leadership may have decided that jamming the relevant satellites to forestall, or slow, any intervention was unnecessary. Meaning 'as a result, possible anti-satellite weaponry such as employment of radar sites for satellite jamming, was not attempted and those assets were quickly destroyed during the opening air campaign'.[35] Iraqi intelligence capabilities regarding the finding and fixing of the correct satellites as targets remain unknown, but as an illustrative example on the potential of Earth-based anti-satellite capabilities it serves spacepower theory's purpose.

Earth-based weapons matter for spacepower, like weapons, installations and forces based on land matter for seapower, which is at odds with public rhetoric and debate on space warfare that tends to focus on space-based weaponry at the expense of Earth-based weapon systems.[36] Being able to command space from Earth is not focused upon in other spacepower theories. This principle provides a materialist corrective to the techno-determinism and the centrality of space-based weapons encountered in much space warfare literature. This reinforces the argument of Proposition III that it will be difficult to command Earth from space due to the ability of terrestrial powers to contest the command of space. Space-based weapons should not be excluded from calculations, but rather placed into a larger 'coastal' or adjacent astrographic context when space-based weapons will share the vulnerabilities of 'normal' satellites. The technical gains of space-based weapons are still debated, especially when the costs of development and deployment are taken into account. The most promising space-based weapons technology, beyond jamming, is solid-state lasers for space-to-space firing, but this remains an emergent and unproven technology for weapons-grade purposes. Earth orbit, and the command of space, can be contested without deploying space-based weapons because earth orbit is a proximate and littoral environment. Callwell claimed that strategic success or failure at sea can be decided by land power with no battle at sea itself. He argued that:

> at sea there may be no field of battle to be held, nor places to be won. But even the purely naval issue may not be decided at sea. The final object of attack in maritime warfare should always be the organised forces afloat of the enemy, but those organised forces may be afloat in harbour.[37]

This passage is useful to consider satellites as the targets of celestial coastal weapons – or Earth-based anti-satellite weapons. Ships too close to the land and coastal fortifications are vulnerable – much like satellites that come into range of terrestrial anti-satellite weapons. Terrestrial operations could help to decide the command of space in a time and place like seapower sometimes yields a decision over the command of the sea to land operations. Although spacepower cannot 'come to grips with itself in combat',[38] it may be wrong to argue that as more space powers emerge and mature, the need for space-based weaponry to negate enemy space infrastructure, particularly at altitudes far beyond LEO, will grow. Systems such as Brilliant Pebbles, which were considered by the

United States in the 1980s, may indeed be feasible, but they have not been developed. Concerns over the debris-creation may place normative restraints on their use, though the risk of the increased debris collision remains a threat for the long-term future, rather than the immediate conflict, sparing other satellites for the near future. Should effective space-based lasers come to fruition, they may still struggle to defend themselves from hostile fire from Earth. Contrary to orbital weapons platforms, terrestrial space weapons may be hardened, hidden and deployed en masse to face off against a range of physical attacks.

States can employ countermeasures against space assets to affect the military prowess of any modern spacepower-augmented military, and use space assets against the interests of other powers who may be located on the other side of the globe. Large space-powers will need to use terrestrial operations to help secure their space infrastructure, like land operations supporting the actions of naval forces and infrastructure. The ground segments may be fixed, but space-based infrastructure is inherently global as it orbits the planet, even though its services may only be required on a more regional basis. This means that space warfare capabilities can be useful even for states without global terrestrial power projection ambitions. Regional and smaller powers, not only global powers, have an interest in space warfare capabilities, particularly as smaller states become more dependent on spacepower themselves. That said the capability to fire is one thing – target acquisition is another. A space surveillance network (SSN) with dispersed observation sites will still be useful, if not essential, for 'space deniers' for any method other than an indiscriminate high-altitude nuclear detonation. A rudimentary ground-based tracking and identification system is not beyond the reach of determined small states with modest resources and intelligence capabilities, let alone larger ones, and open source intelligence and amateur observations of satellites populate the internet.

Viewing Earth orbit as a hostile coast integrates with Piotrowski's concept of the 'cone of vulnerability' that anti-satellite capabilities can create. It is a zone that extends from a specific area on Earth and widens up towards various altitudes in outer space based on the operational ranges of anti-satellite weapons.[39] Satellites passing through this zone may be targeted by terrestrial counterspace weapons. Different weapons may be limited in their altitudes, with LEO being within reach of a full range of soft- and hard-kill capabilities, whilst satellites into MEO and GEO may be harder to strike with kinetic weapons whilst maintaining the element of surprise, requiring multiple space-based weapons platforms with loitering capabilities to ensure timely kinetic strikes or laser weapons which do not suffer degraded beams over the vast distances involved in reaching MEO and GEO from Earth. This reinforces the value of appreciating the particular characteristics of Earth orbit and the weapon systems placed within it. Sheldon, drawing on Piotrowski's work, described a 'cone of vulnerability'

> that encapsulates the battlespace [that] can protect friendly terrestrial forces from enemy satellites by engaging those satellites as they enter the cone. The cone is inverted; being at it's [*sic*] narrowest on Earth, yet covering the area of the battlespace, and at its widest in orbit. As enemy satellites approach the cone, ground-based [anti-satellite] weapons at the edge of the cone engage and destroy them. The cone of vulnerability in effect becomes a sanctuary from enemy satellites.[40]

In effect, the cone of vulnerability produces a hostile coast to the targeted satellites based on the reach and accuracy of the deployed weapons, meaning that hostile cosmic coastlines are not necessarily global, indiscriminate or omnipresent and re-stresses the need for detailed knowledge of the operating environment as argued in Proposition II. Just as space-based weapons do not herald the age of certain death from above, Earth-based weapons do not mean certain death from below. China can project a hostile coast above its territory to American satellites through its road-mobile SC-19 direct-ascent anti-satellite missile system. Conversely, the United States can make any orbital location on Earth above its anti-satellite weapons a hostile cosmic coast for Chinese satellites from the locations of its Aegis-equipped destroyers and ashore facilities. Electronic warfare platforms are even more flexible. Hostile coasts are not fixed in time and place: a space power's cosmic coastline extends to where its useful satellites travel and where enemy weapons effects can reach them. This variable nature makes all of Earth orbit a potentially hostile coast. The routes of crucial satellites, such as GPS and Key-hole, transit a hostile coast when within range of Chinese counter-space weapons systems.

The cone of vulnerability works both ways – from Earth up to space and from space down to Earth. Gorshkov determined that a primary task of the Soviet Navy was to conduct fleet-to-shore logistics and amphibious operations, and were generally more decisive than fleet-to-fleet operations because they directly assisted in winning territory.[41] Combat fleet operations aside, Gorshkov nonetheless is analogously correct to highlight the role of space-based services in assisting more significant terrestrial military operations in war. This assistance from space down to Earth is compatible with the cone of vulnerability generated by space systems. Terrestrial forces caught in the crosshairs of enemy space-based observation and terrestrial weapons platforms must take measures to adapt to them if they cannot engage in counterspace activities against satellites or parry the incoming munitions with interceptors or close-in weapon systems, especially if the cone of celestial lines of communication-derived support from space augments enemy terrestrial forces in that region. This is developed further via the pressure of dispersion on terrestrial forces in Proposition VII. For example, Iraqi forces in 1991 and 2003 were caught within overlapping cones of vulnerability produced by space-based communications networks that supported coalition forces in the Persian Gulf.

The cone of vulnerability visualises how 'coastal space defences' from Earth can localise firing lines or arcs on specific orbital paths, and how space-based sensors and infrastructure can impose a hostile coastal flank for terrestrial military forces. 'Coastal space warfare', envisioned through cones of vulnerability, localises some effects. An indiscriminate debris event will still spread out in its orbits and related altitudes – but not all altitudes – over time around Earth. There may be no easy escape from the hostile cosmic coastline for valuable space systems comparable to ships retreating to the high seas and away from a hostile coast. There is no direct geographic corollary to coastal forts or safe ports within which spacecraft can seek refuge – that is if we restrict the use of space to Earth orbit, or the ranges of terrestrial space weapons. Callwell believed that the ships of a weaker fleet should retire to coastal fortresses and await a better opportunity to put to sea, rather than risk certain defeat and an end to any pretence of seapower.[42] This analogy of fleets and satellites retiring to a coast may not be a helpful one given the lack of weapons-grade spacecraft and a general vulnerability to hostile fire from Earth. There may be no fixed or obvious 'ports in the storm' in orbit; but the relative measure of some safe orbits over others will depend on the capabilities of specific adversaries.

In interplanetary space, spacecraft may find ample opportunity to hide and set ambushes, unlike in the close orbits of human-developed planetary bodies that may be within range of counterspace weapons. Earth orbit is not the only cosmic coast in space; any orbit of a celestial body can potentially be considered a celestial shoreline. With such a visualisation, the solar system becomes a collection of continents or islands (planets and large asteroids) separated by seas and oceans (inter-satellite and inter-planetary space), and the necessity of grasping the peculiarities of outer space as stressed in Proposition II returns once more. However, for such a future to arrive, the solar system must become economically viable to enable power projection to defend deep space trade routes. Today, astroeconomic warfare is restricted to the commercial infrastructure orbiting Earth alone.

Astroeconomic warfare

Disrupting economic activities that rely on space can provide an additional tool in grand strategy and an effect of space warfare and manipulating celestial lines of communication. Earth orbit is a place to generate wealth, as well as derive military advantages – any post-war economic calculations involving space powers will involve the trends and governance of the global space economy and where the wealth it generates will flow. The command of space not only allows for the use or denial of spacepower for military purposes, but also decides who can continue to use space to generate wealth and provide services during war. Governments, commercial actors and non-governmental organisations pay for the services and information that satellites provide, generating a taxable space economy. This celestial part of the economy can be a target in war, as maritime and air travel can be, especially as the global space industry is usually embedded within military–industrial complexes and directly feeds into states' war capacities. It is imprudent to hope that space companies will be spared the horrors of war whilst profiting from providing the hardware and services for it. In addition, the value of the direct space economy does not account for the function it provides in enabling all manner of economic activity on Earth, from authorising financial transactions and e-commerce to enabling precision agriculture, monitoring the environment, enabling rapid civil protection and ensuring domestic order. Commanding space can indeed be used to create economic pressure on the adversary, as Corbett argued. The capture of private property was usually one of the early acts of maritime wars, and military 'conquest' or interference with sea lines of communication translated into economic pressure due to the economic uses of the sea.[43] This observation from Corbett, at its most fundamental point, is also true of the command of space and celestial lines of communication. Private property in space cannot be assumed as immune to the effects of space warfare. Like economic warfare at sea, astroeconomic warfare not only creates economic pressure, but also reduces the enemy's power of resistance.[44]

Despite the basic similarities that the sea and space are used for commercial as well as military purposes, analogising from one to the other is not a simple logical leap as witnessed in Proposition IV. Sheldon argues that the relative disparities in the strategic value of seaborne commerce and spaceborne commerce make any analogy between them fatally flawed. The sea transports energy, industrial good, and foodstuffs, whereas outer space transports data and provides services. Sheldon critiques many spacepower theorists for assuming, 'explicitly or implicitly, that Mahanian and Corbettian descriptions of the economic vitality and importance of the seas also applies to space commerce'.[45] This is an understandable criticism given the apparent differences between maritime and space-borne commerce. Nevertheless, it is wrong to dismiss insights from naval economic warfare, particularly as decisive battles may be difficult to impose, so commerce may provide alternative targets.[46]

Critical dependencies in some areas of maritime traffic relying on space systems – in navigation for example – may still create significant upsets in global supply chains.

Concepts of maritime economic warfare transpose quite well to spacepower. Astroeconomic warfare (targeting commercial celestial lines of communication rather than purely military and intelligence space systems) only makes strategic sense when contributing to a strategic manoeuvre. The efficacy of astroeconomic warfare will vary, but it will always need to contribute to the overall war aims if it is to be attempted at all, like maritime economic warfare. The most valuable outcome of a *guerre de course* campaign, according to Castex, was its potential to divert the enemy battle fleet and other resources away from a primary theatre of operations to allow temporary disputes of the command of the sea to occur in more strategically vital areas, thus tying commerce raiding into a larger strategic manoeuvre.[47] Castex praised such a strategy as a valuable component of a general manoeuvre to trigger a preferable redistribution of enemy forces elsewhere, but not as a complete maritime strategy by itself.[48] The advantages from successful *guerre de course* operations had to be translated into tangible benefits by making offensive naval action more palatable in another theatre and lamented that *guerre de course* had generally not been integrated into wider war plans in this way.[49] However, astroeconomic warfare in space must not repeat the same mistakes as the naval debate in the late nineteenth century, where

> in France [Mahan] restored the sound military principles of Jomini and Clausewitz, which the *Jeune Ecole* had completely forgotten. His insistence on battle and the importance of the organized force was a necessary corrective to the *Jeune Ecole*'s extravagant enthusiasm for the latest technical wrinkles and their hopes of gaining a cheap victory by attacking only non-military objectives.[50]

It is not unreasonable to imagine space warfare directed against targets to impose economic effects as helping to force a distribution of resources or forces favourable to the attacker or raising the costs of resistance to the victim. Attacking communications satellites could not only cause economic costs, but their lost communications bandwidth could also hinder or even stall the operations of a space-power-supported and information-dependent terrestrial force. This weakened force might attempt to compensate on Earth by changing dispositions which may benefit enemy terrestrial forces in some places, levelling the playing field or at least giving more hope for a successful resistance against a first-rate space-supported military machine. This would be conducting astroeconomic warfare under a strategic manoeuvre to combat the opponent's spacepower-derived advantages. A previously dispersed terrestrial military force, having lost its celestial lines of communication, may have to respond by concentrating its forces to remain effective, as explored in Proposition VII. This would present a bigger target for adversaries that then could launch a well-timed salvo of precise munitions, and exemplifies how secondary theatres can support the primary theatre or become a liability.

Castex argued that commerce raiders had a choice between focal zones where communication routes converge, or disparate regions that have little definable traffic routes. The former has higher risk but greater rewards, and the latter less risk and fewer rewards.[51] This resonates with Mahan's comparison between dispersed British seaborne trade and concentrated Spanish treasure ships. This does not mean that either historic case is predictive of economic warfare on space systems. Not many states on Earth may be as vulnerable to *guerre de course* as Britain was to seaborne trade routes[52] and the concentrated wealth of the Spanish treasure ships may not be repeated. It remains difficult to discern ahead of time exactly how decisive economic warfare can be. The character of space commerce changes with the type of actor, technology and economics in play. One way this diversity can be seen is how commercial space networks can be dispersed or concentrated. The changes in the physical distribution of satellites and ground stations modulate between dispersal and concentration. Iridium's constellation of sixty-six communications satellites in LEO is an example of a highly distributed satellite network. Some space-dependent communications systems may use less than a dozen satellites in GEO, like Inmarsat's, and some commercial space systems are more resilient than others in part due to dispersal and redundancy in the space and ground segments.

Although the Inmarsat constellation has fewer satellites to provide redundancy, it also requires fewer satellites for complete coverage because of the greater altitude of its satellites. This serves as a basic illustration of the complexities of economic space warfare, and each consideration of using astroeconomic warfare must be made by a net assessment of whether an Earth-bound state could ever become so dependent on celestial lines of communication for bare life, as Britain was and still is, on the sea for energy and food since the late nineteenth century. Castex's insistence on using *guerre de course* as part of a general war plan to force a favourable redistribution of enemy forces to tip the balance of capabilities elsewhere, therefore, may be the most practical rationale to utilising astroeconomic warfare. This depends on whether the loss of targeted systems are so severe that they warrant a redistribution of satellites in space and forces on Earth. Despite these uncertainties, it is a useful principle to think and apply critically. Strategic manoeuvre is a way to begin to answer the question of how effective astroeconomic warfare could be, because successful astroeconomic warfare is part of a strategic manoeuvre that triggers reactionary manoeuvres by the opponent. This helps strategists anticipate and think about how the use of and responses to astroeconomic warfare may play out to their own advantage.

The economic consequences of blockading or *guerre de course* will depend in part on the target's economic composition. Castex argued that if the target of *guerre de course* has secure internal communications, and if it is not too dependent on the sea for basic existence, then it may be able to weather the storm. The only recourse for a more strategically significant result would be attacking the enemy's core territory and most valued possessions.[53] Menon argues that effective blockades take time to produce any result, and for the necessity of the government or people targeted to depend on the highly valued commodities and communications that are denied.[54] However, the expectation for economic warfare to become costlier or damaging to the victim over time may not necessarily be the case. Mahan's narrative of French economic warfare against the British during the French Revolution was that the initial shock and surprise inflicted heavy losses on the British. But over time, the surprise and efficacy of the offence was succeeded 'by the more regular course of maritime war'.[55] The British established preponderance and commercial convoys, with opponents resorting to piecemeal commerce destroying with no great strategic result. Mahan examined French attempts to stifle British trade in the mid-eighteenth century, and commented that 'such a mode of war is inconclusive, worrying but not deadly; it might almost be said that it causes needless suffering', and only a dominant navy should expect to conduct an effective or meaningful economic warfare campaign. Even then, the results may be indecisive and, more importantly, 'only' contributory towards the overall outcome.[56] The effectiveness of economic warfare for each particular case cannot be theorised in advance, especially if the raiders and the victims prove adept at countering each other's strategic manoeuvres over weeks, months and years.

Those who have critiqued the Mahanian analogies of the significance of commerce at sea to outer space are left in a precarious position. Mahan held reservations regarding its decisiveness. There is no reason to assume, conceptually, that spacepower may provide as much of an economic stranglehold on an enemy as seapower did, or still can, because seapower did not always have such an economic stranglehold. Although the details change, the basic concepts of economic warfare and its place within seapower are useful to consider when planning astroeconomic warfare. Seapower does not provide a one-sided record of successful commerce destroying or blockading at sea – in that sense spacepower should inherit the same ambiguity when thinking of economic warfare within seapower.[57] Perpetuating the resonance between continental seapower and modern spacepower, these concepts are also applicable to the situation of small or middle space powers in the same way that continental seapower included second- and third-class (but not weak or helpless) sea powers. Even a small space power can impose military and economic costs in the cosmic coastline. In orbit, commercial activities created and underpinned by a web of satellites will be at risk from the arsenals of weaker and regional powers with anti-satellite capabilities, and electronic warfare capabilities in particular.

Any decision on whether to conduct astroeconomic warfare should depend on the enemy's relative vulnerability to such astroeconomic deprivation in the short and long term. This in turn is determined by its dependency on the space economy, the distribution of that commercial activity, and the links to other communications assets and integrated allied capabilities. The enemy's responses to economic losses in other sectors and theatres must be taken into account as one strategic manoeuvre begets another. Commercial actors and activities will not necessarily be immune from political and military conflicts in space, and there are powerful strategic incentives to hold the commercial sector hostage. Corbett and Mahan are as one on this point. Corbett perceived the pointlessness of banning the interception of commerce, meaning that he also was balancing his views between the general inefficiency of economic warfare at sea and its useful attrition towards the enemy.[58] This underscores the need for good judgment on how and when to apply economic warfare – through raiding or blockade. Even when no specific astroeconomic warfare may be planned and sanctions alone are used, wars on Earth can have significant impact on the space economy. An example is the opening up of Ukraine's space economy to the West and away from Russia, and the American dependence on Russia for RD-180 rocket engines for essential military and intelligence space launch vehicles.

If militaries continue to use critical infrastructure in orbit that also perform economically significant tasks, such as the GPS constellation, astroeconomic warfare will remain a consideration within the entire gambit of space warfare. Astroeconomic warfare may have more direct military consequences for a campaign on Earth than Castex may have ever imagined possible for *guerre de course*'s contributions to continental wars. In a crowded and contested environment, astroeconomic warfare may be a more democratic affair in the growing global space economy, and there is a myriad of neutral actors and third parties risking being caught in the crossfire because they offer a range of strategically significant space capabilities which increase the efficiencies of terrestrial military and economic power. Importantly allied and commercial space systems allow states to enjoy mass in terms of space assets and to weather the blows of a concerted counterspace campaign against it, developing an attritional capacity and strategic depth in space warfare.

Third parties and neutrality

Neutral or third parties must find their place between securing an armed neutrality and suffering an abused neutrality if they are not party to a conflict. There is no reason to assume that commercial space assets and infrastructure will be immune in a time of war, in large part due to the dual use nature of space technology and the integration of space industry with military industrial complexes, which blur the lines between civilian and military users and equipment. The dual-use and globalised character of space activity make non-warring states, companies, corporate interests and the global space economy significant features of space warfare. Other than attempting to remain neutral, third parties may seek to commit to a party of a conflict. Such opportunities could be lucrative if the winning side is chosen – and such aid may contribute to strategic manoeuvres by the warring parties. Continental seapower theory allows these dynamics to be theorised in detail for spacepower. Like the oceans – and especially busy coastal zones – space is populated by dozens of states companies, and non-governmental organisations. Regardless of their type, their neutrality cannot be taken for granted, and astrostrategists should consider a range of persuasive and coercive options for third and neutral parties in the space sector in any modern conflict.

It is naïve to expect commercial and neutral actors to be spared the trials of modern warfare in the twenty-first century, given the prevalent nature of the military–industrial complex in space industry. Reflecting on the 1905 Russo-Japanese War, Callwell remarked that 'the rights of neutrals are still liable to be trampled upon if those neutrals are unable, or unwilling, to defend them'.[59] Neutrals risk being caught up in warfare, political–economic intrigue or espionage if their trade, orbital locations or interests carry them towards the areas, capabilities or interests of a conflict, if the warring parties have reason to use or deny third-party assets and when their neutral guarantors cannot or will not protect them. Castex went further and said that

> some now claimed freedom of the seas to be valid in wartime . . . [N]aval war has no point if enemy property can travel without hindrance and if neutrals can supply the enemy or conduct his trade . . . In

wars during which there are many powerful neutrals, one cannot proceed in the same manner of seizing/attacking neutral property at will.[60]

Space warfare would be pointless if celestial lines of communication could be used by all without fear of a curtailment in their use in war. The command of space therefore has commercial and economic rationales and consequences that will affect the wider terrestrial economy. Commercial actors must prepare for this possibility if they are providing critical infrastructure, intelligence and military services. Any asset in orbit may be considered a legitimate target under the right political, normative and emotional conditions, or even simply caught in the crossfire should the element of chance in war decide to wreak havoc. Specific rules of engagement, ethical considerations and legal interpretations in warfare will be determined alongside cultural and political values, therefore theory cannot rule out action that may not be permissible under today's prevailing political conditions. Two initiatives are ongoing to interpret the laws of armed conflict with regard to space infrastructure – the Woomera Manual and the Manual on International Law Applicable to Military Uses of Outer Space (MILAMOS) – but there is no guarantee that these interpretations will be adhered to in practice.[61]

What constitutes as 'innocent passage' or non-military traffic or information is a highly particular and contentious classification that fluctuates with time and with the ethics and perceived threats of the relevant polities involved in any war. It may be difficult to separate data and satellites relevant to the war effort from those which are not, given the ubiquitous and dual-use nature of satellite communications and the integration of commercial communications satellites into military communications. An example of the pervasiveness of this dual-use nature is how the Hubble Space Telescope is virtually a Keyhole reconnaissance satellite that looks away from Earth with a spherical aberration problem on the lens. The value of the technological secrets on Keyhole's systems were so great that certain problems on Hubble were not corrected by the American authorities which did not want to declassify the necessary technical information to engineers outside the intelligence community. Indeed, 'the Hubble and its military sisters, the Keyhole series, had their lenses made by the same company, separated only by a curtain'.[62] A Keyhole satellite was instrumental in the crisis response to the first Space Shuttle mission in 1981, which was used to observe the damage caused by lift-off to the undercarriage of *Columbia* orbiter.[63] Given the use of civilian and commercial systems for military ends (like Iridium), and military systems for civilian and commercial ends (like GPS), it may be that the dual-use problem is more acute in space than elsewhere. This not only increases the scope of astroeconomic warfare, but also increases the ability to impose abused neutrality through the intimate relationships between commerce and the state in the dual-use dominated technology of outer space.

Neutrality for commercial actors is not impossible. In addition to deterrence by denial (making any attack ineffective), neutrality based on deterrence by punishment (inflicting heavy retaliation) is another means to protect a neutral position that is not at the mercy of warring parties. Menon, writing with reference to smaller navies in the shadow of the US Navy, is alert to the reality that 'much of the apprehension that modern naval strategists feel in going in for a blockade is the uncertain nature of the response by larger neutral navies'.[64] Conceptually, neutrality in international space commerce would be facing the same concerns. A neutral party must either be of marginal or no interest to warring parties, or can deter and inflict massive costs on any factions that attempt to abuse or infringe its neutrality. If a war occurs between two smaller powers, and third-party vessels enjoy the protection of a stronger power, then neutrality, profiteering and political distancing from a conflict may be more feasible. In the absence of 'armed neutrality' – the ability to inflict or threaten severe punishment in retaliation for molestation – 'abused neutrality' is always a possible threat to third parties at the side-lines of a war between stronger belligerents. Abused neutrality can mean the loss of trade and assets, or co-option into facilitating the demands of a party to the conflict. A Chinese space warfare manual warns its readers against incurring the wrath of an otherwise-uninvolved space power by inflicting 'mistaken wounds' upon its space systems or those of companies it is responsible for. In addition, it advocates Castex's argument that blockading the enemy in space and imposing such costs should be viewed 'from the high perspective of the overall strategy'.[65] In other words, such actions should only be undertaken if they contribute to the overall war plan and that they do not unnecessarily escalate the conflict to bring in unbearable third parties or generate international opprobrium, harking back to the days of unrestricted submarine warfare. This takes the plane of thought about the consequences of astroeconomic warfare into the realm of international politics and post-war grand strategies regarding the global political-economy, going beyond the scope of spacepower theory's epistemological limits.

Third parties, including allied states and companies registered within, may complicate some matters as inter-allied dependence on space systems and the transparency provided by more eyes and ears in orbit increases. During Operation Allied Force in the Serbian war in the 1990s, Eutelsat initially leased communications bandwidth to North Atlantic Treaty Organization (NATO) countries and Serbia, before Eutelsat was persuaded to suspend service to the Serbian government.[66] Open source information and analysis from satellite imagery proliferate and contribute to public debate on matters of defence, security and foreign policy. However, commercial laws and interests may hinder the dissemination of commercial imagery, even within the same military. In Operation Desert Shield, the US Army could not afford the royalty fees of France's *Satellite Pour l'Observation de la Terre* (SPOT) images bought by USAF, and thus, they went without SPOT imagery throughout the war.[67] The United States must adapt to varying degrees of strategic transparency that even small space powers can impose, which develops into dispersion on the battlefield as explored in Proposition VII.[68] This is not an unprecedented concern. In 1990, the Soviet Union began to sell satellite imagery on the open market – allowing any buyer to access images with greater resolution than anything else that was available at the time.[69] Sheldon notes the subsequently constrained political environment if one seeks to disrupt the spacepower of an enemy through third-party service providers – repeating the Chinese sentiment of inflicting 'mistaken wounds'.[70]

Mahan provides an illuminating illustration of the illusions of maritime commercial neutrality between Britain and France being shattered during the Austrian War of Succession (1740–8): the comte de La Bourdonnais, a commander of French ships in Indian waters:

> obtained from the [French] East India Company a squadron . . . with which he proposed to ruin the English commerce and shipping; but when war actually began . . . he received orders not to attack the English, the French company hoping that neutrality might exist between the companies in that distant region, though the nations were at war . . . Their company accepted the proffer, while saying that it of course could bind neither the home government nor the [R]oyal [N]avy. The advantage won by the forethought of La Bourdonnais was thus lost; though first, and long alone, on the field, his hand was stayed. Meanwhile the English admiralty sent out a squadron and began to seize French ships between India and China; not till then did the company awake from its illusion.[71]

Another example would be Mahan's case of the 'Armed Neutrality' of Russia, Sweden and Denmark in 1780, in the context of Franco-British maritime warfare during the American Revolutionary War. Britain threatened Russian, Swedish and Danish maritime trade because of London's intent to seize 'enemy' goods in 'neutral' ships. The eventual Dutch decision to join this Armed Neutrality led Britain to take Dutch possessions and trade.[72] Hopes, expectations and policies for commercial immunity are not new to the twenty-first century, and neither are the risks of such hopes being trampled upon. The point here is to articulate conceptual political precedents. If the political object of the war is serious enough, it can override existing normative restraints towards non-combatants. A poorly armed neutrality can lead to an abused neutrality, or the end of it utterly if a previously neutral power becomes a party, through accident or design, to the conflict.

Despite the problems posed by commercial entities, Michael Smith listed three possible options to handle the commercial space sector's data and services during war. First, to buy out satellite capacity to prevent enemy commercial access. Second, to negotiate on agreed constraints on image distribution. Third, to take direct military action against space systems that threaten military operations.[73] There may also be a fourth option: to neutralise or intimidate – short of violence and within legal limits – any 'problematic' individual or organisation. Legal prosecution and the liquidation of private assets – in the interests of national security – are potential options for states. The difficulty of counterspace operations, the sensitivity of space services and the multipolar character of space activities makes unilateral action more daunting in political, technological and economic terms. But political conditions can change overnight, given a potent-enough mix of events, circumstance, leaders, surprise and alarm.

From the perspective of a neutral state with potentially useful space systems, the four options on dealing with the commercial sector are useful to structure astrostrategic thinking. A neutral or non-combatant state can still take action in the global space economy and manage information flows in ways it deems useful for its interests, taking part in the war by proxy. Commercial operators may face pressures from state interests if they have an influence (whether intended or not) in a conflict. A company will need the formal approval of some state authority to operate in space, raising questions of power relations between commercial and state interests, if they are ever at cross-purposes, not least as Article VI of the Outer Space Treaty makes states liable for the activities of all non-state entities registered within them. In addition, another aspect of commercial actors is that many of their staff, owners and principal shareholders may have allegiances – coerced and voluntary – to the registered state and may not pose a problem to a state's goals. Interests may even converge. The commercial sector should be seen neither as inherently neutral nor as never wishing to have a hand in profiteering from conflict; business and economics are still political. Such an open attitude can help to identify assistants to one's aims, targets in the commercial sector to co-opt, or companies to prosecute, infiltrate and conduct espionage against. These are merely avenues for strategic manoeuvres to utilise in a war effort.

Despite the potential for non-state actors in space, any commercial operator will likely be at some point answerable to a state. If political–economic consensus between major space powers can be achieved during a war, a belligerent enjoying that consensus may likely keep out third parties from intentionally assisting enemies. Third parties participating in a war against a cartel of major spacepowers risk incurring the wrath of that cartel. Despite this, managing commercial interests may be difficult. Hertzfeld qualifies his views about commercial interests being subordinate to the state when he says:

> no longer can a nation such as the United States even rationally plan for control of the [commercial communications] systems or capabilities. In time of conflict, it would be almost impossible to interrupt services because businesses and governments as customers depend on them. In fact, the government is one of the major users of commercial communications networks.[74]

In the absence of 'rational' plans, perhaps ad hoc solutions to the commercial sector is the best approach. Indeed, with the commercial sector and spacepower characteristics perpetually in flux, such thinking is apt for spacepower theory. There are always possible tensions between state interests, especially in a time of war, and the interests of commercial entities. This will be true as much as within a state as between states and foreign commercial entities. What determines who carries more weight in these interactions can only be examined as individual cases, as every incidence of commercial and state interests in a particular scenario will vary. Spacepower theory sharpens critical thought by exploring these possibilities and subsequently making astroeconomic warfare relevant to long-term grand strategy through strategic manoeuvre. Exploiting the promises of, or eliminating the threat from, the commercial space sector and third parties are strategic manoeuvres that will influence the rest of the war effort and the peace that follows.

The issue of third parties, either as benefiting from or supplying space support, is not new. The Cold War saw a handful of alleged examples, such as Soviet reconnaissance provided to Egypt in the 1973 Yom Kippur War, Soviet space-derived information being used in the 1978 Somalia–Ethiopia war, and Argentina receiving Soviet data with Britain receiving US satellite intelligence in the 1982 Falklands War.[75] In 1991, it may be that SPOT imagery was cut off from Iraq after its invasion of Kuwait only because no other company would impose opportunity costs as at the time, the only other agency that could have made such a decision to sell to Iraq was the Earth Observation Satellite (EOS) Company that operates Landsat. According to Phillipe Renault, deputy director-general of SPOT Image, if EOS had sold Landsat images to Iraq, SPOT Image would have done likewise in the interest of business competition.[76]

In the 2003 Iraq War, the Iraqi Army had access to Russian GPS jammers, and used them with very limited localised success.[77] The war in Ukraine has seen attempts by NATO to use satellite imagery to prove the involvement of Russian forces in eastern Ukraine.[78] The same is true for the use of spacepower in Russia's operations regarding Crimea and the separatist regions in eastern Ukraine. Allies can also cause problems in space. The European Galileo system, according to Beidleman, challenged American space dominance because of signal security issues and third-party access to Galileo's encrypted and military-grade Public Regulated Service.[79] Today, Galileo is on track to become a backup for the American GPS for the US military, enhancing its resilience and reducing GPS as a potential centre of gravity for US military operations. Grand strategic relations between the United States and European states have not always been the most cooperative in space, and transatlantic space politics challenges some of the expectations made of transatlantic politics more generally with several instances of competition and non-cooperation.[80]

These facets of spacepower's influence on grand strategy and modern warfare do not involve spectacular space battles as blue-water thinking and much of existing spacepower theory may have readers imagine. As a detailed consequence of Proposition II's view of spacepower as infrastructure, spacepower has a pervasive influence in the realm of economic competition, infrastructure, diplomacy and alliance politics. Whilst these topics begin to leave the purview of strategic theory, the strategist must no doubt be cognisant of the non-military aspects and consequences of spacepower beyond any immediate conflict. The astroeconomic and industrial-scale exploitation of Earth orbit are far more significant and real to all space powers than the potential of embryonic space-based weapons capabilities. Space is essential in knowledge- and service-based economies, high-technology manu-facturing and military–industrial complexes. Myriad third-party actors and increasingly globalised space infrastructures populate this complex web of economics and manufacturing. Third par-ties to a conflict must find their place within or apart from the grand strategies of warring space-faring powers. Third parties and commercial actors can be opportune allies or liable threats. Based on the precedents of neutrals in maritime wars, third par-ties and neutrals can be persuaded, coerced or co-opted into one's general plans for war, contributing to a strategic manoeuvre that embraces non-military means in support of a war effort. The non-military aspects of space translate into logistical effects on Earth through the emerging commercial access to outer space and the commercial provision of data and communications bandwidth, and harnessing or denying the logistical support that space can provide can translate into mobility and paralysis on Earth.

Logistics and mutual support

Spacepower is highly amenable to being described like logistical components to strategy, as the 'objective of a logistic effort is the creation and sustained support of combat forces'.[81] This reso-nates with much of what has been said so far about spacepower as infrastructure. Continental approaches to seapower stress that logistics matter not only at sea, but also on land for the exercising and securing of the command of the sea. The same is analogi-cally true for spacepower: logistics matter in space as well as on Earth for fighting over a command of space and exploiting it. Logistical support from celestial lines of communication matters for wars on Earth in a conceptually similar manner to how logis-tical support from sea lines of communication matter for conti-nental wars. Logistical capabilities allow a belligerent to throw its material weight around to where it matters, and sea/spaceborne logistics can help to make up for capability deficiencies elsewhere. Resources mean nothing if they cannot be used at the right time and place. As a subject logistics is something of a neglected aspect in the study of strategy, bluntly expressed in the famous truism attributed to Omar Bradley: 'amateurs talk strategy. Professionals do logistics.'

Henry Eccles described logistics as 'the bridge between our national economy and ... the combat forces in the field ... Sound logistics forms the foundation for the development of strategic flexibility and mobility.'[82] Abstract discussions of 'national' space economies or bean-counting material manifestations of spacepower mean little if the means of production are not logistically geared towards strategic ends. Within continental seapower, Castex considered the importance of logistics when thinking of a coastal theatre. He reasoned that in its own waters, the defender

> will be more comfortable than anywhere else – close to his own bases. Near to necessary resupply and repair, he will be able to take advantage of all his resources, even of ships with a short range of action ... The enemy far from his bases, a bit 'In the air', will be handicapped by the lack of these facilities.[83]

Transposing Castex's argument about coastal defences, terrestrial anti-satellite weapons will enjoy some logistical advantages over their orbital counterparts, and assets in orbit will have limited manoeuvrability and concealment compared to mobile counterspace weapons on Earth. Weapons on Earth may be able to deceive enemy sensors and conceal themselves before firing, as well as manoeuvre after firing, and stop for maintenance and resupply. For example, for targeting satellites in LEO, an air-launched or road-mobile ground-based anti-satellite weapon fired for an orbital interception mission (noting that the missile and interceptor will be on a suborbital trajectory) is more flexible and cost-efficient in terms of basing and launch times compared to the Soviet space-based co-orbital anti-satellite weapons system, which could only launch on demand twice a day to intercept a target above the planet on a stable orbital trajectory matching that of the target.[84] Some coastal defences may need more communication by sea to remain operational. Likewise, some Earth-based space weapons may need celestial lines of communication to remain operational, depending on their design, function and location. Spacepower in the cosmic coastline requires orbital and terrestrial logistical support to function and withstand the attacks of the adversary, and replenish in the aftermath.

A logistical attitude to space reminds the reader that getting into space is still a very hard and expensive thing to do, and harder still to alter orbital flightpaths once 'locked in' to efficient routes. Spacelift requirements to launch and replace dozens, if not hundreds, of space-based weapons and satellites is far beyond what is possible in brute material and logistical terms today, even for the United States.[85] Weapons on Earth will usually be better placed to generate effects in space, and to maintain, replace and resupply. Concealing and accessing a terrestrial laser designed to interfere with satellites in LEO may be easier to specialise, upgrade, maintain and operate than a similar weapon based in LEO. However, some highly niche capabilities may provide some advantages – yet whether they make up for the normative consequences, economic costs, and command and control vulnerabilities remains a highly debatable issue. In the vacuum of Earth orbit, lasers are more efficient because there is hardly any atmosphere to dilute the beam compared to terrestrial lasers. However, the beam does still disperse in the distances involved in targeting other regions of Earth orbit. At a high enough orbit, a space-based laser could generate a wide cone of vulnerability towards other space-based targets. Space-based electronic warfare platforms may also have some advantages, but basing, targeting and counter-jamming of the remote system remain problems limiting their utility. Space-based weapons will be entirely dependent on celestial lines of communication – which can be jammed or infiltrated – to function. These logistical trade-offs provide a practical merit for the continental seapower-derived cosmic coastline analogy described above. Commanding space from Earth may be easier than or at least a necessary component of commanding space through space-based weapons, and the terrestrial source of spacepower's logistical strength means that attacking an enemy's spacepower may involve terrestrial operations, and that space-based destruction may be rare. Still, the 'tools of conflict are interwoven' and should be used as deemed appropriate – when one tool becomes less attractive in a particular scenario, another may become more so.[86] In a littoral zone, there are options available for actors who may not dominate one environment to influence command in it from another environment.

Logistics entails understanding the effects of celestial lines of communication upon Earth as well as how spacepower depends on terrestrial lines of communication and objectives. Callwell's words strike a chord here when he argued that:

> writers on naval subjects sometimes hardly seem to realise the extent to which fleets are obliged to lean upon land forces, and how sub-servient during the actual progress of a campaign the conditions of sea-power must under certain conditions be to operations on shore. If this feature of war be not taken into account, false strategical theories may be arrived at, and a dangerous naval policy may be adopted at a critical time.[87]

Analogically, a spacepower theory – and any derived astrostrategy – that ignores the dependence of the command of space on operations and logistics chains on Earth may promote unwise space-centric strategies that do not take terrestrial events, conditions and capabilities into account. As much as space systems support terrestrial forces, space systems themselves lean on terrestrial systems for support. Launching a satellite is merely the end-process of a long and complicated resource and manufacturing chain which spans Terran continents. Space-centric strategic thought must embrace its dependence and subservience towards objectives and vulnerabilities on Earth, not least on the logistics side. The importance of logistics from, and ease of access to, a medium helps to determine where the major objectives and chokepoints may lie.

Earth orbit may not feature much space-to-space combat relative to Earth-to-space weapons fire, contrary to its prominence in many works of spacepower theory as referred to in Proposition III. Again, continental seapower provides precedents of this, where neither side had the logistical resources for intensive naval or fleet-on-fleet combat. The effects of logistical support from a medium where there was hardly any combat was not lost on Callwell. Of Egypt's wars against the Ottoman Empire in the Levant in the mid-nineteenth century, Callwell chronicled that:

it was a campaign in which there had been no sea-fight of importance, and in which, till just before its termination, naval operations had been entirely of a passive kind; but it was a campaign which nevertheless hinged upon the question of maritime command . . . in which . . . the transfer of naval preponderance from one side to the other exerted a paralysing influence over the prospects of an army.[88]

This shows a case of battle being threatened, but not carried out and still caused an effect on the adversary. The fear of a decisive clash was enough to avoid battle for both sides due to the irreparable damage it would do to both sides' naval forces. This was something of an existential deterrent effect from fleet loss. The lack of battle between fleets is secondary here to the effects that a working command of the sea had on the land war in the Levant. Whomever had command at sea determined success on land because armies could be reinforced and supplied from the sea. According to Callwell, fortunes would flip as soon as one side threatened to act against the other's naval logistics and sea lines of communication. Mahan was also grasping at this possibility in his narrative of British seapower in its struggle with rebellion in North America – that without maritime superiority, British forces ashore struggled to act decisively.[89] British troops faced stagnation and paralysis in the colonies if the French threatened British resupply and transport ships. This is analogous to the paralysis imposed on terrestrial forces if they are denied their space force enhancements and logistics. As efforts to dispute the United States' command of space continue, it remains to be seen whether Callwell will be prophetic in noting how a transfer or change in the command of space will confer tactical, operational or strategic paralysis to the victim. As Chapter 6 shows, A2/AD strategies attack this logistical support from space to modern terrestrial forces, imposing dispersion and paralysis on the adversary. Because of Western militaries' habitual dependence on space-enabled precision munitions and other capabilities, it is not unreasonable to expect that the denial of support from the celestial coastline may exert paralysis that may help to swing (but not decide by itself) the fortunes of battle on Earth.

Continental seapower theory illustrates cases where the main theatre was on land, and where most, if not all, fighting took place.

The most ardent spacepower and 'force application' advocates may have to be content to see such analogous strategic behaviour in orbit. There may be little in terms of direct battle in space relative to the main theatres of war on Earth, where the command of space can acutely influence terrestrial warfare. Castex was thinking along these lines and his words can be transposed to space:

> when the nations at war have common [terrestrial] frontiers, mastery of [space] is, at least in theory, no longer even a necessary condition [for victory], since the issue of the hostilities will finally depend on the result of the combat between the [terrestrial forces]. But the command of the sea will most often have a serious effect on the operations of these [forces] and it will be useful to the power that holds it.[90]

This continental approach unpacks the difficult grey area that spacepower operates within. It can be extremely useful, but cannot be decisive by itself. Such thinking lends itself to the Persian–Egyptian war in the fifth century BC, where Egyptian naval combat and logistical power kept Egypt in the fight against the vastly superior Persian Empire until it crushed the Egyptian navy with its own overdue equivalent.[91] Likewise, spacepower can significantly improve (but not determine) the chances of success in terrestrial warfare and provide opportunities to exploit their terrestrial advantages over those of the enemy, as explained in Proposition III. If satellites continue to provide such useful support for terrestrial forces, one cannot expect every adversary to refrain from neutralising them to improve the odds of success on Earth.

As well as providing a range of support services from space to Earth, spacepower itself has logistical needs 'concerned with the ability to launch on demand without fear of enemy interdiction, and also to freely use datalinks without fear of interference'.[92] As Callwell noted how seapower leaned on the land for support, ensuring the operation of space infrastructure against a determined foe may prove difficult enough without considering the additional difficulties involved in the logistics of space-based weapons. Sheldon raises the logistical burdens of running satellite constellations and SSNs, with ground stations across the world having to be staffed, supplied and connected. Such duties may become burdensome during a time of war, even though they are for the most part Earth-based.[93] As explained in Proposition IV, the term communication within celestial lines of communication refers to the routes of material supply as well the routes of data transfers and satellite orbits. The supply chains in the space economy are complex and often just-in-time and, in the case of Europe and America, transnational, transcontinental and transoceanic. This would make replenishment of lost satellites and rockets, during a time of war where the enemy will seek to disrupt such activities, a daunting task.[94] A comprehensive spacepower and a command of space based on space control cannot function without terrestrial support. Managing a comprehensive SSN is logistically taxing, let alone a string of satellite control stations. The US, Russia, China and Europe manage SSA stations across the globe, inside and outside their own borders. Increasing commercial interests in space surveillance would further accentuate the impact of war upon them, as they become a source of space intelligence.

When committed to action, a space power must fight with the space infrastructure it has and what is due to be deployed in the near future. Strategy and tactical missions are 'always limited and at times are determined' by logistics.[95] Ad hoc expedients and deal-making with third parties or allies may be worked out faster than developing or manoeuvring sovereign space systems, but any extra capability will be restricted to what third parties have and are willing to supply. The inability of space logistics to meet changing demand and respond to crises overnight was apparent in Operations Desert Shield and Desert Storm. General Horner, chief of the air component of US Central Command, requested more reconnaissance satellites to help enable more flexible and responsive air operations with real time data. But it would take six to twelve months to fulfil his request as satellites and space launch vehicles were built to order.[96] Although some emerging technologies – such as reusable rocket technologies, small satellites and three dimensional printing – might provide some flexibility and responsiveness for specific capabilities, for the foreseeable future the bulk of critical space infrastructure is met by large satellites (the mass of which is measured in tons) and with highly intricate heavy rocket systems that take years from the ordering phase to the launch countdown. The length of time required for replacements of large, bulky hardware for spacepower is a similar to that of contemporary seapower. Plans for flexible and manoeuvrable satellites, replenishment and on-demand launches, or 'operationally responsive space' as it is called in the US Air Force, are not new yet may finally see some degree of achievement with the emergence of small satellite launchers, the mass manufacturing of satellites with off-the-shelf commercial systems, and reusable first stage rockets. Still, these are ameliorating rather than transforming logistical problems. A large spacepower with many demands on its space infrastructure may be slow to act relative to the abilities of specialised Earth-based anti-satellite weaponry, casting further doubt on the efficacy of a hegemon dominating Earth orbit. Not only can spacepower be a constraint or a cause of a sluggish military posture on Earth if a major space power is caught unprepared, but failing to defend its space backbone may translate into serious paralysis in its terrestrial warfighting capability.

Manoeuvring satellites is not impossible. A Russian satellite – Olymp (designation Kosmos-2501) – moved in concert with Russian warships on Earth's oceans. In February–June 2015, the Olymp was 'parked' in GEO at 96.4° East (off the western coast of Sumatra), which coincided with the visit of the submarine destroyer *Admiral Panteleyev* to the Indian Ocean, which returned to Vladivostok in August. However, by 25 June Olymp had moved to 18° West, above the Atlantic Ocean and to the south of western Africa. This coincided with the visit of the *Moskva* missile cruiser in a joint Russian–Egyptian naval exercise in July. Olymp began moving again after the *Moskva* returned to Sebastopol in August. Such a satellite may be used to relay data in the Russian Navy, and to manage data from and to precision weapons.[97] The United States, Russia and China have all been conducting 'rendezvous and proximity operations' and inspection missions with satellites in GEO – providing a new SSA capability to determine what specific satellites are doing in GEO and perhaps even eavesdropping on their communications.[98] Such satellites, using low-thrust but high-efficiency Hall plasma thrusters, may be able to move slowly but efficiently and consistently to maintain a lengthy operating lifespan for operations that can wait for satellite movement in GEO that moves by a few degrees over the Earth's surface per day. This demonstrates not only how some aspects of space infrastructure can be flexible, but also how strategic manoeuvre in the cosmic coastline supports terrestrial operations. For optimal efficiency and precision-strike capabilities, the Russian Navy's modernised systems may need such responsive satellites to be in place, if a permanent constellation is not to be placed in GEO. Strategic manoeuvres in the cosmic coastline will rely on cumbersome and pre-planned space infrastructure and physical assets.

Successfully harnessing the logistics chains of spacepower allows for a greater exploitation of its enabling and enhancing capabilities for terrestrial warfare. This essentially contributes to a strategic manoeuvre that rests to a degree on the command of space (Proposition I) which uses or denies relevant celestial lines of communication (Proposition IV). Logistics enable and are determined by strategic manoeuvres, which aim to provide better chances of success in war even though logistics themselves are not concerned with combat. Logistics must be embraced in such theory, as such logistical services cannot be assumed to simply 'work' as needed when operations occur. Secure and efficient celestial lines of communication enhance the capabilities of modernised terrestrial forces, creating a form of strategic depth and more opportunities for strategic manoeuvres. Logistics in a littoral environment are extremely useful for its adjacent environments, but those logistics are vulnerable to hostility from that adjacent environment, as well as the restrictions on the logistics and support provided from there. Spacepower logistics therefore cannot be understood as apart from terrestrial logistics – mutual support between Earth and space is key for modern terrestrial and space power to function at their best.

Strategic manoeuvre captures the logistical realities of space-power based on the continental school of seapower. Just as a stronger space power may want to command space to secure logistical advantages, a weaker one may want to command space locally and temporarily to cut the enemy's space-dependent logistical lines. Strategic manoeuvre with spacepower can help to increase the odds of overall success of military operations on Earth. The efficacious exploitation of a command of space for some degree of strategic result – to conduct a successful strategic manoeuvre in the cosmic coastline – can make up for deficiencies elsewhere. Strategic manoeuvres in space provide strategic depth by increasing efficiencies in terrestrial military forces.

Strategic depth from space

Strategic depth from the cosmic coastline refers to the capabilities a constellation of satellites makes possible for terrestrial military forces. A space control strategy tries to exploit a command of space to exploit the strategic depth provided. Spacepower 'can provide a global presence that can be turned into strategic depth', which is 'the extent to which global access and presence can be translated into tangible military force on Earth'.[99] Spacepower can form strategic depth in an analogous way to seapower in continental wars. Dutch seapower in the Franco-Dutch War in the late 1670s, as told by Mahan, captures the concept of strategic depth from an adjacent medium well:

> Holland . . . lost not a foot of ground in Europe; and beyond the seas only her colonies on the west coast of Africa and in Guiana. She owed her safety at first, and the final successful issue, to her sea power. That delivered her in the hour of extreme danger, and enabled her afterward to keep alive in the general war. It may be said to have been one of the chief factors, and inferior to no other one singly, in determining the event of the great war which was formally closed at [Nijmegen].[100]

The Dutch ability to harness its seapower to support its war against France prevented it from being overrun. Dutch seapower prevented the French from flanking the stalled land fronts via the sea – although they lost some colonial possessions. In addition, the alliances the Dutch had formed ensured that there would be no landward flanking which would have decisively ended Dutch resistance. Mahan's description illustrates the value of seapower as a source of strategic depth making up for deficiencies elsewhere. The outcome was a joint effort, where seapower proved to be a crucial adjunct to dealing with the landward strategic threat. Callwell thought along the same lines:

> The tactical and strategical advantages enjoyed by a military force operating with its back at the sea, in possession of a suitable port, and fortified by naval power, are immense. The flanks are secure. Retreat in case of reverse is assured. There can be little or no anxiety as to supplies. Friendly warships may be able to afford assistance in actual battle.[101]

In the case of the Dutch, retreat on land may not be a feasible option for an entire population, but the point of the sea providing numerous advantages that combine to create some strategic depth to assist in land warfare is still useful. Continental seapower theory thus theorises the connections between the sea and the land to a far greater extent than Corbett's classical text does, although Corbett is of course correct in his observation that people live on land and what you can do to the land is what matters most.[102]

Israel exemplifies the ideal that

> strategic depth may have its head in orbit, but its feet are firmly rooted on the ground. This attribute exploits . . . orbital space in order to augment and enhance strategic depth on Earth, and can apply to states of all kinds of geographical dispositions.[103]

A small state in a tumultuous region where the use of force is common, Israel can make up for its small stature in territorial and demographic size through high-technology armed forces that depend in part on spacepower in the cosmic coastline for strategic depth. The strategic depth provided by various space systems, when used competently in a combined-arms effort, can make up for deficiencies through buying time with more efficient forces, rather than through sacrificing territory. Israel can make its numerically inferior forces more rapid, mobile, responsive, efficient, accurate and survivable through harnessing strategic manoeuvres in the cosmic coastline and making it a hostile coast against its adversaries. This does not translate into omnipotence, however, as Israeli strategic defeats or stalemate against Hezbollah in 2006 showed.

The increased speed of decision from spacepower-supported forces harnesses a faster form of John Boyd's 'OODA loop' (Observation, Orientation, Decision, Action) to outmanoeuvre the enemy and increase the tempo of operations to a pace where the enemy will always be reacting to, rather than setting, the agenda on the battlefield.[104] An OODA loop involves processing cycles of information gathering and decision-making in order to act as fast as possible with the most accurate and timely data about the enemy. The faster the loop is executed, the more effective-per-unit that force is because it forces the enemy onto a constantly reactive posture.[105] Another way of looking at this is through closely integrating and speeding up the 'sensor-to-shooter cycle' by gathering and transmitting real-time data on mobile targets to weapons platforms and deployed forces. Between 1991 and 2003, certain US reconnaissance-to-strike speeds shortened from three days to less than forty minutes, with some specialised units being able to attack targets in less than twelve minutes after identification. Ground-attack aircraft could, for the first time, launch in the general direction of hostilities or target areas and receive target data whilst en route, making for faster and more flexible operations and air sorties.[106]

This greater speed and efficiency of terrestrial assets through space support adds to and creates strategic depth because small forces can become more lethal, rapid, efficient and survivable. But a faster OODA loop or sensor-to-shooter cycle does not guarantee strategic success. Good 'operational art' is not the same as strategic success. Proposition VII examines the adaptations against such spacepower-enabled ways of warfare. Early warning and information capabilities (including but not limited to space-based information) can all build strategic depth. Strategic manoeuvres in space not only concern the assault of enemy space systems, the use of astroeconomic warfare, the problems of third parties, and the mastery of logistical needs, but also exploiting the secondary theatre of Earth orbit's advantages as a form of strategic depth that only has meaning insofar as it influences wars on Earth. If winning a terrestrial war means sacrificing space capabilities, so be it. But the ability to force an adversary to attack space systems imposes resource and disposition costs on the adversary that one may be able to take advantage of in another, more important theatre.

Spacepower can provide strategic depth for offensive and defensive purposes. Space systems may be able to deliver greater force protection through early warning to terrestrial forces, and space-power may enable a more efficient deployment of forces for a general defence.[107] For example, the integration of Defense Support Program (DSP) satellite terminals with the warning systems on Patriot theatre missile defence units in the 1991 Gulf War could have reduced the time taken to assess a threat from five minutes to ninety seconds out of a total Iraqi Scud missile flight time of seven minutes.[108] The advantages gained by strategic depth (be it geographic size, hostile terrain, popular resistance, superior lethality and mobility, unassailable internal or rearward lines of communication) whilst on the strategic defensive is one of the reasons why Clausewitz believed in the defensive as the stronger form of war, with the intent of weathering the initial blows to gather strength from whatever advantages and remaining capabilities one has for a devastating strategic counterattack.[109] This means that spacepower can be made useful for both offensive and defensive grand strategies and military postures, and counters one-sided astrostrategies that extol the virtues of an all-out 'Space Pearl Harbor' offensive as encountered in Chapter 6.

Strategic depth from spacepower can compensate for weaknesses in other areas, such as the numbers of deployed forces and lower ammunition stocks. Strategic manoeuvres are about channelling that strategic depth. Such a strategic depth requires space and terrestrial infrastructure to be correctly placed and integrated in an operational status by the time war arrives, which may not always be the case, as encountered in Proposition VII. The use of spacepower to develop strategic depth enables strategic manoeuvres because the large potential spacepower support provides a polity through the enhanced coordination, warning and precision of organised violence and destruction. Exploiting the cosmic coastline allows terrestrial powers to harness a celestial strategic depth, and turn it into tangible results on Earth that confer advantages on oneself, take advantages away from the enemy, and capitalise on enemy weaknesses. The hostile cosmic coastline, astroeconomic warfare, the corralling of third parties and the mastery of 'astrologistics' contribute to a celestial depth and would be a masterful strategic manoeuvre when brought to bear upon Earth. Taking this strategic depth away – and its logistical benefits – translates into potential paralysis.

Spacepower, like the conscious exploitation of seapower, and airpower, can contribute to strategic depth and chances of overall success as supplements to land power – to influence people and their lives exactly where they live. Harnessing the depth provided by spacepower within strategic manoeuvres relates a large range of space capabilities to grand-strategic thinking and planning when the bulk of today's character of spacepower is in the grey area of enabling combat unit efficiency, information flows and force postures on Earth without invoking the spectre of spectacular and fantastical space battles. Logistics, often neglected in strategy in favour of the 'art' of conducting battles, should avoid a similar fate in space as it is defined by the strategic depth it provides.

Conclusion

All five parts of strategic manoeuvre come together when space is considered an adjacent realm, like a coastline, and a secondary theatre to terrestrial wars. Actions in one geography can affect another both acutely and over the long term, as much or as little as overt and destructive acts, which corresponds to a non-linear understanding of war.[110] Continental seapower, with its emphasis on where seapower meets land-based strategies and powers, has enabled a more in-depth theorisation of the interaction between Earth and space to a degree that bluewater seapower theory cannot match due to its imperial bluewater heritage. The hostile cosmic coast, astroeconomic warfare, the actions of neutrals and third parties, logistics chains and strategic depth through space only matter in the way they act as useful tools against enemy weaknesses in any terrestrial war. Imagining the relevant sectors of Earth orbit as a hostile cosmic coast, and Earth-based counterspace weapons like coastal defences which made close-to-port operations extremely dangerous by the late nineteenth century, raises doubts on the accuracy of imagining Earth orbit as an open ocean as one would with a bluewater seapower analogy. The vision of the coastline undermines expectations of a space empire because Earth orbit is relatively more accessible and vulnerable to would-be challengers to any hegemon seeking to unilaterally dominate Earth orbit. The command of space could still be won to the required degree through an Earth-based space denial campaign, where the relatively weaker or impoverished aggressor need not be concerned with building a comprehensive space-based infrastructure.

Strategising spacepower through strategic manoeuvre can be interpreted as merely a call for spacepowers to be flexible in their use of it and in their logistical management of celestial lines of communication. That is true to a certain extent. However, declarations of flexibility are not enough for competent strategists. For full flexibility to be achieved, commanders 'must have the type of intuitive understanding that results from a thorough analysis of the objective and the mission of the command'.[111] Visualising Earth orbit as a coastal environment and conducting strategic manoeuvres through it helps to build this intuitive grasp of spacepower as we know it today for astrostrategists and decision makers. Intuitive strategic thought about space is improved through a critical engagement with the universal principles of the component parts of strategic manoeuvre in real-world scenarios.[112] Commanding the cosmic coastline from Earth and the five parts of strategic manoeuvre crystallise universal themes that are always relevant to the strategist. Proposition V has theorised the defining aspects of spacepower as a relatively subtle enabler and contributor to modern warfare and the ramification that Earth orbit is nearby littoral and is not a vast ocean separating warring parties. Events on Earth can acutely impact the cosmic coastline as much as a dominant spacepower can consciously exploit the celestial shore against a terrestrial foe. The elements of Proposition V have shown how the command of space can be exploited, further structuring Propositions I–IV to take into account that they are operating within the celestial coastal zone of Earth orbit. All strategic actors and military space services must engage with this cosmic coastline which also generates cultural effects and challenges that resonate with the experiences of continental navies, and is where the next chapter and Proposition VI turns the focus of spacepower theory.

Notes

1. Kosmodemyansky, *Konstantin Tsiolkovsky*, p. 95.
2. Mahan, *The Influence of Sea Power upon History*, p. 209.
3. Corbett, *Principles of Maritime Strategy*, pp. 88–104.
4. Texts used from the 'continental school': Menon, *Maritime Strategy*; Gorshkov, *The Sea Power*; Callwell, *Military Operations*; Castex, *Strategic Theories*.
5. Armstrong, 'Introduction', p. 9.
6. On discussions of airpower's efficacy, see: Clodfelter, *The Limits of Air Power*; Heuser, *The Evolution*, pp. 313–50; Gray, *Airpower for Strategic Effect*, pp. 182–5; Pape, *Bombing to Win*; Kagan, *Finding the Target*; Shultz and Pfaltzgraff, *The Future*.
7. For an imagining of close tactical space support in terrestrial warfare, see the Jayhawk War, in: Niven and Pournelle, *Footfall*, pp. 276–89.
8. Sheldon, *Reasoning*, pp. 123–4.
9. Ibid. p. 21, footnote 25.
10. Deudney, *Dark Skies*; Dolman, *Astropolitik*, pp. 7–8; Johnson-Freese, *Space Warfare*, pp. 165–84.
11. Ropp, 'Continental Doctrines', p. 452.
12. Mahan, *The Influence of Sea Power upon History*, p. 329.
13. Clausewitz, *On War*, pp. 752–3.
14. Ibid. p. 753.
15. Handberg, 'Is Space War Imminent?', p. 418.
16. Oberg, *Space*, p. 4.
17. Castex, *Strategic Theories*, p. 101. Emphasis Castex's.
18. Ibid. pp. 105–21; Luttwak, *Strategy*, pp. 4, 9, 15.
19. Clausewitz, *On War*, p. 760.
20. Gorshkov, *The Sea Power of the State*, p. 148.
21. Luttwak, *Strategy*, p. 17.
22. On Liddell-Hart's 'indirect approach', see: Danchev, 'Liddell Hart's Big Idea', pp. 29–48.
23. Klein, *Space Warfare*, p. 103.
24. Menon, *Maritime Strategy*, p. 30.
25. Ibid. p. 42.
26. Castex, *Strategic Theories*, pp. 345–6. Menon, Gorshkov and Callwell substantiate historical cases and thinking about this, see: Menon, *Maritime Strategy*, p. 85; Gorshkov, *The Sea Power of the State*, p. 242; Callwell, *Military Operations*, p. 164.

27. Till, *Seapower*, 3rd edition, p. 76.
28. Callwell, *Military Operations*, p. 164.
29. Till, *Seapower*, 3rd edition, p. 152.
30. Panikkar, *India*, pp. 40–63.
31. Heuser, *The Evolution*, pp. 233–41.
32. Callwell, *Military Operations*, pp. 132–4.
33. Mei Lianju, *Space Operations*, p. 132. An excerpt of the translated manuscript was kindly provided by Dean Cheng of the Heritage Foundation, Washington, DC.
34. Handberg, *Seeking New World Vistas*, p. 102.
35. Ibid. p. 189.
36. On a critique of 'space weaponisation' debates, see: Bowen, 'Space Oddities', pp. 265–79.
37. Callwell, *Military Operations*, p. 167.
38. Sheldon, *Reasoning*, pp. 277–8.
39. Piotrowski, *Space Warfare*, unpublished manuscript, taken from Sheldon, *Reasoning*.
40. Sheldon, *Reasoning*, pp. 167–8.
41. Gorshkov, *The Sea Power of the State*, p. 214.
42. Callwell, *Maritime Operations*, p. 164.
43. Corbett, *Principles of Maritime Strategy*, p. 97.
44. Ibid. p. 99.
45. Sheldon, *Reasoning*, p. 155.
46. Klein, *Space Warfare*, p. 89.
47. Castex, *Strategic Theories*, p. 362.
48. Ibid. p. 136.
49. Ibid. pp. 348–9.
50. Ropp, 'Continental Doctrines', p. 450.
51. Castex, *Strategic Theories*, p. 365.
52. Callwell, *Military Operations*, pp. 169–77.
53. Castex, *Strategic Theories*, p. 394.
54. Menon, *Maritime Strategy*, pp. 64–86.
55. Mahan, *The Influence of Sea Power upon the French Revolution*, p. 203.
56. Mahan, *The Influence of Sea Power upon History*, pp. 136–7.
57. Discussed further in: Bowen, 'Neither a Silver Bullet nor a Distraction'.
58. Corbett, *Principles of Maritime Strategy*, pp. 91–4, 113, 187, 261–2.
59. Callwell, *Military Operations*, p. 44.
60. Castex, *Strategic Theories*, pp. 37, 39–40.

61. On the Woomera Manual and MILAMOS projects, which are two separate and ongoing projects to interpret the laws of armed conflict to space, see their respective websites: The University of Adelaide, 'The Woomera Manual', available at <https://law.adelaide.edu.au/woomera/> (last accessed 14 January 2020); and McGill University, Manual on International Law Applicable to Military Uses of Outer Space', available at <https://www.mcgill.ca/milamos/> (last accessed 14 January 2020).
62. Handberg, *Seeking New World Vistas*, p. 55.
63. See: White, *Into the Black*.
64. Menon, *Maritime Strategy*, p. 80.
65. Mei Lianju, *Space Operations*, p. 136.
66. Smith, *Ten Propositions*, pp. 62–3.
67. Spires, *Beyond Horizons*, p. 253.
68. Smith, *Ten Propositions*, p. 61.
69. Richelson, 'U.S. Intelligence'.
70. Sheldon, *Reasoning*, p. 322.
71. Mahan, *The Influence of Sea Power upon History*, pp. 273–4.
72. Ibid. p. 406.
73. Smith, *Ten Propositions*, p. 63.
74. Hertzfeld, 'Commercial Space', p. 222.
75. Stares, *Space*, p. 121.
76. McKinley, 'When the Enemy Has Our Eyes', p. 319.
77. Klein, *Space Warfare*, pp. 59, 95.
78. North Atlantic Treaty Organization (NATO) Allied Command Operations, 'New satellite imagery'.
79. Beidleman, 'GPS versus Galileo', pp. 51–8; Bolton, 'Neo-Realism', pp. 186–204.
80. Sheng-Chi Wang, *Transatlantic Space Politics*, esp. pp. 10–28.
81. Eccles, *Logistics*, p. 42.
82. Ibid. p. 10.
83. Castex, *Strategic Theories*, p. 347.
84. Grego, 'A history', pp. 3–5.
85. Handberg, 'Is Space War Imminent?', p. 420.
86. Eccles, *Logistics*, p. 315.
87. Callwell, *Military Operations*, pp. 146–7.
88. Ibid. p. 322.
89. Mahan, *The Influence of Sea Power upon History*, p. 400.
90. Castex, *Strategic Theories*, p. 48.
91. Gilbert, 'Persia', pp. 5, 12.
92. Sheldon, *Reasoning*, p. 173.

93. Ibid. p. 174.
94. Ibid. pp. 175, 318.
95. Eccles, *Logistics*, p. 316.
96. Handberg, *Seeking New World Vistas*, p. 90.
97. Zak, 'Proton'.
98. Detailed descriptions and technical analysis are found throughout Weeden and Samson, *Global Counterspace Capabilities*.
99. Sheldon, *Reasoning*, p. 81.
100. Mahan, *The Influence of Sea Power upon History*, pp. 168–9.
101. Callwell, *Military Operations*, p. 297.
102. Corbett, *Principles of Maritime Strategy*, p. 15.
103. Sheldon, *Reasoning*, pp. 82–3.
104. On John Boyd's OODA loop and its contribution to airpower theory, see: Gray, *Airpower for Strategic Effect*, pp. 205–8; Boyne, *The Influence of Air Power*, pp. 374, 429.
105. Friedman, *Seapower*, p. 131.
106. Shimko, *The Iraq Wars*, pp. 164–5.
107. Sheldon, *Reasoning*, p. 86.
108. Spires, *Beyond Horizons*, p. 255.
109. Sumida, *Decoding Clausewitz*, p. 46.
110. On nonlinearity and Clausewitzian theory, see: Beyerchen, 'Clausewitz'.
111. Eccles, *Logistics*, p. 118.
112. Sumida, *Inventing Grand Strategy*, pp. 104–17.

4. Astroculture and Geocentrism

Proposition VI: Spacepower exists within a geocentric mindset

Proposition VI continues the continental seapower analogy by inferring the cultural effects of the cosmic coastline. It details how geocentrism – the primary importance of Earth in strategic considerations – conditions the evolution and perceptions of spacepower. Like with all military activities, a culture emerges that shapes and codifies the way people think, interpret and act with regard to strategic problems and threats. This is no less true for space. Proposition VI states that astroculture is geocentric in its context and conditioning, and extends to the entirety of spacepower. As astroculture emerges, it is still dominated by terrestrial priorities and terrestrially minded military and strategic cultures. Going beyond Proposition II's focus on astrographic features and its inescapable practical connections to Earth, Proposition VI argues that military astroculture will resemble that of seapower for continental navies and states with land-orientated grand strategies and primary threats. The primacy of terrestrial needs and objectives will shape the influence and manifestations of spacepower. Spacepower will remain geocentric so long as Earth remains humanity's only centre of life and civilisation. What happens in space will only ultimately matter in how it affects life and strategies on Earth. This is geocentrism, as opposed to astrodeterminism. The military services that use space carry their Terran cultures into space with them, and use space with Earth as their reference point. This is the cultural consequence of the continental seapower analogy from

Proposition V – the space powers of today are terrestrial powers that use spacepower for terrestrial wars. Spacepower will have to find its place within geocentric strategic cultures as a secondary source of power and operating environment.

Astroculture is the way humans interpret outer space, or 'the cultural significance and societal repercussions of outer space and space exploration'.[1] Outer space has tended to be 'intimately bound with notions of modernity and utopian visions of human progress'.[2] Astroculture in spacepower theory refers to the cultural consequences of spacepower, as well as how spacepower can be interpreted and manifested through cultural lenses. Unlike Geppert's use of astroculture which includes the infinite universe, space exploration and the question of extra-terrestrial life, astroculture in spacepower theory remains restricted to where humanity uses space for strategic and economically significant tasks: Earth orbit.[3] It is true for many that because only a few people have been to space, and fewer still have walked on another celestial object, the 'popular understanding of outer space is chiefly a product of images and representations'.[4] Yet thousands of humans engage with space every day. The United States employs a space manufacturing workforce of around 70,000, Europe around 38,000, and 7,000 in Japan.[5] Thousands more work in launch, operations, research and downstream applications sectors of the space industry and economy. Humans are engaging with the cosmic coastline and are building a syncretic strategic culture based on mundane but ubiquitous infrastructure. A challenge is to increase awareness of how pervasive spacepower is in everyday life as GPS, for example, has become pervasive in almost any military and economic activity.[6] The 1991 Gulf War was a watershed for the visibility of GPS and American spacepower, not least for the Iraqi Army.[7] The widespread use of space technology builds a society that is able to tap into the promises of spacepower, whose cultures and subcultures are shaped by emergent astrocultures as a result.

The state is embedded in 'social rules and conventions that constitute its identity and the reasons for the interests that motivate' them; culture adds another factor for strategists seeking to develop specific war plans and strategies utilising spacepower.[8]

Human traits and the passion, reason and chance of war's nature are still relevant, if not essential, for the strategist's comprehension of space warfare. Culture is not separate from this because any behaviour takes place within culturally conditioned environments[9] to which space is just another environment for strategic and military culture to develop from and operate within. Forecasting the character of war cannot be reduced to its pure material aspects as 'future technology is no more synonymous with future warfare than past technology carried the complete story of war's history'.[10] Likewise, Proposition VI should counter any interpretation of this theory of ignoring non-material aspects of space warfare and spacepower. But culture alone cannot determine strategic behaviour. Geography and humans' approaches also matter in strategy, and therefore the mix of cultural and geographic pressures on human uses of spacepower can be termed 'astroculture'. Despite the fact that spacepower and space warfare are primarily conducted with machines in space, it does nothing to diminish the reality that they are as influenced by cultural and human factors as any other geographic theatre of warfare and source of power. Indeed, satellites can provide images but people must interpret their meaning;[11] humans are always in the loop of spacepower.

Culture 'strongly mediates the effects of the wider security environment on state policy. Culture means that strategic behaviour is not fully responsive to externalities.'[12] In other words, actors bring their own cultures to the strategic table as a discrete attribute and not merely as a response to events. More specifically, 'culture consists of shared decision rules, recipes, standard operating procedures, and decision routines that impose a degree of order on the view of individuals and groups with their environment'.[13] Spacepower's influence in military culture and bureaucratic struggles will be defined by its character as a secondary theatre for Terran powers, in many ways analogous to continental navies and seapower. Astroculture will remain geocentric. Spacepower not only has to compete with 'an ambiguous repertoire of competing ideas that can be selected, instrumentalised, and manipulated, instead of a clear script for action'[14] from terrestrial experiences of parent or dominant armed forces, it itself generates ideas that inform military culture, particularly through the adoption of PGMs, reconnaissance-strike warfare, and the efficiencies it has created in the conduct and management of war which feature prominently in Proposition VII.

Viewed as a toolbox or cognitive shortcuts that can influence the ways that groups and individuals handle a mass of data and make decisions, strategic culture becomes another factor for strategists to ponder considering how to match ends and means, and to anticipate the responses of the enemy.[15] As space powers, militaries, societies and people confront strategic problems, the residual cultural attributes and experiences of those people, societies and institutions may make some courses of action easier to grasp, approve, forestall or more difficult to adopt than others. No entity is a cultural monolith;[16] an ecology of subcultures exists alongside the competition of military bureaucracies; diversity within entities is as important as diversity between them.[17] Space capabilities are not immune from such concerns on the identity, politics and motivations of the actors that constitute spacepower and those actors that spacepower influences in turn. Spacepower theory takes no strong position on values or validities of the positivist versus context debate, or the Johnston–Gray divide, in the study of strategic culture.[18] Proposition VI offers the observation that the cultural quality of spacepower is a secondary concern, and one that rarely engages in large-scale battles, analogically like the continental navies in wider strategic cultures. The continuing marginalisation of spacepower in strategic studies, IR and military cultures may attest to this as discussed below. This assumption can be tested empirically or provide contextual information for understanding.

This observation about astroculture forms a context for the Gray approach to understanding strategic culture as context, and also provides a starting point for Johnston-inspired positivist analyses of specific strategic and military astrocultures. Military space culture, or astroculture, can also refer to the bureaucratic politics and internal development of a space power's space capabilities and organisations, and more specifically the 'career development, education, and training to develop and sustain a cadre of highly competent and motivated military and civilian space professionals'.[19] Engaging with astroculture also includes the way that top-level decision makers and the institutional processes of grand strategy may view and accommodate spacepower's role in warfare, which may or may not be conducive to its utilisation. Whilst spacepower theory mostly focuses on the external environment and interactions that space powers find themselves in, Proposition VI accommodates the equivalent of Waltz's first and second images of analysis: that of 'human nature' and the structure of states and actors themselves.[20] As 'no single image is ever adequate', spacepower theory cannot ignore the internal dynamics of space powers and the agency of humans, and therefore offers the proposition that spacepower's secondary status will shape the organisation and conduct of spacepower within actors.[21] All else may be impossible to generalise in a nomothetic fashion, as the study of individual organisations and cultures would be too idiographic and epistemologically different – though no less valid – a study. The geocentrism of astroculture and spacepower in the cosmic coastline is a cultural complement to the more geographically, technological and strategic propositions featured so far in the theory.

Checking ethnocentrism

Seeking to understand how the enemy and oneself may think and act with their cultural 'hard-wiring' is a cornerstone of classical strategic wisdom,[22] though it is fraught with risks of ethnocentrism, stereotype and prejudice. Ethnocentrism is the perception of one's own group as being the most important, capable, superior or the 'normal' yardstick by which to measure others, which often disguises diverse actors by imposing a false perception of homogeneity on them.[23] American spacepower should not be seen as a gold standard by which to imagine what a comprehensive space power should look and behave like. Yet cultural diversity can only go so far when faced with the universal challenges of astrography and strategic logic. Any application of this theoretical proposition must balance the 'quirks' of culture that operate against the real-world limitations of technology, physics and strategy.

Cultural or identity-based analyses must also be wary of ignoring similarities when they occur. There is the risk of viewing the

enemy as different but in pejorative terms that may reflect prejudice, and at worst may exhibit social Darwinist tendencies. Sometimes, culturally and economically distinct strategic actors may
mimic one another's behaviour in war or conform to a system-
wide style of warfare, such as the Welsh kingdoms against the
invading Anglo-Normans through the eleventh–thirteenth centuries. Much commentary has erroneously exhibited views of the
Welsh military culture and institutions as those of a 'noble sav-
age' on the periphery of medieval Europe.[24] Perceiving medieval
'Celtic' kingdoms as a 'fringe' of Europe as possessing different
methods of warfare to the 'centre' of medieval Europe is not only
historically problematic because it overlooks military imitations
and homogeneities, but is also an expression of the geopolitical
gaze. The cultural turn in strategic studies, or the quest to dismantle the apolitical and acultural 'strategic man', should not
accentuate cultural differences between military organisations for
its own sake and end up replicating the problems of the geopolitical gaze.[25] Similarities and differences between actors must be
recognised as further variables in understanding warfare and the
spread of power, influence and techniques in any political system.
Applying an uncritical and unfounded assumption of 'they are
different to us' is merely another form of ethnocentrism.

Abhorring views of homogeneity among actors disguises the large
degree of unity among many strategic theorists that were separated
in time and place. Handel saw more commonalities than differences
between strategic theorists from diverse cultures and eras in his own
magnum opus on strategic theory.[26] The persistence and recurrence
of the ideas are a testament to their utility and a common universal understanding of the logic of strategy to an extent that is independent of culture. The USAF's adoption of certain values from the
Army indicates 'that though the material and surface components
of the service, uniform and technology for instance, have changed,
the embedded cultural wiring remains largely intact, and traditional
concepts, taken from the army, still flow strongly through the system'.[27] Imagining strategic and military cultures as prevailing ideas
and conceptual toolkits that hard-wire people and groups to think
and act in some ways more than others is as useful a definition of the
cultural element of militaries in warfare as one is likely to find. The

cultural legacies and heritages of military services – and all actors that use space – will inform behaviour in space warfare and in making spacepower a constituent and consequence of strategic cultures. They too, however, may in turn be influenced by their experiences of using space.

Connected to ethnocentrism are concerns that the very study of strategy is a Western-centric or Anglo-centric exercise in the continuation of particular systems and structures of power in the international system. Booth described 'Anglo-American strategic theory [as] a coherent set of interrelated beliefs about international order and its preservation'.[28] However, spacepower theory and all strategic theory is not just for the satisfied powers of a global order. Clausewitz's formative thought on total war and popular resistance were derived from his experiences as a Prussian nationalist whose country was occupied by an imperial Napoleonic France and its Continental System. As seen in the next part, continental seapower theory embraces the agency of weaker or smaller states in spacepower, and not just the dominant or large ones. Spacepower theory itself should not become restricted to or associated with a status quo mentality of international politics.

There is no universally 'right' answer to strategic or military problems, beyond whatever gets the job done. Culture can shape the methods used to do so.[29] Therefore, all spacepowers need to develop some form of rocket vehicles and basic satellite competencies, yet the ultimate objectives, governance systems and priorities can vary whether a power is revisionist or not. In their study of the history of Chinese space policy, Handberg and Zhen are adamant that

> the Chinese space program is best understood as one analogous to those developed earlier by the original space participants . . . There exists no nationally unique route to the stars; the laws of physics still rule. There are only unique national programs reflecting domestic conditions and their general role in the international system.[30]

Diversity and homogeneity exists. China's motivations for launching a space programme was firstly the existence of external threats which had to be deterred with missile-launched nuclear bombs, and the second was to consolidate the personal political power of Mao Zedong.[31] The American genesis of the space programme, whilst similarly bound up in managing the threat from the Soviet Union via reconnaissance satellites and the revitalisation of the missile programme due to the advent of the hydrogen bomb and Soviet missile advances, was not so intimately tied to the personal and political power of American presidents.[32] Space is more than rocket science, as 'the rocket teams in both Superpowers protested that they could have launched a satellite years earlier if left to do so without military or political interference', McDougall concludes, adding that

> the characteristics of the Soviet regime and the advent of nuclear weapons provided the nourishment and climate sufficient for the space technological revolution to occur. Those characteristics included an ideology of foreign relations that ensured distrust and competition whatever the diplomatic settlement after World War II.[33]

These discrepancies may highlight one possible reason why China was relatively slow to roll out a significant reconnaissance satellite programme after its first satellite launch in 1970, whilst the United States took the lead in such capabilities with the NRO from the early 1960s onwards as a means to circumvent the limitations of U-2 reconnaissance, and to establish the right of satellite overflight as a new global norm.[34] Indeed, the prestige aspects of being the first to launch a satellite were not seen as important for the Eisenhower administration as keeping up with Soviet heavy rocketry and promoting the scientific International Geophysical Year (IGY) satellite initiative as a peaceful civilian cover for its reconnaissance satellite efforts.[35] The IGY could be interpreted by some as a way to 'hoodwink' the world into pursuing aggressive space programmes, or as a ploy of 'cagey politicians manipulating the scientific community to provide a stalking horse for the resolution of a thorny geopolitical problem'.[36] For its part, India has always stressed the human and economic development uses of space technology, and has shaped its spacepower assets and innovation accordingly for much of its long and distinguished history, despite space imposing the same techno-physical limitations.[37]

Despite these political, strategic and cultural variances within and among these space powers, all have developed materially comparable space infrastructure.

Spacepower has enabled the capabilities some have interpreted as crucial to an American 'way of war'. Space capabilities are relied upon to provide enhanced speed, manoeuvre, precision and force protection for deployed military forces. Illustrating this, Robert Citino argues that during the 1991 Gulf War: 'the constant updating of real-time intelligence . . . as well as satellite surveillance and GPS, was a quantum leap in the quick flow of information . . . combining maneuver, firepower, attrition, and destruction into one potent and *distinctly American package*.'[38] The American 'way of war', however, has become politicised and polemical in its use; caution must be used in elaborating from any conclusions as to the cultural preferences of any entity or individual, particularly when states can engage in diverse behaviours as strategic conditions demand.[39] The view that American strategic culture is defined by attrition or annihilation in its approaches to warfare, as characterised in the seminal work by Russell Weigley in 1973, is 'not borne out by events'.[40] Spacepower is not only conditioned by geocentrism, but spacepower has already been shaping the culture and practices of warfare on Earth. The relationship between astroculture and geocentrism is not a one-way street. That distinctiveness in technologies and warfighting styles may be eroding given the proliferation of battlefield-relevant space technologies to other states.

Spacepower has not only influenced but enabled a culturally ingrained American desire to increase overwhelming firepower and effects of mass on the enemy and to reduce casualties and deployment size.[41] However, Echevarria's reading of American strategic culture differs, and he argues that rarely was overwhelming force the objective – rather it was to show a credible force. A credible force is that which is deemed to be enough to sustain and project American credibility in a theatre. The US military has a track record of doing more with less, further challenging the view of American strategic culture as one centred upon attrition, excessive logistics and overwhelming firepower.[42] Spacepower enables a far more efficient compression of firepower and effects to a more discriminate area, maintaining a decisive combat advantage and a credible force whilst reducing the footprint required to do so, a feat theorised explicitly in Proposition VII. Cultural attitudes, inter-service rivalry and internal political processes still matter in the high-technology realm of space activity. As spacepower enables some forms of fighting and challenges others, if it produces positive cultural responses within a geocentric mindset it would find a better home in an Earth-bound state despite being a secondary geographic environment. Regardless of one's opinion on American military culture, one cannot deny that space is essential to the conduct of American warfare and what its population expects from its military campaigns and successes with precision and discriminating warfare, remotely piloted vehicles, continuous top-level command and control, and pervasive twenty-four-hour news coverage from the battlefield and press room.

So what? Experiences with spacepower over time could form habitual thinking and a tangible astroculture for better or ill. Experience may reinforce such preferences, or challenge them. Whatever gives one the best chance at the most meaningful command and exploitation of space in any given scenario to support an overall war aim should be the immediate objectives in space warfare, within what is deemed politically and ethically viable by a military or authority's rules of engagement and commitments to laws in war. Propositions I, IV and V are attempts to provide a useful approach to identify what those specific objectives could be in any scenario – regardless of their material and cultural diversity. Proposition VI is a way to stress that part of identifying the solutions to and threats from commanding space, celestial lines of communication and the hostile coast are also subject to cultural attitudes and the ancillary and secondary quality of spacepower.

Strategic and military culture is useful for spacepower theory in two ways, beyond using it as the recognition of a culturally bound toolbox to help analyse strategic problems, make decisions and keep ethnocentrism in check. It is also an opening into examining the internal composition of spacepowers and a starting point for theorising human culture as determined in part by the two-way interplay of geocentrism and astroculture. It must be noted that space policy does not exist in the sense of a coherent or singular state approach to outer space, typified by the fact that there is often no single budget or agency for all space activities conducted by a state. Military, intelligence, economic and scientific space projects are conducted in different government departments and draw funds from different budgets, and reflect different priorities and approaches to space activities. The next section uses the bureaucratic and cultural struggles of continental navies as a base analogy to explore some actual and potential problems facing Earth-bound military space services.

Geocentrism and the continental mindset

Like continental seapower, spacepower today is a secondary source of power that is utilised in a geographic environment of secondary importance. Proposition VI crystallises this feature of spacepower in Earth orbit, which emerges from a combination of Propositions V and III. If space is a secondary theatre for strategic manoeuvres (V) and it does not lend itself to viewing decisive battles as a regular course of operations (III), it may be more difficult to convey the value of spacepower to a terrestrial state or leadership that may have more pressing concerns on Earth's surface rather than above the atmosphere. If much of this geocentric military culture still emphasises combat roles as those fast-tracked for promotion and prominence within a service, spacepower will continue to be handicapped in inter-service budgeting and joint service appointment disputes. Spacepower will struggle to attract resources, promotion and prestige in military cultures as they prioritise combat capabilities over others. Combat is, after all, the *raison d'être* of any military force which executes or threatens violence and destruction in the name of a political entity. Spacepower is mostly about mundane infrastructure, support and logistics to the 'more interesting' questions of combat hardware and fighting troops. Military space services – and by extension spacepower – may struggle to find their place in Earth-bound powers and mindsets due to the fact that logistics often gets overlooked on popular, cultural and prestige fronts. Caught up in such concerns are domestic and bureaucratic politics, as 'all warfare has a domestic hinterland, usually several such'.[43] The cultural impact of spacepower as infrastructure and support in a secondary theatre as explained in Proposition V means that strategic manoeuvres in space may not get the resources or leadership required to carry them out.

Continental seapower can illustrate the similar issues that spacepower faces. The subtle contributions of seapower are sometimes lost on land and battle-dominated strategic cultures.[44] Raja Menon believes that an oceanic or bluewater strategy focused on large battle fleets tends to be less visible or noticed because it is less likely to trigger large battles in the first place if there is a decisive advantage with one surface fleet over another. With such an advantage, the weaker navy will tend to avoid battle or conduct small-scale attacks and harassing operations in a fleet-in-being strategy.[45] It is therefore has less of an impression upon a joint military staff and the civilian leaders of a continental power, despite the fact that moving the enemy regardless of battles fought, rather than being moved by him, is an important part of the art of war.[46] This is a challenge for the primary occupation of spacepower as an enabler in a littoral or flanking environment and the other roles in Proposition V. Navies may struggle to advertise

> the benefits of economic warfare are the same as those with recommending sanctions – no ordnance is expended, no battles are won, and the damage is only visible in statistics . . . the strategy they advocate . . . is unglamorous, uncertain and quite often boring compared to what the army and air force presentations are on the same subject.[47]

The same is conceptually true for space services, and translates into problems of military culture and bureaucratic politics that are resonant with the place of continental navies. Just as continental sea powers was land-centric in thought and perspective, Earth-based space powers are themselves geocentric, prioritising terrestrial needs and perspectives.

The lack of combat operations in the bulk of likely strategic manoeuvres generates cultural and prestige problems for both continental sea powers and contemporary terrestrial space powers. Menon warned of the dangers for navies in a continental mindset of political masters and military planners where the relative lack of spectacular fleet actions failed to communicate the usefulness of navies in continental wars. The navy risked becoming 'just' a transport wing of the military, a logistics corps or an amphibious force alone. This is not to say that all states need or should have ocean-going capabilities, but such tendencies could be, for example, detrimental to India's feasible oceanic strategic possibilities.[48] Having borders in the Himalayas 'loom large' may be a significant cultural inhibitor towards seapower thinking in Indian strategic cultures, posing challenges to Indian Navy advocates.[49] Menon writes that 'for a continental power to see the possibilities of maritime strategy is ... difficult because the problems of the land frontiers are much too immediate'.[50] Analogically, Earth orbit is an adjunct to terrestrial powers' main media of threats and combat capabilities, thus it would not be without precedent that the role of spacepower may be hard to explain and promote in the geocentric strategic cultures of terrestrial states. But with the political-economies of the major powers of the international system increasing their infrastructural dependencies on space systems, there may be increasing 'ammunition' for spacepower advocates and those wishing to see more independent military space services.

Gorshkov observed and feared a vicious circle of reduced visibility and reduced perceptions of the value of navies in continental powers. In the Second World War, the Soviet Navy was hollowed out for the more pressing needs of frontline territorial defence.[51] The repurposing of naval personnel to land operations shows the more immediate need of a land front in a supreme emergency. Today, Gorshkov's and Menon's concerns on the secondary nature of continental navies continue to play out in discussion of India's maritime identity and the place of the Indian Navy in New Delhi's grand strategy and the 'land-bound attitudes, habits, and traditions that inform Indians' outlook on strategic affairs'.[52] Spacepower is pressed into serving the needs of terrestrial warfare among the most developed and modernised states, which may handicap attempts to develop a space-centric approach, service culture and force development programme. This shows a risk to space services if it is not seen to be contributing to primary threats or immediate needs, and could fall victim to a vicious circle of funding cuts and reduced capabilities. This raises the need for coherent thought about strategic manoeuvres in space and how operations in the secondary theatre of the cosmic coastline impacts wars on Earth.

Gorshkov also maintained that common efforts were needed between all branches of the armed forces for 'complete victory'.[53] Raoul Castex had preceded this line of thought and attempted to make French seapower relevant to the land-dominated strategic culture of France, dealing with similar problems at the level of grand strategy that Gorshkov would later face. Gorshkov argued that

> it is false to try to build a fleet to the model and likeness of even the strongest sea power and to determine the requirements for the building of ships for one's fleet merely by going on quantitative criteria and ratios of ship composition. Each country has specific requirements for sea forces which influence their development.[54]

Castex and Gorshkov show a land-centrism in their approaches to seapower, and show how a geocentric approach to spacepower should be done. The geocentrism of astroculture is not in itself a problem, as it is not impossible to integrate the secondary status of spacepower into mainstream grand strategies. Rather, its geocentrism merely raises some hurdles to the untrammelled manifestation of spacepower. It must be sensitive to and embedded within the needs of geocentric strategic cultures and wars.

In addition to outlining the geocentric mindset of spacepower, continental seapower theory also allows theory to emphasise its applicability to second-rank or lesser powers, or those who may not be able to match the most capable states in orbit. Continental powers could still hope to challenge ocean-going adversaries. That principle of asymmetric challenge is emphasised through the continental analogy to balance the bluewater approach which tends to focus on the operations of a dominant or the most capable naval powers of the day. Indeed, as the 'father of the Indian space programme', Vikram Sarabhai claimed that

> there are some who question the relevance of space activities in a developing nation. To us, there is no ambiguity of purpose. We do

not have the fantasy of competing with the economically advanced nations in the exploration of the moon or the planets or manned space-flight.[55]

India instead focused on rocketry, developmental and scientific earth observation, and civilian telecommunications capabilities which contrasted with the nuclear delivery, spy satellites and early warning priorities of the Cold War superpowers. Spacepower must be tailored to the needs of its users, and not necessarily always imitated in the image of other, perhaps more established space powers, exactly as Gorshkov and Castex were arguing for their continental navies.

Continental navies with significant combat power have a history of being neglected, even when properly funded as Ropp comments that 'neglected in France, pampered in William II's Germany, the navy was in both instances regarded by orthodox military men in these countries as a stepchild'.[56] Just as continental thinking and culture can hamstring the utilisation of seapower, it can be a boon if argued and managed coherently as aspired to by Castex, Gorshkov, and Proposition V which relates strategic manoeuvres in a secondary theatre or medium towards a main war effort elsewhere. The same is analogically true in space – a geocentric mindset that influences the exploitation of spacepower and the development of astroculture. Spacepower should not be dominated by space-based thinking, as seen in Proposition III, at the expense of ignoring the connections between space and Earth. However, terrestrial space powers should not ignore spacepower's uniqueness and infrastructural quality as described in Proposition II, either – not only in what the utilisation of spacepower brings to the table in terrestrial warfare, seen next in Proposition VII, but how it may impact our own grand strategic perceptions of geopolitics, military services and cultures. Spacepower and strategic manoeuvres in Earth orbit are therefore conducive to terrestrial mindsets.

The human element of spacepower means that a people and its cultures must be attuned to the promises of a geostrategic environment to fully develop its potential. Mahan emphasised the importance of people in his narratives of great sea clashes and in his ideas of seapower.[57] If there is a population familiar with the needs and skills of the medium that is important to warfare, given enough time (and ability to weather the initial blows), a spacepower can turn demography and wealth into a long-lasting strategic advantage. A deep integration of space sciences, engineering and technologies into one's economy and society can create a significant strategic depth to call upon in a protracted hot or cold war. A state can instil a Mahanian drive to make one's people and economy geared towards space in much the same way 'so that when their forces go to war, they go with the best equipment and training that only a nation for whom the medium had become second nature would naturally produce'.[58] A spacepower with time, resources and plentiful experts of this new vista coupled with excellent command skills and an eye for material profits (or leaders that guided them) could be a potent mix. The use of space popularisation, for example through the use of astronauts as ambassadors for European space activities and integration, to generate support for not only space but a political project is a clear example of some efforts to instil an emergent political and instrumental astroculture.[59]

Yet no matter how a state, its people and its culture views space, they cannot avoid the thorny question of how to organise their military forces in a Space Age. The internal political and bureaucratic problems facing continental powers' armed forces, institutions and geopolitical outlook can resonate with spacepower in states or armed groups that are still bound, materially, culturally and psychologically, to Earth. Bureaucratic turf wars, whether in the USAF since the 1950s or in China today, strengthen the argument that spacepower is conditioned by geocentrism and bureaucratic politics.[60] As recent events have increased the visibility of spacepower, they all occur in the context of a geocentric mindset which places spacepower on a secondary geostrategic footing, as Proposition V encourages.

Space organisation and independent forces

Spacepower has a cultural problem. It 'is discrete . . . and does not attract much attention in the way that armies, navies and air forces

173

do . . . One only hears of it when something goes wrong.'[61] Military services are usually geared towards fighting battles, breaking things and killing people in the name of the state. In that sense, it may serve some objectives of the space staff within USAF to seek more counterspace capabilities in order to secure more funding and visibility for spacepower. Although more common in practice, gaining more resources for offensive and aggressive purposes may not be an inherent or ever-present goal of bureaucrats and military leaders.[62] As spacepower and space weapons proliferate, the use of space for military purposes and operations has generated military space units, sub-forces and culture. Unlike nuclear and cyber, space is more geographically determined. Spacepower must centre upon and draw its capability from the exploitation of an environment. Conceptually, a space force is no less ridiculous than having a separate service for the sea and the air. Importantly, however, due to Proposition II's emphasis on space as infrastructure, a space force will be primarily concerned with supporting terrestrial missions and managing logistics and communications infrastructure, rather than combat operations. This may create hurdles in martialling support for truly independent forces for Earth orbit. The US Coast Guard as a safety and constabulary force also features in debates on models for a space force, and it has its merits as well as being a custodian of waterways, though celestial lines of communication are inherently global, not territorialised like home waters or Exclusive Economic Zones. Still, the primary questions of a space force should be who could manage space infrastructure and its protection best, and which branches of the military should engage in counterspace missions, most often involving terrestrially based weapons. This is an increasing concern for smaller space powers, and not only the 'big three' of Russia, China and America.

Australia and the UK are two important allies for the United States – not least in space, nuclear and intelligence activities through the Five Eyes partnership. Through their integration with America they have many reasons to imitate its spacepower organisation. The British state has recently taken a greater interest in the military and commercial dimensions of outer space with a string of institutional moves and its first published space policies.

The Ministry of Defence has decided to return the operation of its Skynet military communications satellites to uniformed and in-house personnel, has revised its Air and Space doctrine according to British spacepower capabilities in allied and joint warfare, and is mulling a defence space strategy.[63] The UK's military space capacities are housed within UK Strategic Command (formerly Joint Forces Command) and the Royal Air Force, mimicking the American air-led yet joint character of spacepower organisation. Furthermore, the UK's space doctrine is in alignment with the fundamental truth of spacepower regarding the command and exploitation of the medium in wartime.[64] The UK may form its own National Space Council and a new Strategic Command to coordinate and oversee all of the British state's space activities and military space operations, respectively. Australia has also been active in space policy with the foundation of its own space agency in 2018, and has purchased one of the flagship American military communications satellites, the Wideband Global SATCOM (WGS). Australia also jointly operates ground stations such as the Joint Defence Facility at Pine Gap with the United States, a Skynet ground station for the UK, and runs a joint-level office for space operations and services for the Australian Defence Forces – the Australian Space Operations Centre which mirrors the US Combined Space Operations Center (CSpOC). France has also recently announced its intentions to set up a military Space Command, and an increased space situational awareness and undisclosed active 'defensive' capabilities to protect satellites.[65] This underscores not only the importance of increasing allied integration as their capabilities increase, but also that space culture is developing through practice beyond the United States. Britain, Australia and France, due to their relatively small size in military space personnel and assets, may find compelling reasons to develop solely joint commands for space in future, rather than overburden their air forces as all terrestrial services move ever further into fully joint warfare capabilities in a multi-domain battlespace.

China's PLA in recent years has undergone some transformation beyond its core geographically focused services. The PLA Strategic Support Force (SSF) was set up in late 2015 to integrate and repurpose existing organisations for the purposes of cyber, electronic and space warfare. 'The SSF appears to be wholly constructed from the operational units and organizations from the former general departments', John Costello writes, 'particularly the General Staff Department (GSD), General Armament Department (GAD), and General Political Department (GPD) units responsible for space, cyber, and electronic warfare, the SSF's main missions.'[66] The SSF has brought together much of the PLA's strategic-level capabilities in space, electronic warfare and cyber into domain-specific structures (as opposed to mission types), which has created the moniker of 'Space Troops' within the PLA.[67] The SSF should ease integration and jointness between these domains, and enhance centralised civilian control over such capabilities.[68] Russia, meanwhile, reformed the Russian Space Forces as part of the Russian Aerospace Forces in 2015, re-establishing some degree of expertise and sub-service identity in Russian space infrastructure management, protection and exploitation, as well as missile-based space warfare operations and providing nuclear and ballistic missile information to the Strategic Missile Forces.[69] The merging of spacepower with the air force in Russia[70] should not necessarily mean it is the best way to organise spacepower for the United States or China, as the ultimate question is which framework of organisation in practice enables spacepower to develop and be exploited to its full potential. Back in the late Cold War Norman Friedman noted how US and Soviet approaches to integrating spacepower and disseminating space data in the 1980s differed (the former being more delegated down the chain of command and the latter more centralised), despite the basic satellite technology principles being the same.[71] Differing command cultures may be better or worse suited for the opportunities provided by strategic manoeuvres and support from the cosmic coastline, and the second-order military services of spacepower.

Despite the technical principles being the same, Chinese reconnaissance satellites, such as the Yaogan and Gaofen series, have not necessarily created a similar bureaucratic structure as America's NRO. The NRO is a defence agency and an element of the civilian intelligence community, whilst the uniformed PLA controls most, if not all, of Chinese space infrastructure. The Yaogan series of satellites are built on universal technical-economic principles of digital space-based photography, which are inherently superior to space-based cameras that must send film to re-enter the atmosphere and be picked up by terrestrial vehicles. The structures governing the use and analysis of these systems are bound in the practices and internal politics of the Chinese leadership and its military and intelligence community, which differ from American practice. This reinforces the value of not assuming too much homogeneity between military and strategic astrocultures despite strong techno-physical forces imposing similar technological capacities on diverse actors. Despite these differences, both China and America appear to be taking similar approaches to integrating and conducting space operations as the PLA's views on 'system of system operations' appears to be in line with American equivalents, which emphasises treating 'all space assets, both classified and unclassified, as part of a single constellation'.[72]

The US has re-activated United States Space Command (USSPACECOM) as a separate combatant command on the same level of authority as the regional commands and United States Strategic Command (USSTRATCOM), and Congress in 2019 legislated a US Space Force as a semi-independent corps within the USAF into being. The US Space Force took over the duties of USAF Space Command. The Joint Space Operations Center, which among other things conducts space surveillance, offensive and defensive 'space control' and specific SSA missions, providing on-demand reconnaissance about the space environment as opposed to persistent and routine surveillance, has now become CSpOC, which increases allied and commercial involvement and interoperability in US military space operations, and integrates the American military with allied space capabilities.[73] With the vertical proliferation of spacepower among America's allies, tapping into these assets will help the US build resilience and redundancy in its spacepower backbone, challenging notions of the centre of gravity as discussed in Proposition III. The success of this in part depends on the ability of American space personnel to work with allied forces, and the political will to do so. US military branches have space offices and units in addition to USAF. The inter-service quip from a US Navy admiral that '[o]ur idea of a joint program is one the Air Force pays for and the Navy uses' may be somewhat outdated.[74] With spacepower filtering through every branch of the Pentagon, every service must have space-specific personnel to integrate with USSTRATCOM and USSPACECOM, which incurs financial and human resources costs. But Army and Navy space commands generate non-air force astroculture as well as geocentric pressures that instrumentalise space infrastructure for their specific terrestrial needs that will not match the needs of air forces. 'Space cadres' are being developed in all US services and bring various needs and subcultures to the table.

What this landscape shows are efforts across the board to integrate spacepower for the needs of terrestrial warfare, with USAF having the most institutional control over its development and platform acquisition through senior commands and the implementation of the Pentagon's space budget. This current landscape will now change in the years ahead as the US Space Force will take on a greater degree of autonomy and control over budgeting and hardware acquisitions. This is perhaps a response to a historically lethargic space acquisitions process from USAF. Now, the semi-independent corps within USAF has command and control authority over all US Department of Defense satellites and launch operations. Smith's anecdotes of non-space specialist USAF leaders placed at the helm of the USAF's space activities is one manifestation of a terrestrial mindset failing to grasp accurately what spacepower can and cannot do.[75] This not only shows a pervasive geocentrism in American spacepower, but an air-dominated geocentrism at that. Although astroculture may be developing within the services that 'do' space in an organic fashion by simply engaging with space technologies and services, creating an independent space force or corps would have to be a conscious choice, is never a foregone conclusion, and will have politico-bureaucratic motivations and consequences in any space power.

Despite being the most advanced technological power of the time, spacepower was not an inevitable policy course given the dominating cultures and practices of America's government, society and armed forces in the late 1940s and 1950s. Somewhat fittingly, debate on an American space force mirrors the experience of creating an independent air force. Finlan observes that 'it is surprising that the nation-state that witnessed the first powered flight in the history of human evolution . . . should be so slow to develop its potential in the military sphere'.[76] A similar start can be seen in America's entry into the Space Age, of which its satellite and intercontinental ballistic missile projects enjoyed a 'brief flurry of enthusiasm after the war, followed by budget cuts and cancellations, followed after some years by sudden revival in reaction to Soviet progress'.[77] Prior to the 1940s, the 'U.S. government stood relatively aloof from science and technology' and was quite different to the technocracy that the Space Age ushered in to American national security culture.[78] It must be remembered that there is nothing 'natural' or preordained about the way different parts of spacepower are divided in the United States. At one time, there were two American astronaut programmes – National Aeronautics and Space Administration (NASA) housing the civilians, and the uniformed astronaut corps working with USAF's plans for the Manned Orbital Laboratory (MOL). At the time of MOL's demise, Chuck Yeager – a USAF test pilot – commented that 'no bluesuiter wanted to surrender space to NASA'.[79] Indeed, USAF's crewed space programme predated NASA itself, and was eventually transferred to NASA as Project Mercury. However, the 'real' threat to USAF's astronaut corps via the MOL was the NRO whose development of advanced film cameras and later digital cameras for reconnaissance satellites in the Keyhole series eliminated the need for people in space to process imagery in orbit.[80] The NRO's success in remote photography resulted in the cancellation of MOL in the late 1960s. This demonstrates that a bureaucratic landscape, particularly in the division of military and civilian capabilities, for space which may seem 'natural' today is anything but.

The question of a more independent space service has stalked USAF since its inception in 1947. From its infancy, it had to 'claw its way aggressively, and often against significant Army, Navy, and civilian bureaucratic resistance' towards its status as the executive agent for space.[81] USAF has been placed in a dilemma regarding its double-hatting as an air and space service, as explained by Benjamin Lambeth:

> should it move *too* fast toward expanding its percentage of funding support for space, it will run the danger of further undercutting its

support to its equally important air obligations. Alternatively, should the Air Force be perceived as dragging its heels with respect to funding the nation's military space needs ... it will ... run the danger of eventually being asked to turn over its stewardship of space to a separate Space Corps or Space Force.[82]

The Air Force strongly resisted attempts by the Navy and Army to gain more rights in the space domain, and Thomas D. White coined the term 'aerospace' in the late 1950s 'to portray air and space as a single continuum'.[83] From the viewpoint of 2019, the Air Force seems to have failed in this balancing act with the creation of the Space Force as a corps within USAF. An unrestrained USAF culture transposed into space could transfer strategic bombing logic to spacepower, as a mechanistic approach to the utility of bombing is 'still strong and visible in contemporary USAF doctrine'.[84] Until space-based weapons make orbital bombardment a reality, particularly with a non-nuclear kinetic version of the Fractional Orbital Bombardment System, strategic bombing and its associated airpower thinking will continue to have little to no resonance in outer space.

Doctrinal documents show a subtle difference in tone between the Air Force and the joint service level. USAF doctrine begins its annex on space power with space superiority as a 'primary concern', meaning the USAF needs the ability to engage against targets in space and destroy threats to space systems on Earth.[85] Resonating with Proposition V, joint space doctrine stresses the services and benefits of space throughout, where combat missions or 'fires' are embedded within, and its introduction notes 'the operationally limited' character of space operations.[86] These differences may be symptomatic of the Air Force's continuing culture which privileges flying and combat roles above 'support' or logistical functions as well as the belief that air superiority is needed to conduct all other operations.[87] This transposition of air superiority for land and naval operations to space superiority over terrestrial operations was performed by White in the 1950s.[88] However, the spread of a 'warrior culture' to base personnel, particularly after the experience of counter-insurgency campaigns in Iraq and Afghanistan may have enhanced the prestige of non-flying personnel within the Air Force.[89] The role of the new Space Force in joint doctrinal development remains to be seen at this early juncture.

Many years prior to the recent establishment of the Space Force, Michael Smith contended that American spacepower demands a centralised outlook because of its global nature and the regional demands of the military's services, as well as demands from civilian departments, the Intelligence Community and the Executive branch.[90] Arguments over contrasting theatre and global perspectives of US spacepower with systems such as the CCS are illuminating examples.[91] The CCS consists of two USAF squadrons, soon to be under US Space Force authority, that are deployed in-theatre to jam adversary satellite communications in the localised area of operations, in support of terrestrial military operations. This highlights how spacepower is influenced by cultural, political and bureaucratic elements, and is by no means a subject reduced to technical considerations alone. As only Nixon could have gone to China,[92] perhaps it is only a USAF officer that could say the following:

> The idea that an airman with a *theater* perspective should ever control space assets, which are properly 'tasked and assigned from a *global* perspective,' should send shivers up the backs of military leaders . . . Just as the expanded mind-set of airmen drove their need for centralized theatre-level control of airpower by an airman, so too, the further expanded mind-set of space professionals drives their insistence that spacepower must be centrally controlled by a space professional.[93]

The geocentric airpower mindset may be a severe problem if the USAF persists in culturally dividing personnel between those who fly and those who do not, and specifically with fighter pilots sitting at the top of the former group,[94] especially as spacepower is strategically relevant with virtually no requirement for a human presence in space itself. Furthermore, if USAF's 'key criterion for ranking within the institution, as with soldiers and sailors, revolves around the issue of combat',[95] it may be difficult for spacepower to be appreciated in its own right as a medium and theatre where they may be little to no direct violence. This may create some operational issues with regard to tasking space assets when a combat operation may not need space support to make a crucial difference, but a terrestrial non-combat mission may fail without it. Would a combat-focused air force make the correct space tasking decisions? Smith argues that spacepower is represented without the filter of a parent Air Force. Smith continues:

> it makes little sense to organize space units as if they were flying units, or space personnel as if they were fliers, but this is what is done today. The Air Force even assigns the heraldry – unit logos, patches, customs, traditions, and histories – of famous flying units of the past to today's space squadrons, groups and wings. The message is not subtle: the Air Force does not value space, space power, or its space professionals. It does, however, value the space budget's contribution to air power.[96]

In principle, USAF's traditional counterargument before the Trump presidency, that setting up a space service would de-integrate spacepower when it should be integrated further, falls foul of Proposition VI's claim about geocentrism shaping astroculture and spacepower.[97] The question about military space organisation is who will nurture it best to exploit the space environment and spacepower's infrastructural quality to its fullest, realising Proposition II? As of yet, there are no firm plans for any acceleration in space weapons technologies in line with new military space organisations. 'Space warfighters' will still mainly refer to technicians and engineers sitting in windowless rooms and bunkers, starting at computer screens, managing satellite operations and data. This is a clear manifestation of Menon's observations of how difficult it can be to 'sell' these activities when they rarely involve battle and visible effects, which translates into cultural and bureaucratic struggles over identity and resources. As such a debate on space force has happened within USAF and Congress for decades, Trump's desire to create one is neither new nor especially foolish.[98] It is still unclear what problem the Trump administration is trying to solve by reorganising its military space bureaucracy and combatant commands – whether for cultural development, acquisitions or something else. Whether this USAF culture will transpose to the Space Force will determine the amelioration or exacerbation of spacepower culture issues in the US military. In its infancy, the Space Force will after all be composed of 'former' Air Force personnel.

A ham-fisted implementation may indeed bring about USAF's worries but practical concerns only go so far in debates that may involve strong emotive and conceptual elements. A serious issue is what organisation should train and equip America's spacepower capabilities (a military service branch), and what organisation should command space assets during a campaign (such as regional or functional commands like Pacific Command or USSTRATCOM). This reinforces the presence of geocentrism in shaping military astroculture. A unique concern about the organisation of a state's space capabilities, relative to terrestrial forces, is that spacepower refers mostly to using, protecting and denying infrastructure. An independent space service will take over a fleet of platforms and services, whilst terrestrial forces are primarily focused on weapons platforms and fighting units. This raises significant issues for the conceptualisation of a space 'force' where much of what it does will be infrastructure and logistics support, as Proposition V makes clear. To what extent infrastructure such as GPS and space situational awareness should remain within military hands at all as opposed to civilian ones remains an open question. A separate military space service may become 'merely' a logistics and enabling corps, potentially victim to Gorshkov's vicious cycle.

Lambeth argues that USAF's space personnel may be uniquely positioned to rise above the divisions among military services (including against air personnel in USAF) and the intelligence community because American spacepower is inherently valuable in how it enhances and enables joint warfare across service boundaries. Contrary to Smith, Lambeth maintains that USAF seems like the best place to let military astroculture grow if USAF allows it to happen.[99] The institutional landscape is in flux in the United States as space increases in importance in both military terms and in the perceptions of policymakers and the media, whilst USAF now adapts to the creation of a semi-independent corps which will relieve it of much of its space mission. The American implementation is important as its organisation and experience will inform the organisation of its allies, many of whom are increasingly capable space powers in their own right.

The debate illustrates the conceptual forces of military culture at play in the context of spacepower. A core problem in this debate is that some issues with regard to space acquisitions within USAF will not be fully transparent for the present, although budgets are public knowledge. This is a particular problem if the NRO is seen as possessing a space acquisitions model worth imitating, as the NRO is less transparent in its processes than USAF. In public, symbols and emotive narratives about space may trump debates on USAF's actual track record in nurturing American spacepower and military astroculture. Even if the US Space Force was a separate service, it does not mean spacepower and its advocates will overcome the terrestrial or geocentric perceptions and priorities of strategy within civilian leaders and inter-service disputes on acquisitions, budgeting and war plans. The inter-service struggles of continental navies and the concerns of continental seapower theorists attest to this.

Spacepower theory's propositions highlight both reasons for and against the creation of a more independent space force, which may create a more distinct astroculture within existing strategic cultures of states and their societies. Proposition I argues that achieving the command of space requires a proper interface between grand strategic or political objectives and what spacepower can offer. Managing expectations whilst not underplaying the full potential of spacepower requires specialists, given the forms commanding space can take and its range of effects on Earth. Commanding space is conceptually on the same footing as commanding the sea and the air; an equivalent space force is a rather intuitive institutional move. Closely connected, Proposition II argues in favour of an independent service because it is a unique geographic environment which requires specialists unconditioned by unwarranted geocentrism cultural influences, yet it must take into account the needs and influence of all terrestrial environments equally – not just the air. Proposition III encourages a more joint outlook and perhaps is an argument against a space service, but individual services in most militaries do not preclude successful joint warfare, particularly in Western states. The question would still remain as to which terrestrial service should be the custodian of spacepower and military astroculture, as air forces have no natural authority over it. Proposition IV would entrench aspects of Proposition II by asking organisers whether an independent service is needed to fully control and exploit chokepoints and positions of value in space, increasing the need for dedicated space operators. Proposition V stresses the supporting nature of spacepower: that spacepower will remain a secondary form of power that supports primary terrestrial theatres. Whilst at a glance this does not augur well for an independent space service and may encourage a more joint organisation, this logic would also have to apply to independent navies and air forces relative to land, yet their institutional independence seems assured.

Conclusion

Proposition VI is the codification of the secondary and proximate nature of spacepower in Earth orbit into a geocentric mindset which necessitates a grounded approach to spacepower as a secondary component of grand strategy for Earth-based military cultures. An independent space service may have more freedom to develop military astroculture, but it will still be shaped by geocentrism, only on different terms to a sub-element of a terrestrial military service such as an air force. Proposition VII challenges an air-dominant approach to spacepower because all terrestrial military services and theatres require and benefit from spacepower in diverse ways. Air forces are not the sole beneficiaries of spacepower. Spacepower imposes dispersion on the terrestrial battlefield, as argued in the next chapter, and this is not restricted to the employment of airpower. Therefore, it raises the requirement for a more space-centric approach to take on board all terrestrial requirements but also to make space more accessible and useful for all terrestrial users. However, the presence of spacepower and astroculture in all terrestrial services simultaneously helps and hinders in the challenges of creating a space service: it will find supporters and detractors in every service as the existing military space enterprise is taken from terrestrial military services. Spacepower's unique feature as a pervasive enabling infrastructure where space-based combat platforms are not the predominant concern also raise the possibility that such infrastructure may be best placed in civilian hands, or an ostensibly space-centric space logistics corps.

Conceptually, spacepower theory argues that spacepower is as varied, geographically distinct and equally important as the sea, and the air. All are adjuncts to where humans live – the landmasses of Earth. To put it more bluntly in Ropp's words, seapower, airpower and spacepower are all ill-favoured 'stepchildren' next to land power. This should not be taken as support for the institutional dominance of a military force by its army, however. Spacepower will always be a secondary grand strategic concern because as a strategic geography it is where support and strategic depth are found, where strategic manoeuvres are created, but not where humans live nor most major combat operations take place. Spacepower exists within a geocentric mindset, and until humanity dethrones Earth as the primary – let alone the only – political–economic node in its civilisation this will not change. This is a pressure spacepower will continue to face, regardless of the uniforms worn.

Propositions II, III and V generate a cultural reality for spacepower codified in Proposition VI: it exists within a geocentric mindset and will remain a secondary tool of grand strategy, resembling seapower of continental navies rather than the relative primacy enjoyed by the oceanic navies of island powers. We remain a Terran species, and Terran powers will use space as a helpful but never primary tool of war and strategy. Military cultures can 'hardwire' people and organisations to approach strategic problems in certain ways, and this is no less true of the emerging astroculture within military forces. These people and organisations, as the vanguard of military astroculture, must compete with others within geocentric states for resources and prestige. Space has plenty of room for cultural baggage. This is not to say that geocentrism is misplaced – it is merely outlining the abstract cultural context. Spacepower theory must appreciate how cultural attitudes and bureaucratic politics in military space may shape perceptions and decision-making tendencies in whatever relevant actor in whatever contingency they face. Different actors may develop and exercise spacepower according to their needs, but also according to their own subcultures. Examining the cultures and internal political divisions of friends as well as foes is not only an exercise in recognising diversity but also in accepting strategic unity in dealing with geostrategic environments. Another common homogenising force of spacepower is the material consequences of the successful realisation of Propositions I, III, IV and V on terrestrial warfare: dispersion. No matter the organisation of space powers, the technical systems being deployed in space and integrated into military forces for highly networked and precise warfare capabilities generates a universal dispersal force on friend and foe alike. This is the subject of the next and final proposition.

Notes

1. Geppert, 'Introduction', p. 8.
2. Ibid. p. 6.
3. Ibid. p. 9.
4. Ibid. p. 13.
5. Organisation for Economic Co-operation and Development, 'The Space Economy', p. 51.
6. Easton and Frazier, *GPS*, pp. 187–8.
7. Ibid. p. 117.
8. Katzenstein, 'Introduction', p. 23.
9. Waldman, *War*, p. 89.
10. Gray, *Another Bloody Century*, pp. 100, 106.
11. Porter, *Military Orientalism*, p. 7.
12. Ibid. pp. 10–11.
13. Johnston, *Cultural Realism*, p. 35, taken from: Finlan, *The Royal Navy*, pp. 3–4.
14. Porter, *Military Orientalism*, p. 15. Emphasis removed.
15. Bloomfield, 'Time', pp. 451–2.
16. Ibid. p. 452.
17. On distinct 'air' and 'space' communities in the USAF, see: Estes, 'The Aerospace Force', pp. 165–74.

18. Bloomfield, 'Time', pp. 456–7.
19. McLaughlin, 'Military Space Culture'.
20. Waltz, *Man, The State, and War*, pp. 225–34.
21. Ibid. p. 225.
22. Sun Tzu, *The Art of War*, p. 53; Musashi, *The Book of Five Rings*, p. 13.
23. Booth, *Strategy*, pp. 14–15.
24. Davies, *Welsh Military Institutions*, pp. 89, 260.
25. Porter, *Military Orientalism*, p. 10.
26. Handel, *Masters of War*, esp. pp. 41–80.
27. Finlan, *Contemporary Military Culture*, p. 62.
28. Booth, *Strategy*, pp. 22–3.
29. Gray, *Modern Strategy*, p. 259.
30. Handberg and Zhen, *Chinese Space Policy*, p. 13.
31. Ibid. pp. 82–3.
32. McDougall, . . .*The Heavens*, pp. 97–111.
33. Ibid. p. 62.
34. Ibid. pp. 117–18.
35. Ibid. p. 123.
36. Launius, *Reaching*, p. 20.
37. Sheehan, *International Politics*, pp. 146–51.
38. Citino, *Blitzkrieg*, p. 290. Emphasis Citrino's.
39. Echevarria, *Reconsidering*, pp. 10, 17, 166.
40. Ibid. pp. 166–7; see also: Boot, 'The New American Way'. On the classic text of American strategic culture, see: Weigley, *The American Way of War*.
41. Mahnken, 'US Strategic and Organizational Subcultures', pp. 69–84.
42. Echevarria, *Reconsidering*, p. 169.
43. Gray, *Another Bloody Century*, p. 91.
44. Menon. *Maritime Strategy*, p. 21.
45. Corbett, *Principles of Maritime Strategy*, pp. 166–8.
46. Sun Tzu, *The Art of Warfare*, pp. 89–91.
47. Menon, *Maritime Strategy*, p. 70, 83.
48. Ibid. p. 172.
49. Holmes et al., *Indian Naval Strategy*, pp. 22–3.
50. Menon, *Maritime Strategy*, p. 21.
51. Gorshkov, *The Sea Power of the State*, pp. 146–7.
52. Holmes et al., *Indian Naval Strategy*, pp. 10, 6–21.
53. Gorshkov, *The Sea Power of the State*, p. 148.
54. Ibid. p. 254.
55. Indian Space Research Organisation, 'Dr. Vikram'.

56. Ropp, 'Continental Doctrines', p. 446.
57. A major theme throughout Sumida, *Inventing Grand Strategy.*
58. Brown, 'Space', p. 240.
59. Sheehan, 'The Crucial Role of European Space Popularisation'.
60. On USAF turf wars: Hays, *Struggling towards Space Doctrine*, pp. 25–30, 66–101, 113–27, 210–11; Lambeth, *Mastering the Ultimate Highground*, pp. 9–59. On China's bureaucratic turf wars: Stokes and Cheng, 'China's Evolving Space Capabilities', pp. 44–5.
61. Sheldon and Gray, 'Theory Ascendant?', p. 7.
62. Kier, 'Culture', pp. 186–211.
63. Bowen, 'Better the devil you know?'
64. Bowen, 'The RAF', p. 63.
65. Mallet, 'France follows US to set up military space command'.
66. Costello, 'The Strategic Support Force'.
67. Ibid.
68. Kania, 'PLA Strategic Support Force'.
69. Russian Ministry of Defence, 'Space forces'.
70. Bodner, 'As Trump pushes for separate space force'.
71. Friedman, *Seapower*, p. 181; on the operational turn in US space support, see: Spires, *Beyond Horizons*, pp. 209–11.
72. Pollpeter, 'Space', p. 725.
73. Hirsch, 'Departing Head of Space Ops Center'.
74. Hays, *Struggling towards Space Doctrine*, p. 442–3.
75. Smith, *Ten Propositions*, pp. 75–9.
76. Finlan, *Contemporary Military Culture*, p. 54.
77. McDougall, . . .*The Heavens*, p. 99.
78. Ibid. p. 133.
79. White, *Into the Black*, p. 38.
80. Ibid. p. 44.
81. Lambeth, *Mastering the Ultimate Highground*, p. 136.
82. Ibid. p. 156. Emphasis Lambeth's.
83. Ibid. pp. 9–10, 34.
84. Finlan, *Contemporary Military Culture*, p. 60.
85. United States Air Force (USAF), 'Annex 3–14'.
86. US Joint Chiefs of Staff, *Joint Publication 3–14*, p. I–1.
87. Finlan, *Contemporary Military Culture*, p. 68.
88. Hays, *Struggling towards Space Doctrine*, pp. 121–2.
89. Finlan, *Contemporary Military Culture*, p. 70.
90. Smith, *Ten Propositions*, pp. 53–6.
91. See: Evans, 'Space Coordinating Authority', p. 7; Schuler, 'It Isn't Space', pp. 71–3.

92. A Vulcan proverb from the *Star Trek* franchise.
93. Smith, *Ten Propositions*, pp. 54, 56. Emphasis Smith's.
94. Finlan, *Contemporary Military Culture*, p. 68.
95. Ibid. p. 69.
96. Smith, 'America needs a space corps'.
97. Swarts, 'Air Force'.
98. Hunter and Bowen, 'Donald Trump's Space Force'.
99. Lambeth, *Mastering the Ultimate Highground*, p. 135.

PART III

The Influence of Spacepower
upon Warfare

5. Dispersal, Concentration and Defence

Proposition VII: Spacepower is dispersed and imposes dispersion on Earth

Proposition VII explores the dispersing nature and effects of spacepower and what it means for the concentration of military forces and effects on Earth. Integrating spacepower's services into the operational and tactical levels of war imposes dispersion on its users and the opposing force. This allows the beneficiaries of spacepower to disperse whilst retaining an effect previously only gained through massing forces into large concentrations. The opponents of such a force must disperse, counter spacepower, intercept precision munitions in response or face annihilation. This proposition builds on Sheldon's prior work on dispersal and spacepower and breaks dispersal into its constituent elements, relating it to spacepower theory as a whole. It also draws on insights from airpower, and Clausewitz's observations on concentration, dispersion and experiences of modern warfare as they speak most explicitly on the battlefield impacts of precision-strike warfare and the 'hard edge' of spacepower's influence on terrestrial military power. By examining the influence of spacepower upon terrestrial warfare through the lens of dispersion, the responses to the threat PGMs and the geographic and strategic pressures of war continue to demonstrate inherent strengths in the defensive form of war, as weaker military actors respond to the hostile coastline US spacepower has generated in orbit towards its adversaries. Although spacepower is known to have facilitated the stunning offensive successes of American military forces since the end of the Cold War, they disguise the options still available to defenders – themselves with or without their own command of space – in the Space Age and do not necessarily herald an era of offensive conventional dominance.

Proposition VII is the conceptual answer to the 'so what' question of spacepower's influence for terrestrial warfare. The conditions of dispersal and concentration of forces on Earth in the Space Age is the consequence of exploitation of the relevant degree of the command of space (Proposition I), brought about by successful strategic manoeuvres to manipulate celestial lines of communication for the terrestrial war effort (Propositions IV and V). To contest or exploit the influence of spacepower upon modern warfare, combatants must attack, deny or adapt to the technologies that allow terrestrial forces to be dispersed yet retain a coherent effectiveness. Dispersal is the lens through which strategists should view the role of spacepower in campaigns and engagements, because it must be exploited, denied or attacked and doing so influences conventional warfare. Spacepower theory now comes full circle with the final proposition outlined, as it takes us back to Proposition I – why the command of space is so important for modern strategy and geopolitics in the first place. This proposition triggers thought on the dispersal and concentration of three things: (a) the assets and infrastructure in Earth orbit; (b) space-enhanced forces that can concentrate or disperse with great speed, precision, mobility and synchronicity; and (c) the risks and opportunities of concentration and dispersal for forces and actors that fight and react against a space-enhanced enemy, with or without their own space support.

This is no axiomatic declaration that a particular form of dispersal or concentration of forces holds the keys to success in warfare in an era of orbital spacepower. Rather, Proposition VII argues that the command of space and strategic manoeuvres in orbit influence the manner in which terrestrial military forces may concentrate and disperse to impose and resist terrestrial firepower effects. Both parties may be continually reacting and adapting to each other's abilities to exploit and resist the dispersing influence of spacepower through the successful conduct of strategic manoeuvres in the cosmic coastline. Dispersal is the inherent impact of spacepower upon warfare. Yet concentration is not impossible; spacepower merely changes the way in which the effects of concentration in time and place are achieved with tolerable levels of risk and force survivability. Using and resisting the dispersing influence of spacepower is central to thinking of modern warfare capabilities, and is demonstrated as a useful lens to assess strategies in the next chapter.

From the sensor to the shooter: Dispersal

The concentration of force does not translate well into the space segment of space infrastructure due to the relative difficulty and inefficiency of mobility in orbit compared to air and sea platforms. The inherent characteristic of satellite constellations in Earth orbit is dispersion due to the realities of orbital motion and Newtonian and Keplerian dynamics; they are defined by their ability to communicate over long distances and to patch together terrestrially dispersed users. Sheldon states that:

> satellites, due to the inherent nature of orbital mechanics, are unable to mass and concentrate in the same way, and thus are only able to mass in time due to their ubiquity in orbit, or can mass effects vicariously through land, sea and air power.[1]

This normally dispersed quality of satellites reflects how their services impose dispersion on modern warfare. This runs counter to usual conceptions of strategy where the most effective force and strategies concern how and when to concentrate forces upon an objective. However, as seen in the next section, concentration is still a useful principle to understand warfare under spacepower's influence.

Understanding dispersal cannot be done without referring to concentration, much like offence and defence are meaningless without one another. One influences the other in a mutually interacting dialectic between intelligent and reacting opponents. Mahan noted that concentration itself is 'reasonably understood [as] not huddled together like a drove of sheep, but distributed with a regard to a common purpose, and linked together by the effectual energy of a single will'.[2] The distributed sources of an effectual energy of a single will aptly describes how satellites are dispersed in orbit, yet the effects of their signals and celestial lines of communication can be concentrated in time and – on Earth – in place, expressing the pursuit of a single goal. Conversely, anti-satellite weapons on Earth could be distributed but coordinated into overlapping kill-zones and communications jamming arcs towards orbit into cones of vulnerability. Despite its dispersed condition, spacepower can still be concentrated in terms of its effects in space and on Earth. Dispersal is the declarative theme for this proposition because spacepower's physical condition in orbit is inherently dispersed, and the threat and use of spacepower encourages dispersing behaviour on Earth. Dispersion occurs in two places: in orbit through dispersed satellite constellations, and the dispersing effects of spacepower on Earth. Some spacepower theorists have alluded to the concept of dispersal through space-power, but not the same extent as Sheldon.[3] Space capabilities can make the world relatively smaller and more transparent through the greater speed, visibility and scope that space-based C4ISR systems enable when they allow for rapid and precise long-range terrestrial bombardment; an efficient response to it is to disperse those targets and deny any effective bombardment.[4]

The proliferation of space-based communications, reconnais-sance and surveillance systems integrated into operational-level commands and mobile tactical combat units, encourage targets to resort to dispersal, concealment or flight from head-on battle – involving large degrees of coordination and deception. With the advent of satellite field communications and human-portable satellite user terminals such as satellite phones, inflatable dishes and vehicle-mounted apertures, space-enabled forces can disperse more easily without completely sacrificing lethality, secrecy, secu-rity and firepower. This dispersal mimics the dispersed nature of satellite constellations. In space, satellites of the same constella-tion generally do not cluster together and tend to be dispersed. Although all satellites in GEO may appear to cluster together around the same orbital band across the equator, the satellites of a single GEO constellation such as Skynet will still be dispersed along the belt providing coverage around most of the planet. Any kinetic action against one of these satellites will pose high risks of collateral damage to nearby GEO satellites, but not necessarily to the rest of the Skynet constellation in the short term. Transparency from space surveillance systems, and the threat of it, encourages dispersion, concealment and deception on Earth because high-technology militaries with reconnaissance-strike systems or locally deployed spacepower-integrated terrestrial forces can potentially attack whatever is in 'sight' within and beyond the terrestrial horizon.

Connecting such advanced and over-the-horizon sensors to shooters on Earth were most notably demonstrated in the 1991 Gulf War. The effects of the war were clear for a global audience of defence professionals and planners and:

> demonstrated the potential of an entire suite of [satellite] technologies developed since the 1970s and weaved together in war for the first time. This . . . emergence of a 'guided-munitions battle network' or 'reconnaissance-strike complex' with three basic components [comprised]: sensors locating and tracking targets; platforms, weapons systems, and munitions able to attack with precision, often from great distances; and command, control, and communications assets linking sensors and 'shooters'.[5]

These military forces can shoot what they 'see'. A natural and instinctive response to these dispersed but highly lethal and efficient forces is to scatter; to disperse and complicate the tasks of the sensors and the shooters supported by the silent yet devastating pressure of spacepower from the hostile coastline. Concentrated forces are easier to detect and harder to move. Such precision-strike capabilities led many to believe an RMA was underway, based on technological superiority, precision warfare and the ability to create the effect of mass whilst retaining relatively more dispersed forces.[6]

The United States has no monopoly on such networked warfare systems, though it leads the way in integrating spacepower towards terrestrial warfare. The Soviet Radar Ocean Reconnaissance Satellite is an example of an early tactically and operationally relevant reconnaissance-strike space system. This Soviet electronic intelligence (ELINT) system could potentially make US Navy surface vessels 'acquired targets' for terrestrial Soviet anti-ship weapons systems.[7] The European Copernicus programme is a more contemporary example of using a diverse range of satellite sensors to form a comprehensive surveillance architecture that can be integrated into strike weapons systems.[8] As another example, satellite technology since the early 1990s, and today, Japan has deployed synthetic aperture radar (SAR) and is increasingly geared towards its modernising military forces.[9] The Chinese *Qu Dian* military network system now underpins the PLA's long-range precision-strike capabilities across the Asia-Pacific. Dispersion is being imposed by multipolar sources of spacepower, and not just from the United States.

The effect of increasing degrees of transparency from the proliferation of intelligence, surveillance and reconnaissance (ISR) systems – whether real or perceived – at strategic, operational and tactical levels will influence behaviour by imposing dispersion. Although targets may not be always caught in the act by spy satellites, it may force them to take elaborate measures to avoid detection.[10] Actors that cannot afford to be seen to be doing something must conceal their activities or conduct diversions. For example, India succeeded in surprising the US intelligence community in 1998 by foiling American space-based reconnaissance efforts to predict nuclear tests.[11] Although much of this proposition focuses on operational and tactical consequences of Earth observation from space, the grand strategic and political effects of the degrees of transparency provided by space systems should not be forgotten. Indeed, transparency was first achieved on the strategic level through strategic space-based reconnaissance during the Cold War. Commenting upon seeing images from the NRO's Keyhole reconnaissance satellites revealing the smaller-than-expected extent of Soviet strategic missile developments, President Lyndon Johnson remarked in 1967 that 'our guesses were way off. We were doing things we didn't need to do. We were building things we didn't need to build. We were harboring fears we didn't need to harbor.'[12] Today, that transparency and the need to deceive overhead sensors has migrated into the tactical and operational levels with evermore intrusive ISR capabilities.

Fewer bolder or overt actions can be taken on the Earth's surface (or in space) without being detected, and concentrated forces can be more easily spotted and targeted by their potential victims, as well as by third parties. This creates problems for achieving total levels of surprise on the enemy and complicates any Space Pearl Harbor strategy,[13] discussed in the next chapter. Enemy eyes from above and the pressures of dispersion may not be a pressing concern in wars where the enemy has been politically isolated and has no significant third-party support, such as for the United States in both Gulf Wars. In other words, the United States did not need to worry about enemy space systems beyond conducting a strategic manoeuvre to cut off third-party imagery as explored in Proposition V in its campaigns against Iraq. Additionally, they did not need to be overly concerned with Iraq cutting the tethers between satellites and their users and control stations, especially as Iraq had no major sponsor to provide space support to it.

These C4ISR systems impose dispersion on the terrestrial targets of the United States whilst US military units can disperse and retain their firepower and ability to rapidly mass and coordinate firepower effects. US forces must now disperse not only because they can, but because they must in response to the proliferation of comparable systems to the other Terran military powers. China's growing reconnaissance-strike capabilities makes it important for 'the U.S. and Japanese militaries [to] develop the means to wage a "blinding" campaign against the sensor and communications networks that are foundational to PLA missile operations'.[14] Failing that, American forces must be ready to scatter or 'go dark'. The kind of dispersion imposed upon terrestrial forces can differ based on the kinds of satellite systems in use, the kind of targets they are searching for and the terrain they are in. To analogise from a limitation of airpower's influence on land warfare, spacepower can be of varying effectiveness in providing support for operations in different landscapes. Targeting can be much easier in desert and naval warfare than in mountain, forest or urban warfare. Ground forces can deny easy pickings for reconnaissance-strike systems by taking advantage of terrain that produces cover from satellite signals lines of sight, and threaten unacceptable collateral damage by using human shields or holding useful infrastructure at risk.[15]

It is not impossible for satellites to concentrate and orbit closely together. Dispersion is the general condition of satellites in orbit unless a major techno-economic shift occurs to overcome the cost and physical constraints on space-basing and manoeuvring in orbit.[16] In GEO, the relative level of dispersal may not be as great because they are in relatively fixed altitudes, and basic global communications coverage only requires a minimum of three satellites in GEO. Satellite constellations may have different degrees of dispersal and resiliency according to orbit and function, but this must be tempered with Proposition IV where many satellites congregate in their orbital paths in LEO over the poles to form a potential chokepoint and a place for terrestrial counterspace fire to be concentrated. A highly populated constellation provides fewer points of failure that could threaten a system. There is some limited scope for manoeuvre in orbit, as seen below with GPS satellites during the 1991 Gulf War, and with manoeuvring satellites discussed in Proposition V. The concentration of satellites is possible, if not essential, if they must fly over specific ground stations, targets or orbital waypoints and in the process forming paths of heavier traffic. A theory of spacepower must be open to space systems becoming more agile and responsive – if they do, the opportunities for the concentration of satellites will increase. There would still need to be a compelling reason to cluster the satellites of a single constellation together – satellites' unique contribution are their wide fields of view and ability to network communications over vast distances. Concentrating satellites to increase persistent coverage from lower orbits would impose costs elsewhere.

Spacepower will rely on space infrastructure configured for peace as well as war. This places limits on how far physical strategic manoeuvres in space can conducted. There will be a limit as to what extent an existing space capability can be turned to immediate military needs. The dual-use nature of much space infrastructure means that any spacepower wishing to build a space network useful for both wartime and peacetime military and civilian needs will not be as flexible or optimised for every demand. Space surveillance and reconnaissance systems do not appear in wars on demand – they are deployed regardless of rapid political changes on Earth. Satellites are built with a calculation of long-term needs in mind because of the long design and construction processes, and long lifespan of many satellites. Consequently, the loss of some space systems in war may influence peacetime activity for many years to come because of the long development and deployment times-cales for satellites. Small commercial satellites have not replaced the functions of very large military and intelligence satellites yet, though rocket launches are anything but routine and would be a bottleneck on any fast satellite manufacturing capability. Small satellites and military-grade commercial 'off-the-shelf' technology may assist military forces to develop such 'operationally responsive space' capabilities, but even then logistical constraints mean that satellites cannot be scrambled from the ground to space at anything like the speed of local aerial ISR assets.

Sheldon observes a 'paradox' that only increases in its importance with the proliferation of space systems. He argues that:

> having to face space-enabled forces may actually encourage adversaries to transform themselves similarly, leading to a situation where the inherently dispersed nature of [spacepower] is reflected in the disposition of forces on Earth. Dispersed forces require robust command and control and synchronisation.[17]

This may be more of a circular or reinforcing logic, rather than a paradox. Satellites responding to dispersed Earth-based anti-satellite weapons must answer dispersion with dispersion; and terrestrial forces must respond to the dispersing influence of spacepower with their own dispersal to complicate the targeting systems for PGM strikes.[18]

As more states can enjoy the benefits of strategic manoeuvres from orbit and turn it into a hostile flank for adversaries, more terrestrial powers' forces and strategically valuable activities will suffer and exploit the dispersing influence of spacepower. This puts the pressure on otherwise-concentrated terrestrial forces during campaigns to disguise mass manoeuvres and dispositions and to prevent an opportunity to launch a crippling volley of PGMs.

PGMs and long-range precision strikes create the effect of mass and concentration without having to concentrate and mass in a physical fashion to the same degree as before. The same mass effect of firepower can be achieved with forces deployed in fewer numbers and further away from each other, patched together and enabled by spacepower and satellite infrastructure in the cosmic coastline. Deception in the Newtonian world as well as in the electromagnetic spectrum will be necessary in wars that require mitigating the space-based ISR capabilities of an enemy. Full battlefield transparency is a fantasy and the 'fog of war' will remain, but the effects of proliferated space reconnaissance capabilities cannot be dismissed despite the promises of RMA advocates in the 1990s and early 2000s.[19] The compulsion to disperse that may be caused by the exploitation of spacepower and a command of space will only increase if space-to-Earth weapons and reusable spaceplanes or hypersonic strike vehicles are ever deployed en masse. With ELINT satellites proliferating, more pressure will accrue for high-technology and concentrated forces to either disperse from space-enabled foes or develop ELINT deception and concealment techniques, or mitigate electronic emissions through reducing the use of wide-area electronic communications. The point here is that this dispersal logic can be in effect. Whether or not it is, and how it effects the situation at hand, is a task in the critical and intelligent application of this proposition. The threat of the hostile coast of Earth orbit will be one of many factors war planners must take into account.

Learning from and adapting to spacepower's dispersing influence can be observed. The experiences of the United States' spacepower in Afghanistan and Iraq may have accelerated defence modernisation drives in the PLA and the civilian leadership.[20] With spending in the PLA being directed in part towards modernisation and professionalisation, joint operations and increased C4ISR,[21] the PLA might move away from traditionally large ground forces and onto a smaller, space-enabled dispersed and networked professional force. Previous Chinese attempts in the 1990s to modernise missiles with GPS support highlights American control over the system and explains the necessity for China to build its own GNSS system for terrestrial force enhancement. In 2009:

a retired People's Liberation Army colonel told a reporter that since the 1996 missile crisis in the Taiwan Strait, China had been committed to building its own GNSS. During the standoff the Chinese army fired three GPS-guided missiles toward Taiwan as a warning against seeking independence, and the second two missiles went awry. Military officials suspected someone disrupted the GPS signals, and the retired colonel called the incident an 'unforgettable humiliation'.[22]

If civilian GPS signals were 'spoofed' or denied to the PLA, Taiwan in this instance may not have suffered too much from the pressures of dispersal on its terrestrial forces from Chinese attempts to harness (American) spacepower against it should the crisis have escalated to a general war. However, with Chinese space infrastructure increasing in quantity and quality, including the deployment of its own satellite navigation system, Chinese missile forces need not be as concerned about dependence on GPS for accurate strikes. As the reinforcing logic of dispersion works, the PLA – as it modernises and integrates spacepower into its planning and capabilities – may become more vulnerable to disruption and attacks on its own celestial lines of communication for military operations, with that vulnerability increasing with distance from the Chinese mainland and any particular strategy's reliance on long-range and over-the-horizon PGM strikes. Because of matured American reconnaissance-strike systems, dispersing and hiding in rough terrain, and concealing its maritime forces is evermore important for Chinese units as they plan for contingencies with the United States. This in turn makes space communications even more useful because orbital fields of view knit together terrestrial units that cannot easily see or hear each other on Earth. Not only does dispersion increase the pressure to scatter terrestrial forces, but it increases their dependence on celestial lines of communication so that the ill-effects of dividing forces can be minimised.

Without commanding space to a sufficient degree, and conducting strategic manoeuvres to exploit celestial lines of communication, such networked and dispersed forces cannot hope to maintain an ability to create the effects of concentration whilst remaining physically dispersed. This increases the potential pay-off of engaging in space warfare against China, and of cutting off their own celestial lines of communication between sensors and shooters, given their now highly dispersed terrestrial forces on Earth. Without the connecting mesh of celestial lines of communication such forces may be far easier prey to other terrestrial forces that may have just tilted the tactical and operational balance in their favour. By making outer space a hostile coast for any modern military, the transformed force normally 'capable of subduing larger less advanced opponents becomes just a small military force, overburdened with expensive but now useless equipment'.[23] This is a worry for both the United States and China and features in the next chapter.

Dispersion is not the whole story, but it is the central influence of spacepower on tactics and operations because it alters how concentration is achieved. Spacepower plays a role in the risks and opportunities of concentrating forces on Earth, and spacepower's effects in and from orbit can be concentrated whilst its physical infrastructure might be dispersed. However, if spacepower imposes dispersion on a military that is only effective when physically concentrated, that military will have even more incentive to assault the enemy's spacepower and celestial lines of communication to enable it to concentrate and dispel the dispersing effects of the hostile cosmic coastline.

A single effectual will: Concentration

Concentrating forces to achieve a decision through battle and dispersing to deny that battle is an old canon in strategic theory.[24] Whilst concentrating force to win decisive battles does not translate well into space, as Proposition III discussed, it is still a relevant and useful concept for terrestrial modern warfare. Although spacepower tends to be dispersed, its effects can be concentrated in place and time. Spacepower's integration into terrestrial warfare has merely altered the scale and efficiencies with which concentration is achieved with space-supported mechanised warfare. Confronting concentrated forces that have integrated the effects of spacepower into their combat capabilities means that dispersal, concealment, parrying (i.e. active defences and close-in weapon systems), absorption and fleeing are the only immediate responses to escape a 'hammer and anvil' assault. Ground forces engage the enemy in battle and pin them down – the anvil – to prepare for an airstrike or for heavier ground forces to destroy them – the hammer. Remaining concentrated in the open is an invitation to disaster whilst the hammer of modern warfare can be rapid and precise, particularly when the hammer can itself remain dispersed as munitions are launched from over the horizon from multiple platforms from different directions. Spacepower enables these kinds of PGM and missile salvos that can devastate obvious targets. The coordination of airstrikes and land battles depends today on space technology's integrations into communication systems and precision weapons.[25] Carrier strike groups and naval forces require space support for their over-the-horizon targeting and air superiority missions. Air forces rely on space systems for targeting data as they are en route to the theatre and provide final munitions guidance in most cases. The concentration of spacepower capabilities is still possible and is achieved through a concentration of their effects (signals, command and control, data gathering and dissemination, and information analysis services) into specific times and places on Earth and not necessarily through the concentration of satellites.[26] Concentration is still a useful principle, but it does not take the same forms as in other media, like the sea or the air.[27] Because of the unique characteristics of outer space, satellites can have a congregational tendency to cluster at popular orbits, such as in geosynchronous orbit, which can form advantageous positions and chokepoints as described in Proposition IV.[28] This proposition triggers thought on spacepower's dispersed nature and its dispersing effects on modern warfare, which is still concentrating force and effects to varying degrees at decisive points. The effects of mass can still be delivered on Earth if strategic manoeuvres are conducted to form the cone of vulnerability – discussed in Proposition V – towards terrestrial adversaries from coordinated space support to provide excessive advantages in lethality, efficiency and precision for one's own terrestrial forces.

Concentrating forces against decisive points is not a dogmatic maxim that must be followed to assure victory. Even Antoine-Henri Jomini, known for popularising the precept of throwing the mass of an army against the enemy's decisive points, allowed for a concerted yet dispersed effort to resist an enemy.[29] Clausewitz agreed in terms of the abstract principle – that 'the greatest possible number of troops should be brought into action at the decisive point of the engagement'.[30] Concentration is only an important principle of strategy in the abstract sense – when other factors of reality are taken into account it is not such a straightforward or even prudent thing to do. Clausewitz argues that massing the strongest possible forces is not a truism, although it sounds like one.[31] It takes skill to deploy the available resources where needed at the appropriate place and time;[32] spacepower's influence does not change this nature of strategy and warfare, but it has changed its scope and character in so far as spacepower-enabled forces can retain a high degree of dispersal whilst creating the effects of mass and concentration upon the enemy. Being able to concentrate forces and deploy a relatively overwhelming strength at the correct '[coordination] of time and space', requires adherence to the view, as far as it is possible owing to the total resources available, that being able to concentrate forces into a single great mass and deploy it where it can be used most effectively usually results in favourable outcomes.[33] However, it is never a necessary condition of victory and should not be seen as a silver bullet because a relative superiority in a concentrated force is contextual. If you deploy a superior concentration of force against an enemy weak point using surprise, then that local superiority matters a great deal even though your total forces may be dwarfed by the enemy's in the conflict as a whole.[34] Before the advent of long-range precision weapons, massing physically larger forces into battlefields was the way to ensure this concentration of force and ensure a reasonable chance of success. Today, small terrestrial forces can be evermore efficient in creating intense firepower effects due to their range and accuracy with standoff over-the-horizon weapons. Firepower can be concentrated to a sufficient degree with reduced physical mass of troops and weapons platforms in the combat zone. Should space systems become less reliable, then the extent to which terrestrial forces can disperse will decrease and tend towards concentration and heavier forces. Yet the increasing likelihood of enemy PGM capability increases the desire to disperse. The general principle outlined by Clausewitz still concerns the concentration of force in the Space Age because it has changed the degree to which terrestrial forces need to be physically concentrated in-theatre to achieve the same end – an effect of concentrated firepower that was hitherto only achieved via massing people and platforms in a smaller-sized theatre of operations.

Clausewitz was emphatic that the most important law for strategy was to keep the forces concentrated and only divide them when there was a good reason to do so.[35] He was responding to a tendency by many commanders in his experience deciding to disperse forces for no good reason. Concentrating a mass of force and firepower in place as well as time with all available forces is a cardinal law for Clausewitz in strategy, and would be the more complete the more it can all be compressed into one moment. However, 'there is nevertheless in strategy an after-pressure and a successive action' where new forces are brought to bear in subsequent engagements.[36] Such comments qualify his claim to trace the enemy's strengths back to as few centres of gravity as possible, if not one, and then to concentrate the attack against those targets with as few concentrated masses as possible.[37] Clausewitz anticipated such difficulties to concentrating forces and claimed that if the first priority of strategy is to mass forces against a decisive point, as Jomini would suggest, dispersing forces would make sense if the dispersal would not sacrifice the chances of success in a main theatre, or that the basing of the forces heading into theatre were widely dispersed already, or that attacking via separate lines of travel may in this instance lead to greater results, or the breadth of the theatre was too large for forces to concentrate and attack or defend at any one point.[38] The challenge of finding targets in great oceanic expanses and continent-scale theatres of operation could only be met through the integration of spacepower into operations, not least with radar satellites to scan the oceans. Overcoming the vastness of the ocean, long-haul communications connect widely dispersed sources of information and their users. Quite naturally, then, the 'new style of space-oriented warfare with dispersed forces yet concentrated effects in time across vast distances began with navies' in the 1980s.[39] This increasing scale of targeting and precise weapons shrinks the scale of time and space, enhances the geographic scale at which forces must disperse, and follows wider historical trends in increasing firepower and dispersing forces.

From the Napoleonic Wars in the early nineteenth century, increasing artillery accuracy, fire rates, mobility and anti-infantry capability led to increased pressures to disperse infantry and units to a more decentralised form of tactics, to spread out forces working together for a general goal. With increasingly accurate small arms, physically concentrated mass – like Napoleonic shock columns – was no longer needed to the same degree to create its firepower effects on enemy lines by the European wars of the second half of the nineteenth century. Prussian tactics from the 1860s onwards emphasised dispersed skirmishing tactics as opposed to ordered columns to take advantage of increasing rifle accuracy and lessen the impact of anti-personnel artillery rounds. Concentrating fire imposes dispersion on the enemy, and puts a premium on coordination, delegated initiative, manoeuvre, and cover and concealment. With increased dispersal and manoeuvre, more pressure is placed on intelligence and timely information to move and re-acquire targets.[40] When thinking of PGMs and precision-strike infrastructures – if deployed en masse with plentiful ammunition supplies – and their role in modern warfare, the principles of dispersal and concentration are illustrated by a comparison of how the nineteenth century also went through such sweeping changes. By the early twentieth century, 'a modern brigade of 3,000 men with artillery was able to spew more shell and rifle fire in a single minute than had Wellington's entire army of 60,000 in the day-long battle of Waterloo in 1815'.[41] Firepower had dramatically increased in effect, focused in area, but widened the theatre so forces could disperse to minimise its effects on themselves.

This is not, however, a simple forecast of a new or inevitable type of manoeuvre warfare. This highlights the dispersing influence at work and how Proposition VII and space-enhanced warfare is not a complete break from the past. Effective countermeasures through innovative tactics, the equipment and resources available, and exploiting geographic features can bring back relatively static warfare as the 'Miracle on the Marne' in 1914, trenchlock in the Iran–Iraq War of the 1980s, or the battle of Tora Bora in 2002 showed. The next section highlights general principles of resistance and adaptation to spacepower's influence that can undermine the pressure of space-enabled precision-strike warfare. Resisting spacepower can bring about the degradation in spacepower's influence on the battlefield, particularly in longer wars where increasing numbers of satellites may be taken out of action or terrestrial precision-strike platforms may have been expended or destroyed without replacements, only for low-technology reserves to take their places. If both sides enjoy force enhancement from space, then the relative mobility and efficiency gained per platform is decreased, putting a new premium (or return to 'normal') on numbers and mass. Spacepower is changing how dispersal and concentrating the effects of mass can be achieved. This may be the latest variation in a continuing trend of imposing dispersal on the enemy and increasing the scale of the battlefield. Its effects are not permanent, especially as major powers will seek to directly undermine or resist its dispersing influence on warfare, once again swinging the pendulum away from mobility and back to attritional, positional warfare.

The other propositions should provide a wider intellectual and grand strategic context to Proposition VII's hard edge of spacepower on the battlefield and theatre of operations, usually related to tactical and operational considerations of targeting strategies. It is unwise to equate a 'targeting strategy with the whole strategy for a war' because it overlooks the logistical and intelligence capabilities of airpower that combine to provide strategic effect.[42] Spacepower theory, and Proposition VII specifically, must avoid such a fate. Propositions I–VI provide more strategic and non-military observations concerning spacepower.

Knowing when and how to exploit spacepower's dispersing influence on oneself or the enemy puts a greater premium on strategic manoeuvres to conduct this exploitation, of embracing Proposition V and all the support that space has to offer the terrestrial battlefield. This harks back to Napoleon and Clausewitz's views that 'the army's military virtues are directly connected with the quality of its strategic manoeuvres' and the correct assessments of the points upon which pressure from concentrated firepower and force should be applied.[43] Forces should not be dispersed or concentrated just for the sake of it – they must be so at the right time and with a common goal in mind, according to the opportunities of their relevant geographies.[44] Conducting strategic manoeuvres with spacepower, as theorised in Proposition V, to support mobile and precise terrestrial manoeuvre warfare is the most constructive way to view the application of spacepower in the violent aspects of grand strategy.

Despite the pressures of dispersal, geography cannot be ignored and political objectives will usually involve the requirement of presence and capability at a focused geographic point on Earth.[45] Geographic features forcing terrestrial concentrations could be a city, trade chokepoints, ridge, mountain passes, narrow seas, or straits. This at first glance poses challenges to modern forces as they will be very susceptible to precision-strike capabilities given obvious defensive positions or attacking objectives. Yet the adversary can adapt to, absorb or attack the enemy's spacepower, or even attempt to parry the blow of incoming precision-guided projectiles and missiles to lessen the vulnerabilities of concentrating terrestrial forces.

Physical concentration in space will be relatively limited, but the effects and services of satellites can be concentrated into a cone of vulnerability for the opposing force, particularly if it lacks its own space support. Indeed, a 'paradox is that space power, itself unable to mass . . . enable[s] the massing and concentration of air and sea power at the last possible moment through its ability to provide a real-time depiction of the battlespace, connectivity, positioning, and timing.'[46] Discussions of maritime strategists on concentration and dispersal, then, do not quite fit as we are usually talking more about mobile terrestrial guns pointing into the littoral of Earth orbit against targets that cannot move that much beyond pre-planned orbits without significantly reducing their lifespans. Concentrating these signal effects simulate concentrated firepower that only mass or concentrated forces could have done in the past, when the effects of a good command of space and the use of celestial lines of communication are combined with terrestrial forces. Concentration of effects can include the direct impact of weapons fire or the massing of celestial lines of communication so that terrestrial forces can themselves mass and fight with greater safety and efficiency. GPS signals, now ubiquitous, enables mass effect through concentrating firepower effects on Earth with precise and synchronised precision-strike warfare.[47]

Cones of vulnerability formed through the overlapping arcs of ISR and fire can form concentrated kill-zones with dispersed points of origin and infrastructure nodes.[48] This concentration of effect must occur in time and place, where everything must come together for a concerted effort and the duration of a critical operation. This is particularly true of lasers which are additive in their effects. Should a beam's intensity and focus be sufficient to cause the required damage or interference, coordinated targeting from dispersed ground-based or space-based lasers with enough overlapping lines of fire can add to the heating effects at the point of contact with the target. Such weapons systems can be made individually redundant if they were to develop networked accuracy and tracking capabilities, and if they are cheap enough to produce and deploy en masse compared to missile-launched anti-satellite weapons. A highly redundant anti-satellite system may make it a difficult one to defeat when it is used for the first time, as any comprehensive system without a single point of failure will take time to locate, degrade and destroy.

Dispersed weapons systems will necessitate coordination and information gathering capabilities, often achieved through dispersed space systems to concentrate fire to form a mass effect. Spacepower concentration can occur through time; it is to attack or disrupt satellites at the most opportune time through a coordinated attack that may be geographically dispersed across various parts of orbit and Earth's surface to undermine an enemy's spacepower infrastructure.[49] This raises the fear of a debilitating Space Pearl Harbor attack which is discussed in the next chapter. The status of the then-incomplete GPS constellation during the 1991 Gulf War is a useful illustration of the constraints that can be put on terrestrial action should a space system not be working to its full potential. During Operation Desert Shield, where coalition forces were assembling in Saudi Arabia, some existing GPS and DSP satellites were manoeuvred in order to increase their orbital times of over the Persian Gulf.[50] Such tinkering with GPS allowed 'round-the-clock two-dimensional coverage (latitude and longitude, needed for ground and ocean-surface operations) . . . three-dimensional coverage (latitude, longitude, and altitude, needed for airplanes) for about eighteen hours a day'.[51]

This demonstrates some degree of ability to concentrate effects in time and place.

GPS service gaps could leave some hours in every day available to exploit against the enemy that depends on it. The incomplete GPS constellation provides a tantalising insight into a possible terrestrial consequence of a successful space denial campaign targeting the GPS service. With less effective forces that would otherwise need GPS for protection, precision, coordination and mobility, gaps – or disruptions to – celestial lines of communications could be an opportunity for an attack. This gap in coverage could be brought about by weapons fire from Earth's surface based on land, sea, the air and through cyber infiltration, turning the cosmic coastline into a hostile zone for specific GPS satellites. Patrick Cordingley, then commander of the British Army's 7th Armoured Division (the 'Desert Rats'), recounted an episode regarding the (foreknown) loss of full GPS coverage during the war. A battlegroup

> got lost when the GPS . . . ceased to work. First thing in the morning, and then just after dark, the satellites that provided the signals would go out of range. As a result every morning and evening for about fifteen minutes we would get lost.[52]

These gaps were not capitalised upon by Iraqi resistance, but it does show the dependence ground forces may have on spacepower in the desert for their operations, and the potential opportunities for organised resistance against forces cut off from celestial lines of communication. Even then, should the Desert Rats have been destroyed the effect on the outcome of the war is another question. Any successful counterspace operation to provide a measure of space denial may provide a window of opportunity to conduct terrestrial operations against modernised forces that may otherwise be unthinkable when resisting a spacepower-supported opponent. Developing space intelligence is necessary to plan and execute a space denial campaign, so that space warfare can be waged in tandem with terrestrial operational needs.

This illustrates aspects of both Propositions V and VII on the back of Propositions I and IV. With an undisputed command of space, through strategic manoeuvres and the manipulation of celestial lines of communication, the GPS satellites formed a hostile celestial coastline above Iraq by enhancing US terrestrial forces and enabling them to disperse and advance through a featureless desert with great accuracy, and more importantly, synchronisation between widely dispersed units. However, this could only be done for set amounts of hours every day. For its part, Iraq failed to make this littoral flank hostile for the United States. The US exploited its command of space to great effect and could perform strategic manoeuvres with its spacepower to increase its overwhelming military effectiveness through integrated spacepower against Iraq, which could not keep its forces concentrated in open ground whilst punishing the opposition for remaining concentrated by conducting 'tank plinking' with accurate air strikes. Though PGMs were in short supply and 90 per cent of munitions used by the US were 'dumb' unguided bombs, the psychological effect of tank plinking culminating with the 'Highway of Death' incident on the Iraqi troops was undeniable.[53] With assured and overwhelming logistics, strategic depth, international political support and control of third-party information, Iraq was paralysed by the spacepower-supported coalition. GPS-enabled Special Forces Pave Low helicopters from the USAF were used to lead eight Army Apache attack helicopters (which did not have GPS receiving devices) on below-radar flights to simultaneously attack two Iraqi early warning radar installations that were forty miles apart but struck within twenty seconds of each other.[54] This demonstrates the ability to concentrate effects in time with dispersed space infrastructure and terrestrial weapons. Without the guidance and synchronisation from GPS that enabled the success of this operation, Iraqi air defences may have been able to offer greater resistance to the main airstrikes on Iraq which immediately followed this Special Forces and Army aviation operation.

Against a hostile celestial coastline in 1991, Iraq was at the mercy of synchronised, precise and rapid forces; any fixed and obvious mobile targets were at high risk of destruction within a surprisingly short time span. New targets were now vulnerable far from the front line, and far more targets could be acquired and struck simultaneously with the support of spacepower, increasing US efficiency whilst paralysing its mechanised foe.[55] This fact leads to new levels of cover, concealment and dispersion under the condition of space superiority in conjunction with deployed terrestrial forces and superiority at land, sea and air. Spacepower done well does not necessarily lead to a helpless enemy. Attacking the Iraqi Republican Guard proved challenging and included close combat. Overwhelming coalition airpower, armour and artillery did not quickly break the Republican Guard's strong defensive positions.[56] However, at the same time, in the Battle of Madinah Ridge between the 1st US Armoured Division and the Iraqi Madinah Division, the detection of hitherto concealed Iraqi T-72 tanks on a defensive high ground allowed them to be destroyed at a safe distance by coalition tanks, artillery and airpower, with 300 Iraqi armoured vehicles destroyed and only two American armour losses.[57] This demonstrates the value of not being seen and failing to disperse heavy forces against a spacepower-enabled foe with precision-strike weapons.

There is no intent here to claim the apparent successes of US airpower and ground forces in striking targets and imposing dispersion as those of spacepower alone. In terms of understanding wars in their entirety, it is wrong to claim that any one form of geographically categorised power was responsible for the strategic outcome. Gray argues that 'coalition airpower achieved control of the air by fatally disabling Iraq's air defense system in the first 24 hours of the war' and the subsequent twenty-six days of aerial bombardment.[58] Neither air nor spacepower alone could have achieved the stunning successes against the Iraqi air defence system. A space-centric narrative does show the influence of spacepower and satellite infrastructure in joint operations in a way that an airpower-centric one may not, so that the challenges of spacepower's geocentric, secondary and adjunct condition raised in Proposition VI can be addressed somewhat. This is to 'fly the flag' for spacepower in the way continental navies need champions and advocates in a land-based strategic culture and bureaucratic landscape. The value of accounting for space systems and their effects are apparent, especially as their effects are not restricted to any one terrestrial military service. Failing a space denial option, elaborate deception will be needed like in waging warfare under a sky dominated by enemy air observation. In addition, terrestrial forces may still need to concentrate on Earth in terms of geographic regions. Spacepower's concentration of effects imposes dispersal and the challenge of resisting spacepower to those on the receiving end.

Adaptation and the strength of the defence

Those on the receiving end of the dispersing effect of spacepower must learn to adapt through thinking of how to attack foes that use spacepower, or how to mitigate the benefits they derive from it through adaptation and denial. Adaptation can mean fighting in a way that undermines the enemy's technological superiority derived from space infrastructure, whereas denial can mean attacking space infrastructure or parrying the PGM attacks with point-defence weapons or other forms of interference with PGMs in their terminal phases of flight. Spacepower does not undermine the Clausewitzian view that defence is the stronger form of warfare, as spacepower may provide more inherent advantages for the terrestrial defender and does not inherently make offensives against an intelligent opponent easier. The possession of a command of space is very important as Proposition I states, but it does not guarantee victory, even if it is a centre of gravity as Proposition III reminds us. Striking at this supposed centre of gravity does not guarantee success, but it may help. Indeed, Clausewitz was concerned that 'if I cannot . . . decide everything by the first success, if I have to fear the next moment, it naturally follows that I employ only so much of my force for the success of the first moment as appears necessary'.[59] All-or-nothing thinking in terms of space warfare inhibits critical and practical thinking about how to concentrate the right kinds of firepower effects in the right places and at the right time. Clausewitz's anticipation of an afterpressure following a large-scale action is still a valid concern today. Things will go wrong and fall short. War can wreak havoc on the best-laid plans. Attacking space infrastructure will increase inefficiencies in combat and logistics – friction – in the primary theatre of Earth allowing terrestrial forces to resist space-enabled military power. Returning to Clausewitz should chip away at simplistic strategising along centres of gravity. This nuance is lost in the 'high ground' American space doctrine, which believes that wars on Earth will be won or lost in space, much like the ideal of a centre of gravity.[60] The caution detailed in Proposition III is warranted because the centre of gravity disguises the messy reality that the influence of spacepower can be resisted and counteracted, but also its temporary or permanent loss can be compensated for and exploited.

If mass forms through the enabling, enhancing and supporting functions of GPS signals, then GNSS networks can be seen as a centre of gravity for users. This helps to explain why GNSS are being invested in by the major military and economic blocs, with the United States, European Union, China and Russia all fielding their own systems, and India simultaneously integrating into Russia's GLONASS (*Globalnaya navigatsionnaya sputnikovaya Sistema*) and augmenting regional GPS signals. This centre of gravity thought is apparent within Lambakis's concerns about American naval, ground and air forces being paralysed should they lose GPS services.[61] To be fair, space support does provide a degree of cohesion and unity to US military forces, and this cohesion allows them to disperse themselves yet concentrate effects, resonating with Clausewitz's description of a centre of gravity. If it is denied in a struggle over a degree of the command of space (Proposition I), it may give enough of a window of opportunity for meaningful resistance as a result of a contributory strategic manoeuvre (Proposition V) that degrades enemy celestial lines of communication (Proposition IV). If spacepower-enhanced forces are widely dispersed, there may be opportunities for concentrated attacks on them if they were to lose their networked support, precision firing and early warning capabilities. Their isolation and distribution without a good enough command of space – or a success in an adversary's space command campaign that uses both control and denial of space systems – would become an immediate source of weakness and vulnerability. This is a path that the seven propositions anticipate when considering resisting a foe with a large space infrastructure and modernised forces at its disposal.

Such thinking can produce hard strategic choices for any actor when thinking about centres of gravity, or at least the most lucrative targets of an enemy. Clausewitz illustrated the dilemmas of strategic analysis and choice through concentration and dispersal when he argued that:

> if on the one hand, the violence with which we wish to strike the blow demands the greatest concentration of force, then on the other hand, we have to fear every excess as a real disadvantage, because it entails a waste of power, and that in turn a *deficiency of power* at other points. To recognize these *centra gravitatis* in the enemy's military force, to discern their spheres of action is . . . one of the principal functions of strategic judgment.[62]

Antulio Echevarria explains that the centre of gravity is found in what allows forces to concentrate themselves and their effects, and what gives them their unified direction and purpose, and not necessarily the concentrated forces themselves.[63] In pure conceptual terms, a declaration of a centre of gravity is not necessarily a source of combat strength or weakness, meaning that if spacepower is a connecting force for an enemy, it is not necessarily a weak point (it may be well-guarded) nor a fountain of strength (connected forces do not mean that they are good in a fight).

Spacepower, then, may be deemed a centre of gravity for the United States with some initial plausibility. However, such a declaration relies on knowing whether the United States could not recover and persist in the 'afterpressure' in spite of a loss of a command of space. This does not mean that American space infrastructure is inherently vulnerable, or the only source of strength for its combat capability. However, if its space infrastructure is seriously damaged there may be systemic consequences. If spacepower is what holds together American military might, then the most significant parts must be targeted if it is possible to strike them. But a strategist's mind cannot be closed to the diversity of potential centres of gravity in existence between belligerents and at different times, bringing Proposition II to the fore again.[64] 'Concentrating force' against space infrastructure should be seen in terms of mass effects and concentrating them in time, as opposed to place given the dispersed nature of satellite constellations. If an enemy's centre of gravity is deemed to be its space infrastructure, and if it is feasible to assault it, the other propositions in this space-power theory help to visualise how it could be done and where to draw priorities in where to assault the enemy's command of space (Proposition I) by examining its celestial lines of communication (Proposition IV) and its means of response to adapting its capabilities to new realities through strategic manoeuvre (Proposition V) and drawing on its strengths in other geographic environments (Proposition III).

Not all approaches to resisting a dominant spacepower's mass effects need to attack celestial lines of communications and make parts of Earth orbit a hostile coastline for both sides. Even if spacepower is so useful that it may be a centre of gravity, the advantages spacepower provides can be nullified or mitigated by terrestrial countermeasures and adaptations. One can adapt to and deny spacepower-enabled heavy blows by assuming a general defensive posture and playing to the strengths of defensive warfare. This can include denying space systems any obvious targets to acquire or intercepting precision munitions with point-defence, theatre missile defence or pre-emptive interception of terrestrial platforms. Together, these show how the defender, with or without support from the cosmic coastline, still has many opportunities to frustrate the general offensive of a space-supported adversary. The integration of spacepower into terrestrial warfare beyond the United States does not herald an era of offensive dominance in conventional warfare, because actors without spacepower support were already adapting to an unchallenged American command of space and a hostile celestial coastline. By the late 1990s in the Middle East, various powers were undergoing a long-term process to adapt to US military advantages across the board.[65] There were three prongs to that process. First was the ability to absorb strikes and preserve crucial military strength in the face of precision munitions. Second was the desire to establish credible deterrence in order to prevent an open war. Third, there was a recognition of the need to move towards an attritional approach to warfare to chip away at the political resolve of Western leaders and populations, rather than seeking a decisive combat victory against US or modernised

Western militaries.[66] Again, airpower provides interesting analogical insights here given the importance of space-based ISR for supporting airpower operations and targeting.[67]

Improvements in survivability, which includes 'the use of protective means (bunkers and especially tunnels), camouflage and deception, scattering military forces, deliberate obfuscation of military and civilian facilities' as well as using 'low-signature forces', threaten to blunt or complicate the tip of the spear of any space-enabled military force.[68] This is in conjunction with investments in better air defences to counter 'the massive dominance of the West's airpower'.[69] Attacking a space-supported foe in a general and direct offensive may be disproportionately difficult compared to alternative defences and adaptations. If defenders can utilise their own spacepower or draw on support from others, spacepower allows them to make a large-scale conventional attack disproportionately more difficult. Spacepower increases the vulnerabilities of the attacker and the options of the defender; whereas spacepower does not help the strategic attacker to overcome the limitations of an offensive campaign if the enemy has also adapted to the attacker's space-derived advantages. Space-supported military offensives have been blunted on several occasions in the twenty-first century, not least in Afghanistan, Iraq, Palestine and Mali due to reactive opponents and strategies. It is important to not over-sell the conventional offensive power of space-supported terrestrial forces based on the Iraq Wars, as Iraq was hardly a conventional match for the United States.[70] Spacepower enables a significant defensive advantage over low-technology opponents thanks to early warning and surveillance capabilities. The defender always has options to undermine strategic offensives that a spacepower-supported foe may conduct, even without space support. The offensive in the era of spacepower is very effective only if the enemy will not or cannot adapt to or disrupt the influence of spacepower upon terrestrial warfare.

Attacking a spacepower-supported foe is extremely difficult without attacking their space support because any concentrated force will be more easily detectable and vulnerable to a mass PGM strike and long-range interdiction. But a spacepower-supported actor attacking a non-spacepower foe is still not guaranteed success – the strength of the defensive is there if the opponent seeks to capitalise on it. This is partly rooted in the traditional strength of the defensive form of warfare. Clausewitz's idealised conception of the strategic defence increases the problems of supply, time, effort and general friction to the attacker, and reduces them to the defender.[71] Strategically, as time passes without result for the aggressor, advantages tend to accumulate for the defender as it organises a response and the aggressor must struggle to keep up the pressure.[72] However, this does not make a war of conquest impossible. It makes offensive wars more risky and difficult to exercise than the defender's objectives as a general rule. Understanding the relative ease at which a strategic defence can be executed informs how a strategic offensive can be better created, as a defensive will always follow unless peace is achieved following the offensive.[73]

A relatively weaker power's actual capability and practical performance still matters at a strategic level against a stronger foe. Sometimes forces must be relatively concentrated on Earth because of the objective sought. For example, if the focal point of a conflict is a city or a small terrestrial theatre, physical forces will at some point have to concentrate to take and hold that territory. This could make it easier for a defender to plan accordingly as it limits the freedom of the strategic attacker to disperse and keep the opponent guessing. Forces and effects would have to be concentrated in time and place, and this would raise the possibility for opponents to conduct counterspace operations and other adaptive measures at the right time to blunt a concentrated attack on a smaller terrestrial focus. This problem is encountered in the next chapter in the Taiwan scenario and demonstrates the options available to smaller powers in modern warfare.

Spacepower influences an increasing amount of wars as it proliferates horizontally, and is the concern and opportunity of all participants. In the Kargil War of 1999, Pakistani infantry had created problems for the Indian Air Force (IAF) in Kashmir by being able to conceal themselves well in the mountainous and wooded terrain and used 'man'-portable air defence systems to reduce IAF dumb-bombing accuracy by forcing the IAF to operate at over 6,000 ft above the highest ridges. However, once the IAF had used only nine laser-guided bombs and begun improving their conventional bombing accuracy with makeshift GPS solutions on their MiG aircraft, Pakistani resolve seemingly broke. Lambeth writes that

> even this limited use against key . . . target sets, including both for-tified bunkers and makeshift structures, dramatically altered the dynamics of the campaign. After the successful [laser-guided bomb] attacks, targeting pod imagery observed by IAF pilots in real time showed enemy troops abandoning their positions at the very sound of approaching fighters. Diaries kept by Pakistani soldiers that were later recovered by Indian Army units amply attested to the demoral-ization caused by the IAF's attacks, most particularly those conducted during the campaign's final countdown once precision munitions were introduced.[74]

This shows how spacepower, in conjunction with other aspects of the contemporary character of warfare that enable sustained oper-ations with precise munitions, instils a dispersing principle on ter-restrial forces. This is not a new principle of war but Proposition VII shows spacepower's hand in influencing modern warfare and tactical, operational and strategic realities when space-supported forces are in play, and consequently, it illustrates the potential gain of disrupting celestial lines of communication, or making them impotent by hiding what the eyes from above are seeking.

These advantages do not always enable a rout of the oppos-ing force, even for the United States. The decision makers in Washington had wrongly assumed that all enemy forces would crumble in the face of a light, precise and rapid force, and that Iraqi forces would not have learned from the experiences of 1991.[75] Spacepower had been integrated to a much greater degree in US military forces by 2003, yet irregular forces, the Fedayeen, continued to harass US forces and supply lines out-side Baghdad with great ferocity and for a time withstood the 'Thunder Runs' in the urban environment, later dispersing and concealing themselves by blending into the Iraqi population.[76] The Iraqi armed forces had learned to put together relatively small and mobile units to intercept Apache attack helicopters. The Apache attack on the Medina Division involved thirty-two helicopters, of which thirty-one had sustained serious damage, and one was shot down and captured by Iraqi forces.[77] This shows how adaptation to spacepower can bring back the need for attritional warfare and depth of numbers as the advantages of space-supported forces are countered. If what has caused dispersion in the past fails to work again, the enemy may find more opportunities for counterattack, and perhaps, the concentration of mass effects of their own. However, American spacepower had another trick up its sleeve that may have finally broken the Republican Guard: multispectral satellite imaging data and GPS allowed American airpower to effectively target and destroy the Guard during a sandstorm, and broke their will to fight.[78] Whether such shock could be achieved in every case remains an open question.

There are limits to space surveillance – there is a dependency on acquiring intelligence about targets that are amenable to being detected by technical means. In the early years of ISR from airpower, ground forces learned to mislead or not give away their intent to air-based observers, as British operations against the Ottomans in Palestine in the First World War demonstrated.[79] Competent foes can hide and conceal their assets, increasing the risks of harming vulnerable political will in the face of casualties, poor target acquisition or moving in to close combat with enemy forces that risk losing more troops in the process.[80] Al-Qaeda forces in Afghanistan in 2001 adapted to American surveillance and reconnaissance-strike capabilities. Biddle narrates that, after the initial shock and surprise of the precision American bombardment, 'with proper cover and concealment, the defenders were able to prevent American commandos from locating the entirety of their individual fighting positions, many of which could not be singled out for precision attack'.[81] The 1991 Scud Hunt in Iraq did not go as well as hoped as a

> result of . . . the time it took for coalition aircraft to arrive at the estimated launch point . . .; the ability of the Iraqi Scud teams to 'fire a missile, drive away, and hide in a culvert all within five minutes'; the difficulty of detecting or distinguishing launcher infrared and radar signatures from those of other vehicles; and the Iraqi use of decoys.[82]

Space surveillance does not provide a panacea for the detection of targets; neither will it provide omniscience to its bearer. Competent and intelligent opponents can blunt the offensives of a modern spacepower-supported foe by adapting to and minimising spacepower's dispersing influence upon them.

Lastly, the PGM capabilities of the adversary can be rendered less efficient through the deployment of point-defence weapons and more sophisticated theatre missile defence capabilities. This is an option for only the best-equipped military forces as intercepting munitions is an expensive and difficult task. Yet a confident ability to input errors into the enemy's terminal guidance systems, or to shoot down warheads and missiles with close-in weapons platforms like modern warships already do, provides a parrying ability to negate some of the pressures of the precision warfare enabled by space infrastructure. Reducing the confidence of one-launch one-kill long-range attacks in the aggressor would demand that it put more forces to launch more munitions to increase the chances of a kill, placing a greater strain on logistics but also enticing the enemy to concentrate more physical assets, countering the inherent dispersing influence of spacepower. This demonstrates how the dispersal influence of spacepower can be challenged in practice. In theory, dispersal should be used as the starting point for analysing the influence of spacepower, as it is this unchecked quality of spacepower that makes conventional warfare easier for the military power that has secured the command of space and enjoys unmolested celestial lines of communication in the cosmic coastline. This immediately complicates any simplistic strategising on attacking the intelligent enemy's centre of gravity in space as both sides in future warfare may be conducting strategic manoeuvres and counter-manoeuvres in the celestial coastline, taxing military leaders in planning and coordination even further.

Conclusion

Spacepower's physical characteristics in Earth's cosmic coastline is usually dispersed, but their effects can be concentrated in select times and places for terrestrial forces. This, in turn, can enable space-supported forces to become more dispersed in their postures and retain their lethality by coordinating efficient and accurate long-range destructive capabilities. High-accuracy targeting imposes dispersion on the enemy – as any superior force may do. This pushes the enemy to adapt to the sharp end of spacepower-supported forces on Earth by either striking at the spacepower of the enemy (a possible centre of gravity) or adapting to it and denying the targets that such systems seek. Another possibility is that militaries that prefer to mass on Earth must do so only after the enemy's spacepower is dealt with through a sufficient level of destruction or disruption, or a confidence in an ability to intercept and blunt the worst of a PGM attack through theatre and point-defences. The reactions to spacepower's dispersing influence complicate the practice of imposing dispersal and dispel the fantasy of space being a centre of gravity ripe for destruction, partly through the continuing strength of the defensive form of war. But the increasing difficulties of continuing to exploit the dispersing influence of spacepower does not mean its influence is not there; if it was not present, adapting to it or countering it would not be necessary in the first place. Again, Luttwak's paradoxical logic is at work in practice and theory.

Proposition VII theorises the basis for answering the tactical and operational 'so what' questions for terrestrial warfare of securing the command of space (I) and using celestial lines of communication (IV) to conduct supporting strategic manoeuvres (V) in support of warfare on Earth (VII). Proposition VII completes the circle of spacepower theory. However, in keeping with the non-linear view of war and politics as outlined in Chapter 3, connections are apparent between the propositions in any number of combinations and particular manifestations. Their elements, however, persist. Proposition VII has explored thinking of spacepower's condition as being dispersed in orbit, and how it encourages dispersal on Earth. Dispersal in space begets dispersal on Earth, and influences how concentration is achieved by terrestrial forces. The effects of spacepower from orbit can be concentrated, and the harnessing of celestial lines of communication at major points of effort can form a mass effect if executed with weapons systems on Earth. Proposition VII is about the exploitation of the command of space (detailed in Proposition I) to use or deny celestial lines of communication (Proposition IV). For any comprehensive space power such as the United States, Russia or China, the means of securing a command of space and making it contribute to the wider war through strategic manoeuvres (Proposition V) is affected by influencing the concentration and dispersal of efforts on Earth (Proposition VII). Without the means to exploit what the command of space provides, a space warfare campaign may lose its value. Securing a command of space for its own sake is not enough – it must translate into effects on the movement of forces and the use of violence on Earth.

Notes

1. Sheldon, *Reasoning*, p. 290.
2. Mahan, *Sea Power*, p. 316, taken from: Corbett, *Principles of Maritime Strategy*, p. 131.
3. Smith, *Ten Propositions*, pp. 44–8; Oberg, *Space*, p. 124; Lupton, *On Space Warfare*, pp. 19–20.
4. Sheldon, *Reasoning*, p. 306.
5. Shimko, *The Iraq Wars*, p. 93.
6. Ibid. pp. 107–11.
7. York, 'Nuclear Deterrence', p. 22; Stares, *Space*, p. 132.
8. The Steering Committee of Global Monitoring for the Environment and Security (GMES)/Copernicus has not been coy about its military applications since the early 2000s. See: Brachet, 'From Ideas to a European Plan', p. 13.
9. Pekkanen and Kallender-Umezu, *In Defense of Japan*, p. xii.
10. Sheldon, *Reasoning*, p. 78.
11. *Los Angeles Times*, 'Indian test deception reported'; Federation of American Scientists, 'India blasts take U.S. intelligence by surprise'; Burr, 'U.S. detected Indian nuclear test preparations'.
12. Oberg, *Space*, p. 14.
13. Handberg, 'Is Space War Imminent?', p. 419.
14. Easton, 'China's Evolving Reconnaissance-Strike Capabilities', p. 20.
15. Gray, *Airpower for Strategic Effect*, p. 129.
16. Sheldon, *Reasoning*, pp. 180–1.
17. Ibid. pp. 305–6.

18. Fox, 'Some Principles of Space Strategy', p. 13.
19. Sheldon, *Reasoning*, pp. 308–9.
20. Lai and Miller, 'Introduction', pp. 7–8.
21. See: Godwin, 'The PLA', p. 55.
22. Easton and Frazier, *GPS*, p. 180.
23. Wong and Fergusson, *Military Space Power*, p. 95.
24. Handel, *Masters of War*, pp. 155–64.
25. Laser-painted targeting can create precise air support for land forces. See: Biddle, 'Afghanistan'.
26. Sheldon, *Reasoning*, pp. 164–5.
27. Ibid. p. 267.
28. Lupton, *On Space Warfare*, pp. 20–1.
29. Jomini, *The Art of War*, pp. 70, 176.
30. Clausewitz, *On War*, p. 415.
31. Ibid. p. 416.
32. Ibid. p. 417.
33. Ibid. p. 418.
34. Ibid. p. 419.
35. Ibid. p. 427.
36. Ibid. p. 433.
37. Ibid. p. 949.
38. Ibid. pp. 950–3.
39. Friedman, *Seapower*, p. 302.
40. Wawro, *Warfare*, pp. 9, 63, 68, 103, 156.
41. Ibid. p. 156.
42. Gray, *Airpower for Strategic Effect*, pp. 294–5.
43. Colson, *Napoleon*, p. 148.
44. Ibid. pp. 156–64.
45. Mahan, *The Influence of Sea Power upon History*, pp. 28–9.
46. Sheldon, *Reasoning*, p. 165.
47. Ibid. p. 266.
48. Ibid. p. 167.
49. Ibid. 166–7.
50. Easton and Frazier, *GPS*, pp. 124–5.
51. Ibid. p. 125.
52. Cordingley, *In the Eye of the Storm*, p. 204.
53. Shimko, *The Iraq Wars*, pp. 68–75.
54. Ibid. p. 118.
55. Ibid. p. 81.
56. Finlan, *The Gulf War*, pp. 62–4.
57. Ibid. pp. 64–5.

58. Gray, *Airpower for Strategic Effect*, p. 212.
59. Clausewitz, *On War*, p. 430.
60. Lupton, *On Space Warfare*, p. 38.
61. Lambakis, 'Space Control', p. 427.
62. Clausewitz, *On War*, p. 786. Emphasis Clausewitz's.
63. Echevarria, *Clausewitz*, p. 181.
64. Ibid. pp. 182–3.
65. Brun, 'While You're Busy'. Brun refers to, among others, Iran, Iraq, Syria, Hezbollah, the Taliban and Al-Qaeda.
66. Ibid. pp. 548–9.
67. Gray, *Airpower for Strategic Effect*, pp. 236–7.
68. Brun, 'While You're Busy', p. 549.
69. Ibid. p. 550.
70. Shimko, *The Iraq Wars*, pp. 78–9.
71. Clausewitz, *On War*, p. 627–8.
72. Ibid. p. 619.
73. Ibid. p. 629.
74. Lambeth, 'Airpower', pp. 304–7.
75. Finlan, *Contemporary Military Strategy*, p. 135.
76. Shimko, *The Iraq Wars*, pp. 153–7.
77. Finlan, *Contemporary Military Strategy*, pp. 135–6.
78. Ibid. p. 141.
79. Preston, *Plowshares*, pp. 41–54.
80. Brun, 'While You're Busy', pp. 546–7.
81. Biddle, 'Afghanistan', p. 36.
82. Richelson, *America's Space Sentinels*, p. 173.

6. A Clash of Spacepowers

Spacepower produces many 'moving parts' for any strategist to consider, and its infrastructural effects are widespread and diverse within military forces and the international system. This chapter projects the dynamics of spacepower onto assessments of a Chinese–American war over Taiwan. Considering the practical aspects of American, Chinese and Taiwanese capabilities from a spacepower perspective should demonstrate why spacepower needs to be taken into account in IR analyses of the balance of power and military strategies, but also how neither side can assume easy successes should a war come. The domination of the celestial coastline of Earth orbit is far from a foregone conclusion. Some analysts are confident of Chinese success in disabling American space infrastructure in the opening shots (Space Pearl Harbor), whilst others are sure of the ability of America and Taiwan to persist in the face of hostile precision weapons fire and use anti-satellite operations at a later time (Counterspace in Being). Both strategies have merits. The application of this spacepower theory and its seven propositions shows how both sides of the debate are grappling with when and how they wish to exploit and blunt the dispersing effects of spacepower. No reader should emerge from this chapter overly confident of either strategy succeeding without great pain or uncertainty, and no prediction is offered on which strategy stands the best chance of succeeding as success will depend on numerous particular details that vary from month to month, and decision-making that must be done in the face of incomplete information. Readers should emerge with a clearer understanding of how spacepower and space warfare fits into modern warfare.

Debate on maritime warfare between China and America tends to gravitate between two opposing strategies of what China will do in the preceding crisis or opening phase of a Taiwan war. The first is termed loosely as a 'Space Pearl Harbor' attack, where Beijing engages in a massive surprise attack against American space and terrestrial assets at the outset of any physical hostilities so that Washington cannot respond effectively to Taiwan's defence, even if it desired to do so. The second strategy is that Chinese, American or Taiwanese counterspace operations may be held off until a critical moment is reached in the terrestrial conflict, and such operations may be graduated or proportionate in their character, rather than an all-out assault. This is labelled as a Counterspace-in-Being strategy, inferring the more latent and threatened nature of such capabilities that may not be utilised at the outset of hostilities, but rather kept in play for continuous vigorous action, especially at a later, more critical opportunity. Spacepower theory demonstrates how the implementation of these two strategies may be influenced by how and when both sides will need to command space and exploit and counter spacepower's dispersing influence on the theatre of operations.

Concepts such as concentration, dispersal, control and denial get at the essence of the effects being sought regardless of the strategy and policy buzzword of the day to describe the latest weapon platform developments and combinations. No matter the language of the day the strategic and theoretical truths espoused by theory are somewhat more robust. As a reminder, the seven propositions of spacepower theory are:

    I. Space warfare is waged for the command of space
   II. Spacepower is uniquely infrastructural and connected to Earth
  III. The command of space does not equate to the command of Earth
  IV. The command of space manipulates celestial lines of communication
   V. Earth orbit is a cosmic coastline suited for strategic manoeuvres
  VI. Spacepower exists within a geocentric mindset
 VII. Spacepower is dispersed and imposes dispersion on Earth

A major flashpoint and continuing source of friction where space warfare may occur is the independence of Taiwan from mainland China, and America's commitment to its defence. This chapter focuses on the conduct of war from the perspective of space-power, and eschews the pre-war, crisis and deterrence phases. Whilst assuming hostile intent for the purposes of the scenario, it is not the case that any party inherently desires war, that a war over Taiwan is inevitable, or that China and America are forever destined to compete in the international system. Indeed, there was a time when the United States greatly assisted China's space pro-gramme, demonstrating an ahistoricism within the 'China threat' assumption applied to contemporary analyses of China's space policies.[1] Chinese military planning also goes beyond the Taiwan Strait, as it must plan for internal and other regional contingen-cies. Space systems will be useful in varying degrees to the People's Republic of China (PRC) and its military forces in all potential conflicts.[2] Nevertheless, Taiwan's military defence against China is an illuminating case for the application of spacepower theory due to the unfortunate reality that it is likely to bear the brunt of space-enabled and supported military power, and is also there-fore one of the most active actors in trying to counter it.[3] Whilst this chapter focuses on the immediate concerns of a Taiwan war, every good astrostrategist must also bear in mind the long-term grand strategic consequences of the campaign for future gover-nance and economic exploitation of outer space. References to the seven propositions demonstrate the nuanced and indeterminate nature of spacepower, and also how the propositions can be used in a non-linear and interactive fashion, demonstrating a way to organise thought about the large number of factors in play during any war and the execution of strategy.

As Proposition I stresses that spacepower and space warfare only have meaning in relation to terrestrial warfare and politics, this chapter is structured according to the three phases of a Taiwan war. This Taiwan-centric approach emphasises the centrality of ter-restrial considerations – or Proposition VI's geocentrism – in any top-level decision maker's mindset, where spacepower's influence may not be as obvious. Spacepower should not over-determine the interpretation or analysis of any terrestrial war. Indeed, the primary objective of the war for the PRC is the ultimate fate of the Republic of China (ROC): its reintegration into Beijing's political control and the end of Taiwan's de facto independence. Taiwan and the United States will seek to prevent that. Every form of power and capability must meet the objectives for determining that fate on Earth. The Taiwan war scenario divides into three phases, listed in Table 6.1. Any exchange of hostilities will take place within the context of these three phases of the campaign on Taiwan and its surrounding islands.[4] The strategies of China and Taiwan are closely aligned, as both sides are focused on respectively triggering or preventing the capitulation of Taipei's government, surrender of military forces and occupation of the main island of Taiwan. Whilst China aims to bomb Taiwan into submission, isolate it from the international system, and hope to avoid a protracted war on the island, Taiwan seeks to impose severe costs on Chinese forces and the mainland, and to hold out long enough for terrestrial American support to arrive. Short of American intervention, Taiwan seeks to impose such an enormous military, human, economic and political toll on China so that it desists in the face of a severe domestic crisis for the Chinese Communist Party and overstretches the PLA's combat and logistical capacities. All parties will need to engage with spacepower support and deny it to their adversaries in order to increase the chances that they can isolate Taiwan from their adversary. China must seek to make it too hard for the US maritime and air forces to approach Taiwan, and America and Taiwan must make the Straits a prohibitively lethal environment for PLA amphibious forces. The command of

Table 6.1 PRC and ROC campaign phases

People's Republic of China (PRC)	Phase	Republic of China (ROC)
Blockade and bombing operations	1	Mobilisation and force preservation
Amphibious landing operations	2	Joint interdiction of PLA amphibious forces whilst embarking
Combat operations on the island	3	Repel invasion; retreat into interior

space will in part determine who can isolate Taiwan from whom – but the proximity of Taiwan to China means that Taiwan still has plenty of options to retaliate, meaning that the Chinese mainland cannot be immune to the effects of the war.

Both sides must struggle over the command of space (Proposition I) so that they can simultaneously exploit and resist the dispersing effects of spacepower (Proposition VII). These propositions act as bookends for spacepower theory that allow the other aspects of the war, stressed in the other propositions, to play out between them and construct an abstract narrative. Any action against space infrastructure must contribute to the command of space (I) through the relevant celestial lines of communication (IV), to conduct strategic manoeuvres in the proximate orbital environment (V). This exemplifies how a targeted, determined and integrated exploitation of spacepower – or its negation – allows resistance against a spacepower (II, III, VI) and creates shifts in the distribution of forces on Earth (V) which blunt the hard edge of the enemy's spacepower-dependent combat power on the battlefield (VII). The purpose of this chapter is to show how to think about and analyse the role of spacepower in a larger terrestrial conflict in a structured manner; and not outline a war-winning strategy. A short narrative of the general spacepower element of a war plan can be permutated in several different ways and combinations using the seven propositions. It is up to the reader to apply them as they see fit to enhance understanding and judgment. This chapter is a demonstration of a propositional spacepower analysis, and not a definitive statement or the final word on spacepower in a Taiwan war, particularly as the research here has been limited to English-language sources.

Phase I: Opening gambits

According to the Space Pearl Harbor strategy, China must strike American assets in space and on Earth early on for it to stand a chance of succeeding in a Taiwan war. Knocking out America's edge gained from space-enabled force enhancement would level the terrestrial battlefield. The hard edge of dispersion from spacepower and networked long-range strike forces (Proposition VII) must be denied to the enemy (Proposition I) to improve the distribution, survivability and chances of success of forces in the primary theatres on Earth (Proposition V). The first stages of the war may be characterised by the deployment and use of standoff long-range strike weapons. Many existing analyses of a China–US war scenario only indirectly consider the effects of spacepower, and the strategy of Taiwan, in their calculations of the opening moves of a war between US and China. This is despite the fact that the kill chains they rely on for long-range weapons, such China's DF-21 and DF-26 anti-ship ballistic missiles (ASBMs) and the United States' very long-range PGMs such as the AGM-158 Joint Air-to-Surface Standoff Missile, rely on spacepower for full capability. Beijing has established a force consisting of over 1,200 short-range ballistic missiles (SRBM) that can easily reach Taiwanese targets, as well as long-range aerial bombers.[5] The United States and Taiwan would face an adversary that not only has a maturing array of anti-satellite capabilities, but also space-enabled networked military systems of its own, providing a more target-rich environment for American and Taiwanese counterspace operations.

The phrase 'Space Pearl Harbor' emerged following Donald Rumsfeld's 2001 Space Commission report. The Commission noted a potential threat to US space systems in the form of a debilitating first strike from an adversary against its space systems. The Commission warned that 'the U.S. could be subjected to serious difficulties if the functions of U.S. satellites were significantly disrupted or degraded'.[6] The notion of a surprise strike against the United States in space – as are the connotations of the Pearl Harbor attack and the pressure in favour of a first strike in the Pacific theatre – is commonplace.[7] Operational and tactical writings from China suggest a preference from some quarters for a crippling first strike against American space systems in order to lessen the threat posed by US power projection and increase the survivability of PLA forces.[8] Whilst there may be ample strategic warning of an attack by China on US space systems, there could be considerable tactical and operational surprise.[9] Some Chinese doctrinal writings go so far as to assert that the initiative in the war as a whole will be determined by whoever seizes the initiative in space warfare.[10] This is not necessarily representative of policy or concluded doctrine, but strategising is occurring along the lines of a first strike in space, which may or may not be drawn upon in war. The PLA is cognizant of the influence of the command of space, in particular through the dispersing effects of American spacepower they would have to face should the American command of space remain unchallenged.

The incentive to strike American space systems early on, and risking a like-for-like retaliation from the United States, may seem like a possibly acceptable cost given China's lighter dependence – compared to America – on spacepower for a Taiwan scenario.[11] The PLA may be tempted to use its ASAT systems, which if several dozen are stockpiled:

> pose a serious challenge to U.S. photographic intelligence (PHOTINT), electro-optical (EO), synthetic aperture radar (SAR), and electronic intelligence (ELINT) satellites that operate in low-earth orbit (LEO) . . . The loss of these EO/SAR/ELINT platforms, which are probably the main targets of China's direct-ascent ASAT weapons, would be a very serious blow to the U.S. at the outset of any conflict.[12]

Additional threats to navigation satellites such as the GPS in MEO and the new WGS and Space-based Infrared System (SBIRS) constellations in GEO and HEO respectively may need to be accounted for as under threat from Chinese space weapons. Even by only considering US satellites and systems within LEO, there is some merit to the view that the United States has something of an Achilles heel through its dependence on spacepower.[13] Though Propositions III and VII caution against such a dramatic description of space systems as a centre of gravity, or space strikes as a fait accompli, American dependence on space systems for power projection across the oceans is still a fact of life. Identifying these space and weapons systems, and how and when they should be denied or destroyed and their celestial lines of communication meddled with, shows the importance of Propositions II and IV. Not all space systems represent similar severity if lost, and not all space systems are as vulnerable as others based on their hardware, supporting terrestrial infrastructure and locations in orbit.

China's dependence on missiles and long-range bombers, which are vulnerable to American space-enabled precision-strike weapons, may create a use-it-or-lose-it situation, or first strike instability. PLA SSF launchers may be vulnerable to an American first strike, unless successful deception, hardening and concealment measures are taken.[14] It is not impossible to locate possible launch sites for a good number of missile units but retaliatory strikes will have to deal with 'shoot and scoot' operations like Iraqi Scud forces in 1991. This adds to the picture of an offensively orientated posture derived from the proliferation of spacepower in orbit and its integration into terrestrial military forces. An American response to sophisticated and effective Chinese air defences would be to use extremely long-range standoff munitions – which are highly dependent on space systems and celestial lines of communication – launched from ships and aircraft to pierce air defence networks, making them extremely useful as a first strike or a 'leading edge' in a campaign.[15] The ever-greater dependence upon such satellites, coupled with a perception of their vulnerability, makes space warfare appear like an offensive-orientated tool or most wisely strategised as an opening gambit in warfare when long-range precision weapons are involved.[16] It is reasonable that 'a central component of China's strategy is to conduct . . . strikes against an opponent by targeting critical C4ISR nodes'.[17] Also enhancing the chances of a Chinese first strike is that it would be a significant escalation for the United States to strike first on the Chinese mainland during a crisis. Yet, as seen below, existing A2/AD analyses neglect Taiwan's strike options on mainland China which complicates the achievement of a Space Pearl Harbor attack.

The most sophisticated weaponry – usually the more spacepower-dependent – may be effectively deployed and used early on in the conflict as anti-satellite weapons, long-range PGMs, and their targets, such as aircraft carriers, would be difficult to replace if ammunition stocks are low, thus providing an advantage to whomever shoots first.[18] If China were to launch its long-range munitions to strike at American targets across the first and second island chains, its dependence on its own growing space infrastructure may diminish without risking its ability to achieve its objectives. Operations on

Taiwan will be less reliant on celestial lines of communication than those in the Spratley Islands, for example. That said, China remains highly reliant on long-range precision-strike weapons, and their supporting space systems, to counter the US Navy and Air Force before they approach the Taiwan theatre.

China's burgeoning space infrastructure now numbers over 250 satellites among government, military, civilian and commercial registries.[19] The PLA manages all of China's space tracking and control, and therefore the data therein can be channelled towards military needs.[20] China's ability to identify, track and target objects in the Pacific in a timely fashion has made significant leaps.[21] The time needed to locate, identify and track naval vessels has been cut by 95 per cent in the past decade through the continuous deployment of four SAR and eight EO satellites of various resolutions, as well as a handful of ELINT satellites within a Naval Ocean Surveillance System (NOSS) in order to cue land-based over-the-horizon radar stations, which provide initial targeting and cueing for China's long-range standoff weapons aimed at the first and second island chains.[22] China has historically enjoyed the most expansive SIGINT network in Asia; however, it is only in the past couple of decades that system has been harnessing the boons of spacepower and the miniaturisation of computer hardware and processing power.[23] Patching together this system of reconnaissance, surveillance and strike capabilities is the *Qu Dian* system – a communications web which includes satellite and airborne sensors that connect sensors with commanders and combat platforms.[24] As well as using dedicated communications satellites, China's satellite navigation system – *Beidou*/Compass – will provide further communications capabilities, redundancies and global coverage as well as its primary precision guidance capabilities.[25]

As China's space infrastructure expands in both quantity and quality, its spacepower presents more opportunities for Beijing to integrate spacepower into its military forces, security practices, and for conducting strategic manoeuvres and developing strategic depth from space. As a result, it is of little surprise that Chinese strategic thought on space refers frequently to the 'command of space', or 'space control', in various forms, embracing the core concepts of Propositions I and III.[26] In a Taiwan scenario, China will be seeking to exploit its own command of space so that it can ensure its long-range strike weapons can threaten key American and allied assets throughout the region, and to annihilate important Taiwanese targets to soften the islands up for invasion through 'key point strikes'. However, this dependence in turn exacerbates a sense of vulnerability to an American first strike against Chinese space infrastructure. But it also raises the payoff for a Taiwanese effort at counterspace operations, in particular in the electromagnetic and 'cyber' realms of soft-kill methods. Yet an increasingly diverse and numerically large space asset portfolio also reduces the chances of single points of failure, increasing the breathing room for a Counterspace-in-Being strategy. The same is true for the United States with its even larger satellite networks. This significantly complicates a picture that some oversimplify with the analogy of Pearl Harbor, demonstrating the need to analyse material factors and spacepower in their own right. Indeed, the Japanese attack on Pearl Harbor did not ensure ultimate victory and shows the case for caution when using historical analogies to inform strategic thought.[27] Additionally, unlike the Japanese at Pearl Harbor, Chinese space warfare in the cosmic coastline may be able to target more pervasive critical infrastructure in a surprise attack against the United States. It must, however, be remembered that due to geographic realities, Chinese forces will be far less reliant in general terms on spacepower compared to American expeditionary forces, increasing the possible desirability in Beijing to engage in space warfare, as retaliation in kind from Washington may not be as serious for its goals and capabilities.

China's reconnaissance-strike regime mirrors long-established American systems, such as the White Cloud NOSS to track and target maritime vessels.[28] This evolving capability to locate, identify and track moving US Navy vessels in the Pacific, as well as to accurately bombard US bases throughout the region, poses a threat in any war planning for the United States and Taiwan. The United States will have to consider the use of ASATs – both hard kill and soft kill – to ensure that American terrestrial forces do not succumb too easily to the Chinese reconnaissance-strike kill chain and suffer from the hard edge of Proposition VII.[29] Neither China nor the US would want the other to enjoy flanking support from the cosmic coastline for the primary terrestrial theatre, yet both sides will want to secure their own advantages from it. A US–China conflict will be one involving competing systems of systems in the cosmic coastline. Such a situation is a 'mature maritime precision-strike regime', where 'the major maritime competitors have advanced ISR as well as precision-strike capabilities all linked together to form a battle network'.[30] This is interchangeably referred to by some as a reconnaissance-strike complex. It is this suite of capabilities that triggers much thought of spacepower as a centre of gravity for the United States. Strategic manoeuvres will be conducted by all parties to maintain spacepower support and degrade that of the enemy.

Such a regime or complex will make ships and aircraft that travel within the lines of sight and ranges of satellite-cued precision munitions more vulnerable.[31] A key calculation in the strategies of China and the US with their opposing reconnaissance-strike complexes is how long naval and airborne forces could loiter within one another's A2/AD zones in order to fire their long-range strike weapons, retreat to relative safety, and use space-based systems to conduct long-range battle damage assessment.[32] Fire and forget is something of a misnomer for guided munitions – commanders need to know if attacks have been successful or whether they need to try again before moving onto the next mission. This is Proposition V's hostile coast made manifest. China's space infrastructure is essential for it to threaten American power projection capabilities in order to isolate Taiwan. US and ROC counterspace operations that undermine the celestial lines of communication of PRC kill chains may provide more time for American and Taiwanese activities in a Chinese 'anti-access' region, exemplifying the deployment of a hostile coast against Chinese satellites to minimise the risk the Chinese orbital flank presents to Taiwan. Any strategy must anticipate the possible use of American and Japanese Aegis-equipped destroyers as potential ASAT platforms, as well as electronic warfare assets. The threat posed to Chinese satellites by the United States is set to increase as the years progress, as Chinese dependence on spacepower for terrestrial campaigns increases and American ASAT systems are developed and deployed.[33] China may be able to reduce its dependency on many space services by building terrestrial alternatives given the proximity of Taiwan to China, again conditioning specific calculations in a Taiwan conflict that may not be applicable in all cases of space warfare.[34]

China's anti-satellite weapon developments, its emerging space-based military infrastructure and the United States' growing anti-satellite capabilities lend weight to Pollpeter's analysis that both China and the US have a strong incentive to strike first.[35] Putting it succinctly:

in the case of the PLA, this is to achieve an asymmetric advantage against a superior [terrestrial] US force in order to delay its entry and keep it away from the conflict zone. For the US military, the incentive is to defeat China's ability to locate, track, and target US bases and naval ships with long-range precision strike platforms in order to create a permissive environment for US forces to operate within or close to the conflict zone.[36]

It is far more difficult for a defender – in this case the United States – to guess to what degree the attacker may be contemplating a bold and decisive stroke.[37] China may wish to realise what Clausewitz called an attack on the enemy's army in its quarters, which prevents the enemy from assembling at its preferred location and buys significant time for the assailant as the victim spends days assembling at a more rearward, safer, position.[38]

Although Space Pearl Harbor is mostly concerned with offensive warfare scenarios defensive aspects should not be maligned, even more so if the military innovator becomes the imitated. Commenting on the disaster of 'trenchlock' warfare and the cult of the offensive in the First World War, Wawro argues that 'after 1870, every European army adopted the Prussian formula . . . [and] the Napoleonic "revolution in military affairs" had lost its punch once every other army in Europe adopted it'.[39] This continuing trend of increasing the ability to concentrate firepower over greater distances in shorter time spans is the realisation of successful combat integration of spacepower into modern warfare. As others imitate this, a new premium may emerge on attritional and positional warfare, with wars being decided on who can weather the most punishing losses and replace lost units best.

Such conceptual thinking fits one way of dispersing weapons platforms or missiles, but coordinating strikes to hit at the same time, providing a concentrated firepower effect whilst military units remain dispersed and saturating local defences with the sheer number of missiles and warheads, still requires space systems to function.[40] As Chinese long-range strike capabilities extend their reach, rearward US bases are directly threatened. Clausewitz maintained that, if an enemy army is not between you and the object of the campaign, then 'the direction of the blow must therefore be not so much on the object itself as on the road the enemy's army has to take to reach it'.[41] This captures how Beijing must assault the relevant American celestial lines of communication that support the naval and air forces that Washington must dispatch to aid Taipei. Increased threats to high-technology platforms and humans should renew emphasis on numerical depth and mass in combat platforms and personnel as well as a willingness to absorb casualties, challenging over two decades of shrinking military personnel totals and deployable assets.

With space technology, dispersed forces can avoid falling victim to the tendency noted by Clausewitz that dividing forces weakens them and makes them less controllable by further relying on spacepower's ability to allow dispersed units to communicate around the world.[42] Dispersion is necessary to deny the superior concentrated foe an overwhelming victory. With spacepower for China and the United States, however, that translates into hardening targets, deception or further dispersing them, which in turn increases the reliance on space systems. This reliance then increases the value of attacking space systems in the first place. This is the reinforcing logic that John Sheldon noted as being unique to spacepower. Dispersing airbases and runways complete with point-defence systems across the region and to a new extent may create more targets than the Chinese can saturate with salvos. Additionally, dispersion through the proliferation of hardened hangars may increase uncertainty for the PLA, and hardening would also force the PLA to strike the actual hangars rather than destroying the tarmac. This complicates a Space Pearl

Harbor strategy and reduces confidence in a successful surprise attack.[43] Other options include campaigns based on temporary and mobile bases, as well as embracing dispersion in operations, within an enemy's A2/AD zone of operations,[44] and using elaborate and multispectral deception and concealment efforts.[45] These parameters depend on the reliability and structures of trust in the precision-strike regimes involved in the conflict, as they determine the actual manifestation of Proposition VII and the hard edge of spacepower in the war. They also depend on remembering the sums of Propositions I and V – that space warfare and the command of space only have meaning when they influence the war on Earth, and the timing of warfare in the cosmic coastline may have more opportune moments to affect the primary terrestrial theatre of war after the outset of hostilities.

There is uncertainty as to what extent such systems can operate effectively if the space segments come under attack from hard and soft-kill methods.[46] Part of understanding such scenarios, however, is not the deployment of weapons systems and bases per se, but to what degree either side feels comfortable under the dispersing pressure and hostile celestial coastline exerted upon them by the other side's spacepower-enabled reconnaissance-strike complex, and how reliably the space components of that system may be targeted and neutralised. On top of this is a parrying ability. Hardening, point-defence or close-in weapon systems, and concealment are attempts to parry, rather than dismantle, the spacepower-enabled PGM salvo, as theorised in Proposition VII. Part of the calculations will be to ensure that ammunition for such defences against PGM salvos are sufficient to meet the estimated deployed PGM stockpile of the adversary. The spectre of attritional approaches to warfare appears again. Dispersing one's own forces can only go so far and alternative plans must be in place should efforts to deny the command of space to the enemy amount to little.

Spacepower in a Taiwan war scenario will feature as a competition between two high-technology space powers swatting visible air and maritime targets and striking key land installations so that neither side can muster their full strength and dispatch it to Taiwan. Whomever strikes first with space weapons may indeed enjoy a terrestrial advantage as the other side scrambles to reorganise terrestrial military assets in the wake of the loss of the command of space in the relevant time and place in-theatre. Yet China's reduced need for spacepower because Taiwan is nearby means that advantages of any American first strike on Chinese space systems may be less significant than a Chinese counterspace campaign. In the midst of this, Taiwan itself will be seeking to counter Chinese spacepower in such a way that China must maintain the element of surprise if it is to decisively disarm Taiwanese forces early on. Despite the incentive to strike first against American space systems, China still needs them to effectively subdue ROC forces so that PLA amphibious forces can embark safely, when they will be at their most vulnerable, especially on the ROC's forward islands. A Space Pearl Harbor attack on America would likely put all Chinese space assets at risk of retaliation. China has as many reasons as America to not have its space systems wiped out early in the conflict.

Taiwan should not be portrayed as a passive actor; Taipei rarely features in A2/AD analysis as an independent agent that can and may resist the PLA fiercely, and will react to any Space Pearl Harbor attack, meaning China risks its element of surprise against standing terrestrial Taiwanese defence forces. Taiwan is also subject to the desire for striking first, against both Chinese space systems and terrestrial sites; however, its plans to resist China's PLA amphibious expedition specifically undermine any simple execution of a surprise first strike. This pushes against simplistic notions that China wins the war if it hits America first in space and with long-range strikes across the Pacific and in space. The ROC Army, Air Force and Navy are planning to conduct their initial phases of the war without significant help from the American military, and with perhaps fewer political constraints as well, given that the political survival of the ROC will be at stake.

Taiwanese defence planning is such that those 1,200 Chinese SRBMs will still be stretched to hit all necessary targets effectively. Taiwan, adapting to the dispersing influence of spacepower and the mass SRBM and guided missile targeting efficiency, has a dispersed and deceptive defence system. A list of 1,000 important Taiwanese targets could challenge the PLA's efforts to concentrate firepower effects, even with space systems.[47] Taiwan has invested in hard and fortified bunkers, not only on its main island but also in its islands dotted off the PRC's mainland coast, such as Kinmen and Matsu, which are hard granite rocks and can host a range of ROC long-range weapons that can strike deep into mainland PRC territory. Whilst China seeks to conduct decapitation strikes and silence Taiwanese early warning radar systems and annihilate airbases,

> these islands are platforms from which the ROC military can launch counterstrikes against bases in the PRC and ships transiting the Strait . . . bristling with long range missiles for sinking ships, intercepting aircraft, and striking targets in China, these islands are apparently viewed by Chinese strategists as a formidable obstacle.[48]

A serious physical assault by China on American space systems early on may persuade ROC forces and the civilian government to fight to the last, triggering a passionate escalation of the conflict in a very Clausewitzian sense. This can be contrasted with 'salami slice' tactics of special forces or unmarked units to change 'facts on the ground' during a crisis with minimal destruction and political opprobrium. This is not to reduce the likelihood of a Space Pearl Harbor, rather it is to highlight its drawbacks and why alternative strategies may be considered. In a Space Pearl Harbor scenario major fighting will be immediately confined to the outlying islands, if Taiwan's defence strategy is initially successful, which 'has long called for keeping a cross-Strait war localised to its offshore islands and away from its densely populated west coast'.[49] A significant number of Taiwan's indigenous standoff munitions, even based on Taiwan and not to mention on forward islands, could engage in deep strike missions against the PRC, particularly against fixed targets and logistical nodes.[50] These are assets in Taiwan's strategies to contest China's command of space (I) and how it intends to turn Earth orbit via supporting manoeuvres into a hostile coastline (V) against the ROC by imposing dispersion on its forces (VII).

The ROC Air Force has invested heavily in runway repair capabilities, makeshift airstrips including the use of highways, and mountain hangars in the main island designed specifically to complicate the task of the PLA SSF.[51] The ROC Navy has to undertake dispersal, hardening and concealment measures to weather the initial strikes from the PLA so that their counterstrike long-range missiles can be deployed at a subsequent time of the ROC's choosing – providing a fleet-in-being effect.[52] During this time, as PLA missiles rain down on Taiwanese bases, forces and government buildings, the ROC will be mobilising its reserve and gearing the population for war. The ROC will be seeking to mobilise the United States to come to its aid, and economic warfare plans may be put into practice by Taipei. The strength of Taiwan's commercial telecoms and information technology industries – which also employ a large degree of workers in the sector in mainland China – could be leveraged to cause economic pain and infrastructure problems for Chinese civilians, which could play out in any number of ways in the court of international opinion, particularly in terms of the interests of third parties, commercial interests and the global population (Propositions V and VI).[53] Coupled with long-range ROC counterstrike capabilities that can hit known PLA missile factories, headquarters and logistical nodes for invasion forces, and also its own theatre missile defence systems that can blunt the dispersing influence of precision Chinese spacepower, the ROC can escalate and demonstrate its will and capacity to resist, perhaps acting contrary to many Western analysts' thinking: that Taiwan has no chance of success.[54] Such hardening and denial of a swift Chinese first strike may buy Taiwan the time it needs to mobilise the population for a defence from invasion.

Spacepower at first glance seems to increase the value of the first strike, particularly for China in these geographic conditions. Yet Phase 1 also shows an incentive by the US to attack Chinese space systems as it attempts to pick apart Taiwanese air defence and maritime interdiction assets and infrastructure so that Chinese strike capabilities are reduced in efficiency and lethality. The need for continuous bombardment – and the eleventh-hour intelligence that America space-based ISR can provide as ROC forces move and adapt – from the PLA warrants caution against analyses that 'military technology and planning are thus creating a bias toward sharp exchange of strikes from the start, with both sides intent on gaining the upper hand or at least denying it to the other'.[55] In addition, the capabilities of the ROC to weather the PLA's major strikes will have to remain an unknown, especially given its highly sensitive and secretive nature. This should caution against overly fatalist opinions that 'it is difficult to escape the conclusion that China either already has or shortly will have the ability to ground or destroy Taiwan's air force and eliminate the navy at a time of its own choosing'.[56] The United States and Taiwan are deploying a resilient C4ISR system, ensuring that the ROC forces have an ability to weather a Chinese first strike and counterstrike with its own missile barrages, enabling Taipei to shoot Beijing's own 'archers and arrows'.[57] The experience of the United States in the Scud Hunt in Iraq should caution against prejudging the abilities of determined forces to conceal their activities from an enemy space power exploiting the hostile coastline of Earth orbit.

China may struggle to 'win' the war in a bold surprise attack along the lines of a Space Pearl Harbor because the best chances of success in Phase 1 requires achieving maximum surprise on ROC defences, as the object of the war is the control and occupation of Taiwan, not disabling American military power for its own sake. A first strike against American assets will surrender any element of surprise on terrestrial Taiwanese forces, which have planned to absorb and withstand 'out of the blue' missile and bomber attacks from China.[58] It also risks triggering a robust will to resist from Taiwan. The PLA will have to engage in continuous and successive bombing sorties to ensure it has hit enough of the correct targets so that it can engage in Phase 2 of its plan, where the bulk of the PLA's forces needed for the eventual conquest of Taiwan will be the most vulnerable, and a tempting focal point for a sustained counterattack from Taiwan, and the United States. Attrition, replacements and reserves can be called in by Taiwan, and China too cannot rely on only the 'tip of the spear' – its most modernised units – to win the war. The primary political objective requires the capitulation of Taiwan's government and military, which requires a complete surprise attack against ROC forces to maximise the chances of that occurring. Yet a Space Pearl Harbor strategy risks diluting, dividing and backfiring on China's efforts on Taiwan and American targets, falling foul of Clausewitz's usual advice to not divide one's efforts. This severely complicates the picture for advocates of a space first strike.

For Beijing, terrestrial surprise against the Taiwanese government may be at a higher premium than catching the relatively more sluggish and distant United States Navy and its supporting space infrastructure off-guard. Sinking the ROC Navy and its long-range interdiction capabilities with an attack out of the blue may well be a higher priority than attacking US forces afloat, as it would take time for American vessels to become relevant to the Taiwanese theatre. This would be evermore the case should the United States expect that any major Chinese offensive would only take place once China had achieved a working command of space because America is expecting a Space Pearl Harbor first. Proposition VI stresses the human and paradoxical nature of war: expect the unexpected and prepare for what the enemy has not. War is a terrifying gamble conducted within a thick, horrifying and paralysing fog of uncertainties.

A strike against space systems at the outset of hostilities or manoeuvres may not be necessary or inevitable because of the needs and conditions of the terrestrial campaign, which in this case has to take into account Phase 2 of a Taiwan war, as well as Taiwan's ability to parry or blunt the dispersing effects of spacepower through precision Chinese strikes. All propositions of spacepower theory can condense Phase 1 thusly: neither China nor America need to threaten each other's command of space and celestial lines of communication at all times (I and IV) to do what they need to do in Phase 1; all sides may wish to avoid escalation and seek to counter and exploit only what elements of space systems that they need (II); and an all-out strike in space and on Earth will not guarantee Taiwan's capitulation (III). Calling the other side's bluff over non-escalation, or to do the unexpected or something out of character (VI) can stall the use of a first strike, as the cosmic coastline need not turn hostile and attack the enemy's dispersion until a more critical moment, which may come in Phase 2 (VII). As the war drags on into Phases 2 and 3, however, third parties and economic costs may come about as escalation occurs and stop-gaps or workarounds by China and the US with allies and private space actors may draw more celestial lines of communication into the firing line in the crowded cosmic coastline (IV and V), threatening other space powers' abilities to command space and exploit its dispersing influence (I and VII).

Phase 2: Peak vulnerability and Counterspace in Being

To invade Taiwan, China will need space systems to retain a credible threat for carrying out Phase 2 – amphibious operations and landing – after blunting and parrying the worst of the ROC's high-end long-range counterstrike capabilities. China has reason not to conduct an all-out attack on American space assets and terrestrial forces so that it can persuade America to stay out of the conflict, and take Taipei with minimal resistance and maximum surprise. China can still control space without necessarily having to deny America's control of space – showing how both top-tier space powers can enjoy significant degrees of the control of space infrastructure as Proposition I considered, should both sides choose not to attack, harass or manipulate each other's celestial lines of communication as Proposition IV detailed. Even should China succeed in forestalling any immediate American actions, Proposition III stands ready to apply the brakes onto any thinking of a fait accompli or easy win for Beijing. Taiwan's war plans specifically undermine the perceived advantages gained by a surprise attack, whether it is in space or on Earth, and the ROC plans to provide an afterpressure and counterstrike following any large action or conflagration. Clausewitz's insistence on the strength of the defensive form of war still provides options for Taiwan's defensive war plans, plans that China must take into account and thus preventing it from focusing all its resources on attacking deep into American support bases across the Pacific. Qualifying his understanding of the ideal attack of an encamped army, Clausewitz cautioned that:

> even when . . . these results are considerable, they will still seldom lead the success yielded by victory in a decisive battle. In the first place, the trophies are seldom as great, and, second, the moral effect cannot be estimated so highly . . . This general result must always

be kept in view, so that we may not promise ourselves more from an enterprise of this kind than it can give. Many consider it to be the *non plus ultra* of offensive activity, but it is not so by any means.[59]

Not only is the defender not so helpless or strategically vulnerable to such attacks under the dispersing influence of spacepower from a hostile celestial coastline as some may believe, the PLA itself is also planning for operations that do not necessitate a Space Pearl Harbor stratagem. Within the PLA, there is strategising occurring over timing acts of space warfare to coincide with efforts, manoeuvres and PGM salvos on Earth. This is a contrast to the opening blows of a conflict in a Space Pearl Harbor strategy where American forces are struck en masse at the outset of a conflict. There is also a strain of thought about persistent and successive rounds of PGM salvos after the first moment of hostilities in the literature on a US–China war, and they provide an opening to conceptualising the use of counter-space operations as one of many options that can be deployed when terrestrial circumstances require it.[60]

The PLA's thinking is not fixated upon a Space Pearl Harbor or use-it-or-lose-it mentality:

> military texts limit the need for gaining air, information, and space superiority to a 'certain time and space' necessary to satisfy tactical, operational, or strategic objectives. Air, information, and space superiority is viewed as a means for achieving campaign (or strategic) objectives – not as an end in itself.[61]

This passage draws out several points. First, it may increase the attractiveness of a Space Pearl Harbor strategy for China, given that it may not be able to win a long war when American strategic depth and its superior dispersing influence is brought to bear on terrestrial PLA forces (Propositions V and VII), thus increasing the time bought through a greater severity and ferociousness of a space assault against American space infrastructure at the outset. However, the counter-current from this dilemma for China is that it may not wish to provoke the United States into such a long war along the very lines of the original Pearl Harbor attack in 1941, and will perhaps reduce its initial space assaults and keep forces in being to generate effects at a more critical moment when needed by terrestrial Chinese forces. Crucially, it reiterates that Proposition I – the command of space – is not an all-or-nothing matter. Selective degrees of command leave open the options of selective space engagements to secure the desired degree of space control and denial, rather than a major comprehensive strike against American space assets.

Both the Space Pearl Harbor and the Counterspace-in-Being strategies are possibilities that must be geared towards the needs of the both sides' space infrastructure and terrestrial warfare. A simple incentive to hold a counterspace campaign in reserve is that its timing can be used to increase the terrestrial consequences of the loss of space support at a crucial time for the enemy. This would be a strong incentive to conduct strategic manoeuvres with spacepower and with assets in Earth orbit to maximise the return on one's efforts in terrestrial theatres, as well as to not alienate the international community and disturb global economic activity (Proposition V). The PLA will still need to use its space assets to maximise its suppression efforts against ROC forces and ensure that they cannot concentrate their firepower on vulnerable PLA amphibious forces which would be massing at muster points on mainland China. The ROC could use uncrewed aerial vehicles (UAVs) and other terrestrial assets as stopgaps for short-range ISR, such as the *Tien Sun* battlespace surveillance system.[62] The PLA plans to force amphibious landings in the face of persistent ROC air and naval threats, and there would be a great deal of pressure on the SSF to provide space-based intelligence on ROC strikes for PLA forces that would have to concentrate on specific beaches and beachheads.[63]

American aircraft, ships and satellites will go near if not through China's anti-access and area denial zones or cones of vulnerability towards the Taiwan theatre. Once US forces have been committed in bulk to Taiwan, they would make for easier targets to find and threaten due to them necessarily being within certain ranges of their objectives on Taiwan. US forces would be more vulnerable the closer they are to Taiwan, especially when amphibious operations to reinforce the Taiwanese resistance take place. Chinese anti-ship missile capabilities – whether ballistic, cruise or 'hypersonic' – are unlikely to be the one-shot one-kill option, meaning that PLA commanders need to maximise the chances of success of hitting an American carrier strike group. The likely limited number of ASBMs and other hypersonic speed weapons available for a salvo and possible US Navy countermeasures and point-defence systems will complicate the missions of standoff munitions salvos. This task should be easier closer to China as other ground and aerial sources can come into play, and if Taiwanese defence and interception systems have been worn down.[64] The Chinese desire to challenge an American command of space through aggressive denial measures will increase as the US task force converges and concentrates in relative terms around Taiwan, opening them up to the dispersing influence of Chinese space control and precision weapons. Denying American spacepower at this time will make US forces easier targets and more likely to suffer losses. This in turn increases the American desire to do the same in return as Chinese concentration is occurring at mustering points to invade Taiwan. Both sides here will have compelling rationales to launch PGM salvos which rely on spacepower, whilst also wishing to undermine the other side's spacepower in order to degrade that salvo and to make them more susceptible to their own PGM barrages in defined geographic areas. This is when terrestrial needs are influencing the potential pattern of space warfare, where all of spacepower and the command of space must be subordinated to Terran politics and strategy, as outlined in Proposition I. It is at this moment of peak vulnerability that US strategic warning satellites may be targeted, reducing ballistic missile warning and tactically relevant infrared data from the SBIRS. This could cause fears of a prelude to a nuclear strike due to the entanglement of nuclear warning systems with tactical ISR space assets.[65]

At this moment of peak terrestrial vulnerability, the PLA forces are mustering for an invasion, which would have to operate under the dispersing influence of a PGM salvo – whether real or threatened – launched by the ROC and possibly long-range American bombers. Preserving, presenting and carrying out a credible threat of being able to do that is the Counterspace-in-Being strategy. This would be a moment of opportunity for America and Taiwan to significantly degrade a Chinese command of space, in particular Chinese space control, to maximise their own dispersing influence of spacepower and poke holes in the Chinese A2/AD zones of fire through disrupted lines of communication and imposing a cone of vulnerability towards PLA forces themselves. This illustrates a strategic manoeuvre in the hostile cosmic coastline. This phase may even witness the kinetic destruction of specific Chinese satellites to ensure that the Chinese flank in the cosmic coastline is definitely exposed, as up until this point it is likely that aggressive yet localised electronic warfare would have been taking place against various celestial lines of communication on all sides, with mixed results.

The elaborate and powerful jamming necessary to target American space intelligence assets would give away the locations of Chinese jammers across the Pacific and merely invite a counterattack from an American PGM salvo or counter-jamming against the Chinese jammers. This leads to the possibility that 'China would either have to abstain from attempting to counter US space-based ISR or escalate to non-reversible effects attacks that it could execute from the mainland without revealing the locations of its naval forces'.[66] Electronic warfare is a dynamic game of cat and mouse or action and reaction, and given its extreme secrecy it is impossible to forecast the balance of capabilities here. However, it is not always clear how the United States may respond, particularly if jamming occurs at a time and in a manner where the effects may be mistaken for accidental or 'tolerable' jamming. Further complicating this, and according to PLA writings, because soft-kill systems cannot permanently destroy physical facilities, one must rely on hard-kill systems to inflict a long-lasting impact on enemy space capabilities. Hard kill is the most reliable way to be sure. Computer network infiltration and disruption is often a one-use weapon highly tailored towards the weaknesses of a particular system and not something that can be repeated or deployed en masse across diverse space systems. Once alerted, the defender can patch the system, reboot or take other countermeasures and not fall to the same hacking attempt twice. Confirming a successful computer network operation may not be as easy as physical weapons fire. Due to the political and environmental risks of hard kill, soft-kill methods are useful in providing more options that may better suit the escalation or effects desired.[67] This stresses the point that the diversity in methods and targets in space warfare makes a strategy seeking to deliver a single decisive blow that may disable the entirety of the US military in the Pacific for a significant period of time, akin to Pearl Harbor, a daunting prospect.

It is at this point in Phase 2, whilst both sides must concentrate their terrestrial forces around Taiwan or at mustering points, that the United States could have a strong incentive to strike at Chinese space assets in order to dismantle, degrade, disrupt or outright destroy essential components of the kill chain supporting China's long-range strike systems and the maritime assets it will require to cover its amphibious forces at their moment of peak vulnerability to ROC and possibly American PGMs and air forces. PLA forces cannot disperse when storming islands, demonstrating that concentration is still an important feature of modern warfare, and one option to respond is to return to excessive mass deployments and absorb PGM salvos. Geography still matters, despite the advent of spacepower. Landing beaches in Taiwan's main island can be reduced down to a small handful of likely locations, further concentrating efforts and challenging the requirement to disperse in the face of a hostile celestial coastline in orbit. Electronic warfare and directed energy weapons may in fact be more useful than kinetic interceptors in parrying the blow of a PGM salvo by increasing the error rates in targeting and guidance systems.[68] Counterspace operations may occur days after the initial Chinese SRBM strikes on Taiwan, and skirmishes between scouting submersible units, UAVs, forward-deployed Special Forces and regular forces in and around Taiwan. Politically, bearing in mind Propositions V and VI, hitting mainland Chinese targets would be a more acceptable action for the United States in Phase 2, domestically and internationally, if they were taken to protect American service personnel as well as Taiwanese military capabilities during Phase 1 of the war. If the body count increases, the relative consequences of destroying machines in space may seem of small ethical consequence.

There may be an incentive not to shoot satellites first if one side thinks they can weather successive rounds of a PGM salvo and exhaust the enemy's supply of PGMs, whilst retaining the ability to meet the objectives of the campaign in the aftermath.

This is precisely how the ROC military intends to survive China's Phase 1 hammer blow and force the PLA into Phase 2 of the campaign, allowing the ROC to bring much of its combat capability and defensive advantages into play. Spacepower's influence upon a Taiwan contingency is most acutely felt through its function as the backbone of a PGM 'salvo competition', of which any space warfare acts must impact to have any strategic or political meaning. Throughout this competition various elements of the Counterspace-in-Being strategy's assets must be deployed as necessary. Successive salvos can continue throughout Phases 1 and 2, and are not necessarily just a feature of the opening blows of a conflict. Gunzinger and Clark argue that

> combatants in a salvo competition will each seek to improve their ability to defeat salvos by using a mix of active and passive countermeasures that degrade its opponent's precision-strike 'kill chain'. A blinding campaign that combines cyber, electronic warfare, and physical attacks on China's weapons and C4ISR networks could greatly reduce the effectiveness of its salvos.[69]

Denying a foe's space support, and their ability to impose dispersion and the effect of mass on the enemy as they need to concentrate physical forces just in time for a coordinated PGM salvo strike when the enemy's terrestrial forces are at their most vulnerable – and concentrated – may be a culminating point of an astrostrategy, and not a desperate all-or-nothing opening gambit. The support from the orbital coastline for terrestrial forces – translated at its hardest and most direct edge as dispersion through the use and threat of a PGM salvo – shows how major space warfare actions may happen at moments of peak terrestrial vulnerability for either side, and not during the opening moves of a Taiwan war. Phase 2 is an extremely dangerous one for the PLA. Amphibious forces are extremely vulnerable to interdiction; the ROC Navy and Air Force, with other strike assets, will take every opportunity to deny the Chinese any early warnings of incoming raids. Just when the PLA needs its space assets most, that is when the US military and ROC forces should deny them that space support and make outer space a hostile coastline for the invaders.

Believing the Space Pearl Harbor strategy to be the only course of action possible shrouds the possibility of an astrostrategy eschewing all-or-nothing first strikes in favour of a gradual escalation, or successive wave of follow-on space attacks. This eventuality is considered by some who favour the United States as a victor in a drawn-out non-nuclear war.[70] War does not consist of a single short blow, and everything is done with reference to the capabilities and preparations of the enemy and the potential counterattacks.[71] Such preparations include air platforms – and in particular UAVs – to act as workarounds, stopgaps or temporary measures for specific ISR services if space systems have been disrupted or destroyed.[72] Striking the enemy at their moment of peak vulnerability – using spacepower's ability to create the effect of mass firepower on the enemy whilst the other side must physically mass for a terrestrial objective – should not be seen as a decisive and finishing blow. Rather, it should be seen as a desirable moment to keep one's counterspace powder dry so as to inflict punishing losses that will help to determine the war's progress. Keeping counterspace forces in being for that moment is a plausible strategy. Chinese long-range missiles are solid-fuelled, road-mobile and concealed, and could be held in reserve on mainland China until called upon by a still-functioning reconnaissance-strike network at a later, perhaps more crucial, moment of the war when an enemy may be more vulnerable and unable to scatter in-theatre.[73] Taiwan and the United States themselves are hardening and dispersing their comparable strike assets.

Whilst Chinese geographic advantage over America is often noted, Taiwanese geographic advantages are often forgotten. Taking Taiwanese agency and geostrategic strength of Phase 2 into account demonstrates the challenge for China to pull off a Space Pearl Harbor attack against the United States, and the value China places on surprising ROC forces in Phase 1, increasing the attractiveness of a Counterspace-in-Being strategy. It is in Phase 2 that the ROC seeks to maximise its fighting power against the PLA and targets on PRC soil, even if it has suffered an attempted decapitation strike against the civilian leadership in Phase 1. Not only would the PLA have to land on Taiwan itself, but it would have to quell opposition on the many fortified islands that stand out in the Strait or near PRC territory.[74] The PLA will have to engage in multiple amphibious landings and operations before touching down on the main island of Taiwan to reduce the amphibious interdiction capabilities of the ROC. Whilst America and China may be mobilising for a significant strike against each other's space assets at the same time as the bulk of their maritime and ground forces are being concentrated, Taiwan here could have its best opportunity to inflict punishing losses on the PLA as it concentrates and musters amphibious forces to transit the Strait. This may encapsulate the most damaging part of the ROC's defence plan – *Gu'an* (solid and secure) – to inflict the greatest direct costs on the PLA before Taiwan succumbs to collapsed civilian infrastructure or starvation.[75] Through channelling PLA amphibious forces into specific beaches that are suitable for mass landings, and also by blocking off certain routes with mines and coastal defences, this would force the PLA to concentrate and fail to disperse in the face of ROC missile and air attacks.

The agency of Taiwanese decision makers in this matter challenges the concept of space as a barrier, as critiqued in Proposition IV. Due to Taiwan's proximity to mainland China, and its proximity to Chinese space systems in the cosmic coastline with soft-kill counterspace systems, Taiwan can ensure China struggles to take 'as much or as little' from the conflict as it wills through wilful escalation and a determination to retaliate until all methods of doing so are exhausted. This is a practical consequence of the littoral nature of Earth orbit as outlined in Proposition V, which undermines the rather imperial hopes of using space as a barrier as detailed in Proposition IV.

The chances of a successful single decisive blow diminish as the abstract absolutist nature of a Space Pearl Harbor assault on space systems is feared and has triggered the mitigation of potential damage of such an attack.[76] Holding counterspace forces in being, and not committing everything at once, is what coordinated space strikes aim to do for maximum effect on Earth. Like Corbett's fleet-in-being concept, a Counterspace-in-Being strategy does not advocate apathy from counterspace forces or that some space strikes should not be conducted in the early phases. Actions equivalent to skirmishes should be pursued if they are deemed feasible and beneficial. Counterspace in Being cautions against launching everything at the outset and encourages the strategist to consider maintaining a large capability until a critical moment approaches at a later time. Their continued existence and threat from deployment at any time, and continued strategic manoeuvring from uncommitted assets in space can affect the conduct of terrestrial wars, even in the absence of battle as discussed extensively in Propositions III and V.

Both approaches to space warfare have flaws and will not guarantee the keys to victory because 'war is no mere mathematical calculation, but an activity carried out in the dark, or at best, in a feeble twilight'.[77] The risks of failure can be great, especially if the forces sacrificed in a surprise attack are forever lost and the enemy recovers in the counterattack. The enemy may then enjoy a disproportionately larger psychological benefit from turning the tables.[78] The tension between seeking a decisive first strike through space warfare and of waiting and responding to the enemy's first moves is notable in Chinese doctrinal writings – but such tensions are unresolved as they are possibilities, not concrete actions.[79] Once war is afoot a prudent commander, 'even at the time he is still yielding ground, may have begun to operate against the communications of the assailant.'[80] Therefore the challenge with realising a Space Pearl Harbor strategy is not only that a complete barrier against ROC deep strike actions is unlikely, but also to succeed in simultaneously applying all forces which are available for the strategic object, 'will be so much the more complete the more everything is compressed into one act and into one moment'.[81] Such thinking also assumes that all enemy space assets are within weapons range – soft or hard kill – at the chosen moment for the surprise attack. Proposition II stresses that not all space systems will be within timely reach of weapons fire to support terrestrial operations, and there will always be the need for successive actions and plans for the 'afterpressure' of any offensive. In a Taiwan war, there are opportunities for successive action if ROC forces hold out during all phases, even should the capital of Taipei fall and they retreat into the mountainous and jungled interior. Such successive action on both sides could benefit from space support, and space assets should not all be recklessly thrown into the fires of war from the outset as a natural or assumed course of action.

Phase 3: Protracted conflict

The perceived calculations, risks and requirements of successive phases influence the planning and execution of the initial phase itself. What is required and expected in Phases 2 and 3 alters what is available and affordable to lose in Phase 1, and vice versa. Clausewitz noted this non-linear nature of war and planning, and warned 'that seeking exact analytical solutions does not fit the nonlinear reality of the problems posed by war'.[82] Before the very last option for defence in Phase 3, the ROC anticipates being able to draw on significant combat capabilities from its Army and what is left of its Air Force, which could still be drawn in at a critical moment, but not for sustained operations.[83] This complicates any linear planning by the PLA. The ROC would have the advantage of being able to focus efforts on PLA landing zones, and make use of fixed hardened defences and the difficult terrain to complicate Chinese space ISR capabilities, if significant assets remain.[84] Additionally, relatively accessible electronic warfare assets can tax the enemy's ISR capabilities by distracting them from their primary functions for target acquisition and forcing them to engage in a tit-for-tat struggle in the electromagnetic spectrum.[85] As ROC forces wage battles on the Taiwanese main island, commanders are taught to not allow PLA units unhindered access to space support, and one can expect significant and continuing electronic warfare and deception measures by the ROC to attempt to ward off and counter the dispersing effects of Chinese spacepower by poking holes in its celestial communications, providing breathing space for insurgency operations against larger and more cumbersome PLA units that cannot take advantage of the dispersing influence of spacepower.

The ROC's defenders are at a significant disadvantage if large numbers of PLA forces deploy on the main island. Once enough physical mass is ashore – divisions and brigades of heavy armour and scores of infantry regiments – the PLA will be able to exploit its superiority in numbers over the ROC and the efficiency gains provided by spacepower become less influential if the PLA can absorb ROC counteroffensives, manifesting one of the forms of blunting the dispersing pressures from the adversary in Proposition VII. That calculation on spacepower changes if American reinforcements are en route. At that time, China will still need a counterspace infrastructure to threaten American maritime and air assets, particularly to impose costs on US forces as they converge and concentrate within strike range on the approaches to Taiwan. If Phase 3 is reached without significant American involvement, the decision to attack an expeditionary US force remains for China in Phase 3. Vis-à-vis the Americans, the PRC will still be in Phase 1 if it has not lashed out at US military assets beyond the theatre before then. Both sides would face strong incentives to attack each other's space systems at this point, with the war well underway on Taiwan itself.

Should the PLA be forced to rely on its strengths in numbers and mass on the ground, it would open itself up to a PGM salvo from the United States. Should space-enhanced PLA forces be sent ashore, they will be smaller in number yet require greater support from Chinese space systems, increasing the payoff towards striking Chinese space infrastructure. Unless it was certain that the United States would not intervene, even the threat of such a strike would continue to impose a degree of dispersion and operational friction on the PLA, providing more breathing space for the ROC to exploit on the ground. This is a manifestation of Proposition V's strategic manoeuvres in space to trigger a more favourable redisposition of forces in the primary theatre. Indeed, the fear of the remnants of the ROC Air Force may encourage Chinese ground forces to plan to 'operate in dispersed groups, moving inland under cover of overwhelming fire support and air defense screens. They could otherwise be caught out on open roads and slaughtered by Taiwanese jets or helicopters held in reserve for final [counteroffensive] action.'[86] In this phase, the most significant spacepower support the ROC will probably be able to draw upon would be whatever tactically relevant ISR and communications systems the United States or other third parties can provide. If the United States is still intent on coming to the rescue of Taiwan, it will do so by having to not only break a Chinese air and maritime blockade of Taiwan but also undermining what remains of China's reconnaissance-strike infrastructure. Some argue that this phase is beyond the point where the Americans could pre-empt Chinese A2/AD in order to avoid such a scenario, and to 'do so would require sustained penetration of defended airspace on a scale that A2/AD will make cost-prohibitive'.[87] Yet the dependence of such capabilities on space systems, and the increase in American counterspace capabilities, should not cause such a case of fatalism if America commits to breaking Chinese maritime and missile forces. Another factor to consider is how much of the PLA's high-technology and most capable forces will have suffered attrition and 'wear and tear' during Phases 1 and 2, only then to face a far more formidable air and maritime foe with a comprehensive space infrastructure in its orbital flank. If the ROC forces can inflict a toll on the ability of the PLA exploit the dispersion of spacepower against the United States after days or weeks of fighting and missile salvos, it would mean that the United States need not be overly concerned with Propositions VII and I in such a scenario. The inability to exploit Proposition VII takes away the sting of an adversary's mastery of Proposition I – of commanding space in the first place – if the enemy's terrestrial forces cannot capitalise on supportive spacepower infrastructure.

The attrition of the PLA Air Force and SSF and the depletion of their precision ammunition stocks would be a significant factor in American chances of success, particularly if a ragged remnant go up against a fresh few dozen fifth-generation US fighter aircraft. Any successful American and Taiwanese efforts to degrade the computer systems managing Chinese weapon systems could also hurt the PLA's trust in their most high-technology equipment and create additional psychological problems. Taiwanese action can still play a role here, as the ROC can use its integrated air defence system – if enough of it has survived – to use 'the SAMs [surface-to-air missiles] to increase the costs of adversary air operations, a force-in-being approach that seeks to add an operational drag on potential aggressors without exposing the SAMs to too much attrition'.[88] However, such attritional approaches works both ways. PGMs can be depleted, but so can interceptor missiles and close-in weapon systems. Emphasising how the mirroring of high-technology capabilities may instil a return to mass militaries after decades of shrinking unit numbers, some analysts estimate that for an effective air defence capability, Taiwan needs SAMs that number in the thousands, and radars in their dozens.[89] As the twenty-first century progresses, the attritional effects Taiwan could place on Chinese air and maritime strike capabilities will be an important factor in American war planning. If the PLA has doubts over its ability to keep enough forces and assets in reserve to face the United States in Phase 3, it may increase the value of striking the United States first in space to impose attrition and friction before they arrive in-theatre in force. Expectations of one phase will inform plans in others. Given the non-linearity of war, strategists should not take the first step without thinking about the last.[90]

Looking beyond the contests of commanding space for battlefield operations on mainland Taiwan, in Phase 3 economic and civilian space infrastructure may increase in salience, as outlined in Proposition V. During Phase 3 some grand strategic considerations come to the fore in this scenario, as the economic and political interests of other space powers may become involved, through design or accident. Though Taipei may be able to inflict some short, sharp and sudden economic shocks on Beijing, in terms of spacepower it may take time for wider third-party and civilian economic and private assets to be commandeered, requisitioned or coerced into either side's war effort and divested from the opposing side, along the contours outlined in Proposition V. Imposing shutter controls could increase longer-term costs to the adversary if they relied more on foreign civilian or commercial imagery for up-to-date data. The pressure on neutral states, third parties and commercial space entities to provide data or services to the belligerents will increase if the space assets of either side are targeted, particularly in a Space Pearl Harbor scenario. The indirect space support that Taipei may be able to garner through international channels, most notably in the US commercial space sector if Washington permits it, could provide the ROC with some assistance in Phases 2 and 3. Phase 1 would be unlikely beyond existing intelligence cooperation agreements and practices as it would likely take time for a state or private company to risk Chinese wrath by lending aid to Taiwan during a time of war. European companies, the European Union and its member states in particular may be caught in a problematic situation of being able to supply information and data to Taiwan but not wishing to sour relations with China. If the United States is committed to the defence of Taiwan, American companies will likely be brought into the fold and used to support Washington's objectives as has been done in previous wars. The dilemmas of abused or armed neutrality will be keenly felt in the other space powers, notably the European Union, Russia, Japan, South Korea and India – if they wish to remain neutral, that is. Whilst China will no doubt be pressuring capable space powers and third parties to remain passive, Taiwan and America will likely wish to bring the support of others in through their own persuasion or coercion.

Should the stakes of the terrestrial war continue to increase as it drags on, there may be an increasing pressure on the United States to impose a space blockade – or at least an attempt to shut down established Chinese spaceports and launch pads. This would impose astroeconomic and direct military costs on China, if the United States could effectively control the most common routes of commerce into and within orbit, as detailed in Proposition IV. But it will not be able to create an impregnable barrier between China and Taiwan, due to their terrestrial proximity. If attacking launch sites is not an option, replacements and replenishments for lost Chinese satellites, or any scheduled to be launched, could be intercepted whilst in transit to the desired orbit or after it has reached its desired position, whereupon the United States could engage in soft- and hard-kill measures. As cautioned in Propositions IV and V, however, a total space blockade would be a gargantuan and novel undertaking, and throughout history many powers both great and small have not always been passive victims of blockades. This is typified by the reality of space as a cosmic coastline where Chinese counterspace systems could simultaneously attempt to neutralise American space systems whilst they are attempting to impose a blockade. This is not to predict the most likely course of action, but rather to include the spacepower element into longer-term and international political considerations of the scenario, which alongside economic costs will become more significant as the war drags on.[91] This kind of strategic manoeuvring in the cosmic coastline – aiming to shift the correlation of forces and tap into strategic depth in space through military, political and economic means to increase the odds of success on Earth – shows the proximate and subordinate nature of spacepower as long as Earth is the only habitat and economic resource of humanity.

Space warfare, and modern warfare on such a scale as could happen in Taiwan, is not something which would happen 'over there', or could be easily contained because one has a dominant command of space, as is implied when engaging with imperially dominated and British–American bluewater seapower analogies alone. The costs and political and environmental consequences of a major and protracted conflagration in modern warfare will affect all because of Earth's relatively shrunken geostrategic size, interconnected global economy, and the reliance of global operations and critical infrastructure in the cosmic coastline to human society and states. Should the worst come to pass in conventional military terms, even before considering a nuclear exchange, the loss of space services will be felt across Earth's economic and service infrastructure through either direct loss or the increased burdening of the remaining space infrastructure. The integration of the 'space coast' to the international system could assist or hinder attempts from either side to draw in external powers to or place pressure on the adversary. Unlike China's weapons systems which may be able to threaten commercial shipping throughout the two island chains,[92] China may be able to threaten astroeconomic warfare on a grander scale due to the global nature of celestial lines of communication in LEO and MEO, and their eventual overflights within Chinese counterspace cones of vulnerability and hostile coastal projections. The same will be true of American counterspace capabilities, threatening Chinese commercial operations in space. The clash of spacepowers over Taiwan may well draw in outside space powers given the proximate nature of spacepower in Earth orbit.

Manipulating shared and overlapping celestial lines of communication is a complex task that not only risks drawing in other powers but is also conditioned by terrestrial events. If merchant shipping in the seas around Taiwan have already been sunk by

Phase 3, it would be remarkable if there was a serious aversion to engaging in counterspace measures against astroeconomic and civilian targets in orbit. The loss of third-party or neutral human life at sea will condition the passions of the conflict as a whole, and will alter the perceived normative costs of beginning to destroy and disable satellites in orbit – which are only machines that generate indirect pain and suffering to humans if lost. If Taiwan, China or the United States behave in such a way that draws in outside powers through collateral damage or abused neutralities, Taiwan's insurgency operations against the PLA on their own soil may take on more global political–economic significance as space systems may continue to be relevant and targeted, enabling or constraining the prospects of strategic manoeuvres (Proposition V) depending on the exact conditions of the war and the way spacepower is used within it (Propositions II and IV). Such factors will shape battlefield successes, and also the tolerance of every side for continued hostilities until one side gives up and accedes to the suspension of open hostilities and the pursuit of war termination.

Conclusion

Whilst some of the Space Pearl Harbor fears can be alarmist, holding counterspace systems in reserve risks not taking advantage of the fact that space systems are most useful in the first two phases of the conflict. American fears of a Space Pearl Harbor may not be realised due to the necessity for the PLA to achieve complete surprise against ROC forces, which pose an immediate terrestrial threat to the PLA, rather than against distant US Navy and Air Force units. A bolt from the blue against American space systems risks putting ROC forces on high alert and the PLA will have lost its chance to impose a punishing surprise missile bombardment on a low-readiness ROC Air Force and Navy. Launching a massive physical strike against American space systems will be difficult to hide. Striking all targets in space, around Taiwan and in the wider Pacific theatre at the same time in a single blow will be harder still. Firing dozens of kinetic ASAT weapons is not instantaneous as it still takes time for missiles to reach orbital targets, especially as not all satellites that need to be taken out will be within range at the same time, and electronic and cyber warfare may not be as reliable a kill method, though it is in principle a faster method. It is not impossible to strike against American space systems whilst also bombarding Taiwan in the opening shots of the war. However, it risks simplifying Taiwan's political calculation and emotional response to fight to the last. It also forecloses a significant later attack on American space systems when terrestrial US would be more vulnerable and dependent on space systems as they approach in-theatre in later phases of the war. Hitting America hard, early on, may solidify American political will to turn its strategic depth from space into its full military–industrial potential, resonating somewhat with the after-effects of Pearl Harbor in 1941.

Conducting such massive strikes against American assets in space or across the Pacific could over-tax the PLA's ability to coordinate its capabilities, not least in the number of available long-range strike systems, to not only strike the very large number of American forces across the vast region at first, but also to conduct a mass bombing of Taiwan at the same time to achieve the desired level of surprise against ROC forces. If China focuses its terrestrial bombing on ROC forces, and also strikes at the same time against US space assets, it loses its element of surprise against terrestrial US forces which, if the political will is there, may be able to adapt or 'make do' with reduced space support whilst en route to the theatre. This would also provide more time for potential replacements or workarounds for space services to be deployed for American needs through allies, commercial providers and any sovereign US backups. This is time that America will have to conduct strategic manoeuvres and adapt to new conditions while its terrestrial forces head to the theatre. This is not to say that a Space Pearl Harbor is not going to happen, rather that it has trade-offs when considering it from the perspective of space-power, and potential alternatives in the way of Counterspace-in-Being strategies must be considered as other possibilities.

The two contrasting strategies examined in the literature are described as different options and possibilities to exploit and mitigate the dispersing effect of spacepower on modern warfare, and hint at far more possibilities of space warfare that will impact the war as a whole. This opens the door to understanding spacepower and the Taiwan scenario on its own terms, which pierces the general and broad nature of existing literature regarding US and Chinese military spacepower integration. Spacepower theory's propositions enable the reader to consider space-centric considerations of modern warfare across the three major phases of a Taiwan war, and how the increasing scale of the battlefield and the need to coordinate concentrated weapons fire – and to resist and blunt its effects – over greater distances is a continued military trend enabled by spacepower integration into terrestrial weapons platforms. Propositions I through VII have qualified the analysis of the campaign phases of the Taiwan war from the perspective of spacepower, and connected the operational considerations of space-dependent precision-strike warfare between America and China to higher-level strategic considerations of a Taiwanese war that can inform generalists. The Space Pearl Harbor and Counterspace-in-Being strategies show the benefits and drawbacks of both strategies as they strive to exploit or resist the dispersing influence and efficiency gains of spacepower. As China and the United States develop newer ways of exploiting and resisting the dispersing influence of spacepower, a continuous reassessment is needed on whether a front-loaded space assault and turning terrestrial warfare to the tempo of a Space Pearl Harbor would pay more dividends than holding a large space warfare campaign in reserve for terrestrial needs. Proposition I will remain valid, however, as any act of space warfare has to be relevant to the war and political objectives at hand, and never undertaken for its own sake. The Pearl Harbor astrostrategy has its strengths, but Clausewitz's observation that the 'vague ideas of sudden attack and surprise, which in the attack are commonly thought to be rich sources of victory, and which in reality do not occur except in special circumstances' should qualify any confidence in offensively minded astrostrategists.[93] Proposition II stresses the need to identify any such special circumstances in space to realise the opportunity for a decisive battle or singular stroke against a centre of gravity, which Proposition III cautions as an often illusory ideal. The phases of this campaign demonstrate a rebuttal of thinking along the lines of a centre of gravity and an acceptance of attrition, imposing costs, continuing to fight in a degraded infrastructural environment, and keeping forces in being until a later, more critical moment. There is no expectation that fighting would end in the face of large strikes against space systems.

Spacepower theory's propositions draw out the geocentric subordination and terrestrial proximity of spacepower. Terrestrial considerations will remain the primary theatre of warfare for the foreseeable future, as elucidated in Propositions V and VI. This geocentrism of strategy in the era of spacepower means that any act of space warfare is about exploitation and denying the efficiencies, strategic depth and dispersion that spacepower imposes on modern warfare. Together, Propositions IV and V assert that the intensity of space warfare should be in part determined by the dependency of meeting objectives on celestial lines of communication, which are never absolute as celestial lines of communication are not the only geographic lines of communication. This secondary and ancillary nature of spacepower in Earth orbit, whilst humanity remains a planetary civilisation, resembles the role of seapower in continental wars as opposed to seapower in imperial, island-based and ocean-spanning powers. Proposition VII highlights how a Space Pearl Harbor and a Counterspace-in-Being strategy are most likely to employed when the dispersing consequences and effects of the command of space need to be exploited or denied for terrestrial effects. A sudden massive strike against space systems may be the opening shots of a conflict if it suits the needs of terrestrial forces at a time of supreme vulnerability or opportunity. The advocates of spacepower must find their place within geocentric strategic cultures, as the requirements of defending or attacking space infrastructure is one strategic consideration alongside those of aerial, maritime and ground force requirements, and Terran needs will influence when, where and how space systems will be used and attacked.

This exercise also shows the more abstract subordination of space warfare to the universal logic of strategy. This instils a Clausewitzian way of thinking about space warfare. Whilst many analyses of counterspace operations in a China–US war tend to favour one approach over the other, any confidence on which strategy is most likely should be qualified by comprehending this Clausewitzian nature of war and the messages of Propositions III and VII which express the uncertainties and action-reaction dynamics in the command and exploitation of space. The seven propositions have shown the grounds on which these strategies can be assessed, and the 'winning' or most likely strategy to be employed is impossible to predict or prescribe, especially as material conditions – such as ammunition stocks and readiness – are in perpetual flux. Yet for analysts, such particular detail can be placed in a larger framework of strategic comprehension and analysis. The nonlinearity and uncertainty of war should remind analysts that this is the business of charting possibilities and probabilities, and not guaranteeing war-winning strategies for decision makers. This is indeed the purpose and essence of strategic theory, and this spacepower theory has hopefully instilled a better way of thinking about space warfare in the twenty-first century. Spacepower theory is about determining the principles upon which space strategies can be built; it is clear that A2/AD warfare, or planning for wars with and against spacepower and in utilising counterspace capabilities, hinges upon the realisation of the dispersing influence of satellites from the celestial coastline.

Notes

1. Hunter, 'The forgotten'.
2. Cheng, 'Prospects for China's Military Space Efforts', pp. 211–18.
3. Easton, *Able Archers*, p. 24.
4. Easton, *The Chinese Invasion Threat*, pp. 95, 201.
5. US DoD, 'Annual Report to Congress', p. 25.
6. Committee on Armed Services for the U.S. House of Representatives, 'Commission to Assess United States National Security Space Management and Organization', pp. 22–3.
7. For example, see: Wortzel, *The Dragon*; Woolf, 'Conventional Prompt Global Strike'; Acton, 'Escalation'; Gompert et al., *War with China*; Krepinevich, *Maritime Competition*.
8. Pollpeter, 'Space', p. 715.
9. Wortzel, 'The Chinese People's Liberation Army', p. 127.
10. Wortzel, *The Dragon*, p. 32.
11. Cheng, 'China's Military Role in Space', p. 73
12. Easton, *The Great Game*, p. 3.

13. Ibid. p. 8.
14. Easton, 'China's Evolving Reconnaissance-Strike Capabilities', p. 5.
15. Woolf, 'Conventional Prompt Global Strike', p. 2.
16. Krepinevich, *Maritime Competition*, p. 17.
17. Pollpeter, 'Space', p. 714.
18. Solomon, 'Maritime Deception', p. 95.
19. Erickson, 'Chinese Air- and Space-Based ISR', p. 110.
20. Hagt and Durnin, 'Space', p. 737.
21. Ibid. p. 757.
22. Heginbotham et al. *The U.S.-China Military Scorecard*, pp. 159–64.
23. Easton and Stokes, 'China's Electronic Intelligence', p. 4.
24. Wortzel, *The Dragon*, pp. 37–40.
25. Erickson, 'Chinese Air- and Space-Based ISR', pp. 90, 106.
26. Cheng, 'China's Military Role in Space', p. 66.
27. Handberg, 'Is Space War Imminent?', p. 419.
28. On White Cloud, see: Easton and Stokes, 'China's Electronic Intelligence', pp. 2–4.
29. Easton and Stokes, 'China's Electronic Intelligence', pp. 14–16.
30. Krepinevich, *Maritime Competition*, p. 12.
31. Ibid. pp. 33–4.
32. Ibid. p. 45.
33. Heginbotham et al., *The U.S.-China Military Scorecard*, pp. 235–8.
34. Cheng, 'China's Military Role in Space', p. 73.
35. Pollpeter, 'Space', p. 726.
36. Ibid. p. 726.
37. Clausewitz, *On War*, p. 867.
38. Ibid. p. 876.
39. Wawro, *Warfare*, p. 225.
40. Gunzinger and Clark, *Winning*, p. 2.
41. Clausewitz, *On War*, p. 861.
42. Ibid. pp. 609, 785.
43. Easton, 'China's Evolving Reconnaissance-Strike Capabilities', pp. 19–20; Heginbotham et al., The *U.S.-China Military Scorecard*, pp. 62–7.
44. Gunzinger and Clark, *Winning*, pp. 13–15.
45. Solomon, 'Maritime Deception', p. 90.
46. Krepinevich, *Maritime Competition*, pp. 72–4.
47. Easton, *The Chinese Invasion Threat*, pp. 183–4.
48. Easton, *Able Archers*, p. 48; Easton, *The Chinese Invasion Threat*, p. 120.

49. Easton, *Able Archers*, p. 48.
50. Easton, *The Chinese Invasion Threat*, p. 222.
51. Easton, *Able Archers*, pp. 52–5.
52. Ibid. p. 47.
53. Easton, *The Chinese Invasion Threat*, p. 7.
54. Ibid. p. 146.
55. Gompert et al., *War with China*, pp. 2–3.
56. Murray, 'Revisiting Taiwan's Defense Strategy', p. 29.
57. Easton, *Able Archers*, pp. 25–7, 39.
58. Ibid. p. 47.
59. Clausewitz, *On War*, pp. 877–8.
60. For example: Cheng, 'Prospects for China's Military Space Efforts'; Cliff et al., *Shaking the Heavens and Splitting the Earth*; Heginbotham et al., *The U.S.-China Military Scorecard*; Erickson, 'Chinese Air- and Space-Based ISR'; Biddle and Oelrich, 'Future Warfare'; Lostumbo et al., *Air Defense*.
61. Cliff et al., *Shaking the Heavens and Splitting the Earth*, p. 49.
62. Easton, *Able Archers*, p. 42.
63. Easton, *The Chinese Invasion Threat*, pp. 98, 125–30.
64. Heginbotham, *The U.S.-China Military Scorecard*, pp. 166–70.
65. Acton, 'Escalation', pp. 57, 64.
66. Heginbotham, *The U.S.-China Military Scorecard*, p. 256.
67. Cheng, 'Prospects for China's Military Space Efforts', pp. 220–1.
68. Gunzinger and Clark, *Winning*, p. iii.
69. Ibid. pp. 11, 13.
70. Heginbotham, *The U.S.-China Military Scorecard*, p. 198.
71. Clausewitz, *On War*, p. 269.
72. Erickson, 'Chinese Air- and Space-Based ISR', pp. 90–109; Heginbotham et al., *The U.S.-China Military Scorecard*, pp. 220–1.
73. Easton, 'China's Evolving Reconnaissance-Strike Capabilities', pp. 6–7.
74. Easton, *The Chinese Invasion Threat*, pp. 113–20.
75. Ibid. p. 198.
76. Clausewitz, *On War*, p. 269.
77. Ibid. p. 861.
78. Ibid. p. 475.
79. Wortzel, *The Dragon*, p. 95–6.
80. Clausewitz, *On War*, p. 863.
81. Ibid. p. 433.
82. Beyerchen, 'Clausewitz', p. 61.
83. Lostumbo et al., *Air Defense*, p. xi.

84. Easton, *The Chinese Invasion Threat*, p. 229–33.
85. Wilgenbusch and Heisig, 'Command and Control Vulnerabilities', p. 61.
86. Easton, *The Chinese Invasion Threat*, pp. 135–6.
87. Biddle and Oelrich, 'Future Warfare', p. 14.
88. Lostumbo et al., *Air Defense*, p. 20.
89. Ibid. p. 69.
90. Clausewitz, *On War*, p. 908.
91. Gompert et al., *War with China*, p. 7.
92. Ibid. p. 44.
93. Clausewitz, *On War*, p. 860.

Conclusion: Spacepower and International Relations

Spacepower's time has come. The deployment and use of machines in Earth orbit influences the conduct of modern warfare and perceptions over the balance of power in the international system. Yet the use of space technology and the 'geo' politics of space continues to be a marginalised material reality in IR. To attempt to redress this somewhat, this book has built on existing space-power theories and provided an original and rigorous theory of spacepower based on seven propositions, the vision of Earth orbit as a celestial coastline, and an application of that theory to demonstrate the influence of spacepower upon a scenario of modern warfare. Regardless of the actor or of the exact space warfare capabilities and basing locations, this theory should structure creative and critical thought about how spacepower influences modern warfare, and how the universal logics of war influence our thought about space warfare itself. Not only does the theory intend to educate the reader in the qualities of spacepower and the dynamics of space warfare on the strategic level, but also to instil a Clausewitzian way of thinking about the conduct of war in the Space Age. Space cannot be reduced to the simplistic 'high ground' as often described in public commentary on military space activities, yet the advantages derived from space infrastructure for tactical military capabilities cannot be denied. The seven propositions and the coastal analogy have instead probed the more nuanced complexities of war in Earth orbit and terrestrial warfare under the influence of spacepower and orbital infrastructures.

It is hoped that the new overarching view of Earth orbit as a celestial coastline, rather than an open ocean, along with the seven propositions have provided something of a 'Mahan for the final frontier'. Mahan himself continues to provide much useful insight through the careful use of strategic analogies. Useful theoretical truths are provided across seven propositions which should advance spacepower theory scholarship on strategy and IR in space by placing it on more robust conceptual footings. Space warfare is political and still 'warfare', wars on Earth may not be decided solely by what happens in space, space may not necessarily be where a war begins, and spacepower will likely continue to be neglected and subordinated in the strategic cultures of Terran states.

Proposition I established that acts of space warfare must contribute to a command of space, which can constitute controlling space infrastructure and/or denying its use. That command of space in turn must serve terrestrial political goals for those who possess it. Proposition II articulated the need to grasp the unique attributes of the Earth orbit environment, how spacepower as we know it is infrastructural in its primary quality (as opposed to combat-platform centric) and is not isolated from Earth. Proposition III pushed against the common notion that commanding space would lead to a domination of Earth and cautioned against an excessive focus on seeking battle or the destruction of space systems as an axiom for strategists and war planners who often seek the enemy's centre of gravity. Proposition IV detailed how celestial lines of communication knit together the components of space infrastructure and where and how commanding space can be achieved by prioritising chokepoints and high-value positions in Earth orbit and from Earth's surface. These first four propositions moderated existing spacepower theories, often drawn from bluewater seapower theories, conjuring the notion of Earth orbit as analogous to an expansive ocean and providing the necessary foundation for the following propositions.

Proposition V projects an analogy of Earth orbit as a cosmic coastline where Earth orbit and the surface are littoral zones where strategic manoeuvres are required to tap into the more subtle supporting effects of spacepower. The insights of continental seapower theory theorise often-neglected aspects of spacepower as supporting infrastructure. As a littoral zone suitable for strategic manoeuvres, spacepower in Earth orbit resembles the use of seapower by continental states rather than maritime powers. Proposition VI continued this continental analogy by theorising the cultural aspects of spacepower in a geocentric reality – what happens in space is only relevant in how it affects Earth. This geocentrism means that terrestrial threats and perspectives tend to override space-centric ones. 'Space forces' may struggle to win bureaucratic and resource struggles against terrestrial counterparts. This is analogous to the strategic cultures of continental states and the oft-neglected status of their navies. Proposition VII brought the theory to a head by drawing out the 'so what' from the strategic level and more abstract discussions of spacepower. It theorised the influence of spacepower on modern warfare as a dispersing influence, continuing a long trend of increasing firepower coordination capabilities with an ever-increasing battlefield size. It also considered how concentration and dispersal are still relevant concepts for studying war in the age of the hostile celestial coastline. The Taiwan war analysis briefly showed how space warfare is not immune to the needs of terrestrial wars. It also demonstrated a systemic way of encouraging geographic-specific thought without undermining the need for 'joint' and 'combined' warfare thinking and placing space strategy in its own silo. The seven propositions demonstrate how two competing strategies for space warfare rest upon a tension between when to exploit and when to deny the dispersing effects of spacepower, and portrayed those strategies as possibilities and ideals, rather than inevitabilities.

The Taiwan war scenario brings the book back full circle to the larger point made in Chapter 1 and the Introduction, which outlined the significance of space activities for IR. Terran politics and the international system shapes the use of outer space, and in turn space infrastructure has become essential to military and economic power and therefore a potential target in wartime. Accepting that space warfare is the continuation of Terran politics gives old theories and concepts regarding human political experience new life in the most novel of environments, and that systemic and unquantifiable political considerations must accompany analyses of space warfare – not technical sterility and mechanistic considerations of space-based weapons. Not only does this allow the canon of strategic theory to be intelligently transplanted into astropolitics, but can also strengthen other efforts to explore outer space with IR theories and its many sub-disciplines. Scholars of strategy engage with the practical considerations of power, should any two actors come to serious blows against each other. Any discussion of balancing, deterrence and anarchy in IR cannot ignore the calculations made and possibilities created by crossing the Rubicon into violent action and destructive measures.

Scholars of IR must grapple with the notion that space has become an adjunct to the security and well-being of states. Only much later it may become an environment worth controlling for its own sake. In the meantime, the most useful and affordable space technologies will continue to spread from where it originated and into the hands of more actors.[1] An 'immediate goal is to gain a greater understanding of how IR theory can (and does) inform our thinking about the near-term space issues, notably how space shapes the power of Earthly states'.[2] Political and strategic discussions of spacepower have to acknowledge that the influence of spacepower upon history and the present is through the relatively subtle and unspectacular supporting space infrastructure, not by cyclically debating whether the United States should deploy weapons in orbit at the expense of every other aspect of astropolitics and spacepower. Brute material forces and capabilities still matter – maintaining energy and food production and distribution systems still matter. Such things are increasingly dependent on space systems, and high-end technological capabilities are diffusing away from the United States and into an increasingly non-unipolar distribution of essential strategic technologies and infrastructure. Across the major states and economies of Earth 'policy goals . . . to utilize space for security, economic development, and prestige purposes have been unremitting'.[3] Scholars of IR ignore such material realities at their peril. Looking ahead, a key agenda for research in IR, its subdisciplines, and related disciplines in the humanities and social sciences is to examine space activities, past and present, in their own right and how they reinforce and challenge our geocentric international system, politics, habits and worldviews. Journals such as *Astropolitics* and *Space Policy* are building a large library of research and argumentation on politics and policy in space, yet space-related articles in 'mainstream' journals and full-length research monographs are rare. Whilst astropolitics is a continuation of terrestrial politics, it is just as diverse and complex as terrestrial politics, and the disciplinary lenses we use will shape research and perspectives on it.

Spacepower is an important and diverse source and manifestation of power in the international system, and previous assessments of spacepower have too simplistically accounted for space capabilities as either 'military' or 'civilian' satellites.[4] Such a distinction is problematic as the exact capabilities derived from satellites can be used for the objectives of war, development and prestige. Through the lens of spacepower, there is perhaps an increasing justification to think in terms of multipolarity, or at the very least not in uni- or bipolarity. A continuing debate in IR is whether America can still be considered a hegemon, and whether the era of unipolarity has given way to multipolarity, or something else. The distribution of power is changing but scholars cannot agree on a current condition of unipolarity or multipolarity.[5] Regardless of polarity, spacepower may exhibit a form of 'soft balancing' where centres of power beyond the US are building 'diplomatic and economic means to counter American power'.[6] Yet as demonstrated throughout this book and more forcefully in Chapters 5 and 6, spacepower also enables 'hard balancing' against the United States. It has allowed increasing amounts of conventional military power and latent economic power to be deployed for the uses of America's most threatening potential adversaries. Military space technologies, once the purview of only the United States, have proliferated for decades and are now being deployed en masse and refined into successive follow-on generations. This has given new, conventional military options for committed powers to contest American influence at specific flashpoints.

This does not mean that an alleged era of American hegemony or unipolarity, in part underpinned by the space-enabled technologies of the so-called Revolution in Military Affairs, is necessarily over. Spacepower does not necessarily overturn or determine terrestrial politics, and to claim otherwise would violate Proposition III's commentary on the decisiveness of commanding space. Space-based weapons are not sufficient to ensure or undermine American power preponderance. Where the US maintains a preponderance of power, the theory goes, 'would-be rivals have strong incentives to accept the status quo of American primacy rather than to attempt to overturn the unipolar order'.[7] With the United States maintaining a significant lead in military capabilities, being protected in conventional military terms with two massive oceans and friendly and militarily weak landward neighbours, as well as not waging war against its primary rivals, talk of multipolarity may still be rather premature. The nuclear revolution means that great powers or rising superpowers would not see a major war as a suitable method to overturn the international system and throwing down American dominance of that system. Rather, that competition with the hegemon would have to happen on economic, diplomatic and cultural fronts whilst nuclear armed states can develop economically and present longer-term challenges to American preponderance.[8] Nevertheless, under the nuclear revolution spacepower is providing its silent yet steady pressure on some states who are now hard balancing the US with long-range precision-strike weapons and force modernisation.

These space-enabled precision warfare technologies, and strategies which exploit or counter such technologies, depend in large part on early warning, communications and guidance systems located in Earth orbit. Yet China and Russia, as the prime (but not only) proliferators of precision-strike weapons that stand to challenge American military primacy, are not only interested in space systems for the ends of modernising their military forces along the lines the Americans have demonstrated to the world since the 1990s. The space infrastructure proliferating within and from Earth's major economic blocs and continent-sized states has wider implications for the global political-economy and not just the military consequences as A2/AD literature focuses on. The ability of the United States to tap into allied military assets or friendly commercial assets and globalised capital to leverage international commercial space capabilities in a time of crisis or war[9] – mirroring Brooks and Wohlforth's arguments on continuing US terrestrial primacy based on globalised American capital[10] – further complicates any simplistic argument about American space hegemony and whether it is in decline. Moltz's point that China is a fast-follower in the development of spacepower, rather than an innovator, can be challenged with Pollpeter's analysis which details innovation as a specific goal of the reforms of the Chinese space industry.[11] Yet 'all countries, firms, individuals, with rare and unusual exceptions, have relied on others to invent, and have imitated more than they have invented'.[12] Whether innovation in and of itself is inherently better than imitation and adaptation is still an open question, or an uncritically adopted assumption in such debates. Spacepower can be interpreted as indicators of hard balancing as well as soft balancing against the United States, and more space-centric research is required to draw out the significance of these material trends for astropolitics and Terran power politics as whole.

Despite the strengths of American power, the spread of space infrastructure and Earth-based space weapons, and the continuing nuclear revolution makes the notions of American space dominance or empire extremely remote in a practical and grand strategic sense. The misplaced nature of these arguments on unquestioned space dominance and the geopolitical gaze in space were alluded to in Chapter 1 and continuously questioned throughout the seven propositions. Whilst it is true in space that 'rivals to the US, particularly China, hope to wear down the US by means of economic competition rather than military struggle' as exhibited by the continuous proliferation of industrial, infrastructural and commercial space activity beyond the United States, the belief that 'the US is so far ahead in terms of military capabilities and advanced technologies that potential rivals understand that a campaign of serious balancing is likely to require decades of onerous military expenditures' is increasingly challenged when delving into complexities of the proliferation of military and economic spacepower today.[13] The increasingly multipolar character of the distribution of spacepower in the international system is not an acute issue – it has been a chronic trend dating back decades and has been continuing silently whilst scholarship remains fixated on activities below the Kármán Line.

The general bipolarity of the Cold War and subsequent American unipolarity since 1991 does not reflect all the contours of the international history of spacepower. Russian and American counterspace and other military satellite efforts are picking up where they left off in the 1980s; yet China's civilian economy-oriented space modernisation and military technological innovation is a result of programmes initiated in the 1980s, after Nixon decided that there was 'no place on this small planet for a billion of its potentially most able people to live in angry isolation'.[14] The seeds of today's increasing multipolar nature of orbital spacepower were sown decades ago; India, China and Japan were early non-Western spacepowers, dating back to the 1970s and 1980s. Key space technologies have been proliferating for decades and preceded the fall of the Soviet Union in 1991 and the American 'unipolar moment'. Indeed, this longer and less polarised space-centric view is adopted by the space historian Brian Harvey, who wrote that:

> the early years of space . . . provided the world with a simple narrative: a life-and-death struggle between the Soviet Union and the United States . . . Barely noticed, other countries had already begun to build their space programs. Japan launched its first satellite in February 1970, followed by China (April 1970), and then India (1980). Israel followed in 1988. Earlier (1965), France inaugurated what evolved into Europe's extensive space program.[15]

Even with only a cursory glance at space history, it is very much a multinational one, if not multipolar, when considering the spread of new strategic technologies and the pursuit of industrial modernisation. Sensitive rocket and satellite technologies have long since spread to Europe, India and Japan, despite initial US technology controls.[16] Many states have sought to join the 'Space Club' of international relations from the Cold War to today, with the USA and USSR serving as its Cold War-era gatekeepers attempting to limit the spread of space technology to an elite club of space-faring states.[17] Today, India is a more independent and autonomous space power than the UK as the former has an established indigenous launch capability, whereas the latter must purchase launches from the open market or allies, creating something of an inverted postcolonial developmental relationship in a sovereign-material sense. Indeed, space technology was central to 'the emergence of a powerful postcolonial techno-nationalist ideology under the leadership of Nehru that signified the pursuit of space projects as normative indicators of the postcolonial state's power, status, and modernity'.[18] Particular geostrategic realities of outer space, now characterised by the spread of entrenched space technologies outside the United States and its allies, are often lost in top-level debates on the balance of power in the international system. Distributions of spacepower do not always reflect terrestrial conditions. The past and present of international politics in space requires far more interrogation from the scholarly community and dedicated astropolitical experts, rather than a casual and fleeting interest from IR scholars whose specialisms are overly geocentric in nature at the expense of not taking space on its own terms – violating Proposition II.

This book has shown how one area of theoretical insight – strategic theory and the question of war in IR – can be usefully transposed into space. Other areas of theory are ripe for the application to outer space as space becomes increasingly democratised and space technology continues to proliferate. No sweeping claim about the end of American security and influence is made here. Rather, it is that, like any specialisation, the waters begin to muddy once a material specialisation is chosen and thought moves on from the systemic-level views of IR theory and generic power distribution analyses. There is a responsibility on Terran disciplines and scholars to recognise the past and present of human activity in space, in how it has and continues to influence our perceptions of the world. This is particularly true as global governance in space, which will in part determine the future of orbital infrastructures that we rely upon, becomes a more frequent talking point in diplomatic and space-industrial circles.

Outer space is a place where human political intercourse continues. Space activities are increasingly influencing military and economic power on Earth. More states and non-state actors are using and developing the uses of Earth orbit. It is time IR acknowledged the material realities of the proliferation of spacepower and accord to it the same conceptual recognition and specialised knowledge it does to the exploitation of other strategic geographies on Earth. Doing so will remain a challenge as space continues to be a secondary environment compared to the primacy of Earth, and decision makers continue to be geocentric. Yet Terran wisdom should not be left at the launch pad. In terms of strategic thought and the conduct of IR, space may be a more 'familiar frontier' in terms of power politics, yet one that may be more multipolar than terrestrial accounts of the balance of power may suggest. Spacepower is defined by its quality as an infrastructure and a place that is used to communicate information and transport materials and effects, like other geographies, which is an inherently geocentric and political activity in relation to Earth. Humanity has only developed Earth orbit so far to play a part as critical infrastructure for the political-economy of Earth; it is merely dipping our species' toes into the cosmic shoreline. Events beyond Earth orbit remain strategically marginal space activities whose effects are mostly felt via propaganda and techno-nationalist symbolism. Theorising the strategic dynamics of spacepower in interplanetary space, with a return to bluewater rather than continental analogies of seapower, may remain the mission of a twenty-third-century Mahan. Yet in the twenty-first century the 'Mahan for the final frontier' is still in large part Mahan himself and the many theorists of seapower who provided insights into coastal-continental aspects of seapower, as it resembles the proximate, contested and littoral nature of Earth orbit which is home to supporting military and economic infrastructures. IR ignores the material consequences of spacepower's continuation of Terran politics by other means at its peril.

Notes

1. Pfaltzgraff, 'International Relations', p. 40.
2. Ibid. p. 39.
3. Harding, *Space Policy*, p. 5.
4. Brooks and Wohlforth, 'The Rise and Fall of Great Powers', p. 19; Posen, 'Command of the Commons', pp. 11–14, 20.
5. Brooks and Wohlforth, 'The Rise and Fall of Great Powers', p. 13.

6. Craig, 'Power Preponderance', p. 28.
7. Ibid. p. 30.
8. Ibid. pp. 46, 44.
9. Moltz, 'The Changing Dynamics', pp. 73–87.
10. Brooks and Wohlforth, 'The Rise and Fall of Great Powers', pp. 29–30.
11. Pollpeter, 'Upward and Onward', p. 406.
12. Edgerton, *The Shock*, p. 209.
13. Craig, 'Power Preponderance', p. 38.
14. Westad, *The Cold War*, p. 399.
15. Harvey, *Emerging Space Powers*, p. xi.
16. Harvey, *Emerging Space Powers*, pp. 24, 28, 70, 164, 253; Sheng-Chi Wang, *Transatlantic Space Politics*, p. 16.
17. Paikowsky, *The Power of the Space Club*, pp. 6–14.
18. Stroikos, *China, India in Space*, p. 112.

Bibliography

Books and book chapters

Al-Rodhan, Nayef R. F. *Meta-Geopolitics of Outer Space: An Analysis of Space Power, Security, and Governance* (London: Palgrave, 2012)

Armstrong, Benjamin F. 'Introduction', in Armstrong, Benjamin F. ed., *21st Century Mahan: Sound Military Conclusions for the Modern Era* (Annapolis, MD: Naval Institute Press, 2013)

Belich, James, *The New Zealand Wars and the Victorian Interpretation of Racial Conflict* (London: Penguin, 1986)

Berkowitz, Marc J. 'National Space Policy and National Defense', in Hays, Peter L., James M. Smith, Alan R. Van Tassel and Guy M. Walsh, eds, *Spacepower for a New Millennium* (London: McGraw-Hill, 2000)

Bolton, Iain Ross Ballantyne, 'Neo-Realism and the Galileo and GPS Negotiations', in Bormann, Natalie, and Michael Sheehan, eds, *Securing Outer Space* (Abingdon: Routledge, 2009).

Booth, Ken, *Strategy and Ethnocentrism* (New York: Holmes and Meier, 1979)

Bowen, Bleddyn E. 'Space Oddities: Law, War, and the Proliferation of Spacepower', in Gow, James, Ernst Dijxhoorn, Rachel Kerr and Guglielmo Verdirame, eds, *Routledge Handbook of Law, War, and Technology* (Abingdon: Routledge, 2019)

Bowen, Bleddyn E. 'Neither a Silver Bullet nor a Distraction: Naval Economic Warfare in Seapower Theory', in Halewood, Louis and David Morgan-Owen, eds, *Economic Warfare and the Sea* (Liverpool: Liverpool University Press, forthcoming 2020)

Boyne, Walter J. *The Influence of Air Power upon History* (Barnsley: Pen and Sword, 2005)

Brown, Kendall K. ed., *Space Power Integration: Perspectives from Space Weapons Officers* (Montgomery, AL: Air University Press, 2006)

Bulkeley, Rip and Graham Spinardi, *Space Weapons: Deterrence or Delusion?* (Cambridge: Polity Press, 1986)

Burrows, William E. *This New Ocean* (New York: Random House, 1998)

Callwell, Charles E. *Military Operations and Maritime Preponderance: Their Relation and Interdependence* (London: William Black & Sons, 1905)

Carr, Edward Hallett, *The Twenty Years' Crisis 1919–1939* (Basingstoke: Macmillan, 1974)

Castex, Raoul, *Strategic Theories*, Eugenia C. Kiesling, trans., ed. (Annapolis, MD: Naval Institute Press, 1994)

Cheng, Dean, 'Prospects for China's Military Space Efforts', in Kamphausen, Roy, David Lai and Andrew Scobell, eds, *Beyond the Strait: PLA Missions Other Than Taiwan* (Washington, DC: US Army War College, 2009)

Citino, Robert M. *Blitzkrieg to Desert Storm: The Evolution of Operational Warfare* (Lawrence, KA: Kansas University Press, 2004)

von Clausewitz, Carl, *On War*, O. J. Mathis Jolles trans. In Carr, Caleb, ed., *The Book of War* (New York: The Modern Library, 2000)

Cliff, Roger, John Fei, Jeff Hagen, Elizabeth Hague, Eric Heginbotham and John Stillion, *Shaking the Heavens and Splitting the Earth: Chinese Air Force Employment Concepts in the 21st Century* (Washington, DC: RAND, 2011)

Clodfelter, Mark, *The Limits of Air Power* (London: Free Press, 1989)

Coletta, Damon and Frances T. Pilch, eds, *Space and Defense Policy* (Abingdon: Routledge, 2009)

Colson, Bruno, *Napoleon: On War* (Oxford: Oxford University Press, 2015)

Corbett, Julian S. *Principles of Maritime Strategy* (Mineola, NY: Dover, 2004)

Cordingley, Patrick, *In the Eye of the Storm: Commanding the Desert Rats in the Gulf War* (London: Hodder and Stoughton, 1996)

Davies, R. R. *The Age of Conquest: Wales 1063–1415* (Oxford: Oxford University Press, 2000)

Davies, Sean, *Welsh Military Institutions, 633–1283* (Cardiff: University of Wales Press, 2004)

Dolman, Everett C. *Astropolitik: Classical Geopolitics in the Space Age* (London: Frank Cass, 2002)

Douhet, Giulio, *The Command of the Air*, Dino Ferrari, trans., Joseph Patrick Harahan and Richard H. Kohn, eds (Tuscaloosa, AL: University of Alabama Press, 2009)

Easton, Ian, *The Chinese Invasion Threat: Taiwan's Defense and American Strategy in Asia* (Washington, DC: Project 2049 Institute, 2017)

Easton, Richard D. and Eric F. Frazier, *GPS Declassified: From Smart Bombs to Smartphones* (Lincoln, NE: Potomac Books, 2013)

Eccles, Henry E. *Logistics in the National Defense* (Harrisburg, PN: Stackpole Company, 1959)

Echevarria, Antulio J. *Clausewitz and Contemporary War* (New York: Oxford University Press, 2013)

Echevarria, Antulio J. *Reconsidering the American Way of War* (Washington, DC: Georgetown University Press, 2014)

Edgerton, David, *The Shock of the Old: Technology and Global History Since 1900* (London: Profile, 2006)

Erickson, Andrew S. 'Chinese Air- and Space-Based ISR: Integrating Aerospace Combat Capabilities over the Near Seas', in Dutton, Peter, Andrew S. Erickson and Ryan Martinson, eds, *China's Near Seas Combat Capabilities* (Newport, RI: Naval War College Press, 2014)

Estes III, Howell M. 'The Aerospace Force of Today and Tomorrow: Transforming the Air Force Control the Vertical Dimension', in Hays, Peter L., James M. Smith, Alan R. Van Tassel and Guy M. Walsh, eds, *Spacepower for a New Millennium* (London: McGraw-Hill, 2000)

Evans, Tyler M. 'Space Coordinating Authority: Information Services from Space', in Brown, Kendall K. ed., *Space Power Integration: Perspectives from Space Weapons Officers* (Montgomery, AL: Air University Press, 2006)

Finlan, Alastair, *The Gulf War 1991* (Oxford: Osprey, 2003)

Finlan, Alastair, *The Royal Navy in the Falklands Conflict and the Gulf War: Culture and Strategy* (London: Frank Cass, 2004)

Finlan, Alastair, *Contemporary Military Culture and Strategic Studies* (Abingdon: Routledge, 2013

Finlan, Alastair, *Contemporary Military Strategy and the Global War on Terror* (London: Bloomsbury, 2014)

Fischer, David Hackett, *Historians' Fallacies: Toward a Logic of Historical Thought* (London: Routledge, 1971)

France Martin E. B. and Jerry Jon Sellers, 'Real Constraints on Spacepower', in Lutes, Charles D. and Peter L. Hays with Vincent A. Manzo, Lisa M. Yambrick and M. Elaine Bunn, eds, *Toward a Theory of Spacepower: Selected Essays* (Washington, DC: NDU Press, 2011)

Friedman, Norman, *Seapower and Space: From the Dawn of the Missile Age to Net-Centric Warfare* (London: Chatham Publishing, 2000)

Fuller, Jr., Joseph, Jeffrey Foust, Chad Frappier, Dustin Kaiser and David Vaccaro. 'The Commercial Space Industry: A Critical Spacepower

Consideration', in Lutes, Charles D. and Peter L. Hays with Vincent A. Manzo, Lisa M. Yambrick and M. Elaine Bunn, eds, *Toward a Theory of Spacepower: Selected Essays* (Washington, DC: NDU Press, 2011)

Gat, Azar, *A History of Military Thought: From the Enlightenment to the Cold War* (Abingdon: Oxford University Press, 2001)

Geppert, Alexander C. T. 'Introduction', in Geppert, Alexander C. T. ed., *Imagining Outer Space: European Astroculture in the Twentieth Century* (London: Palgrave Macmillan, 2012)

Gilbert, Gregory, 'Persia: Multinational Naval Power', in Erickson, Andrew S., Lyle J. Goldstein and Carnes Lord, eds, *China Goes to Sea: Maritime Transformation in Comparative Historical Perspective* (Annapolis, MD: Naval Institute Press, 2009)

Gray, Colin S. *The Navy in the Post-Cold War World: The Uses and Value of Strategic Seapower* (University Park, PA: Penn State University Press, 1994)

Gray, Colin S. *Modern Strategy* (Oxford: Oxford University Press, 1999)

Gray, Colin S. *Another Bloody Century: Future Warfare* (London: Weidenfeld & Nicolson, 2005)

Gray, Colin S. *Strategy and History: Essays on Theory and Practice* (Abingdon: Routledge, 2006)

Gray, Colin S. *Airpower for Strategic Effect* (Montgomery, AL: Air University Press, 2012)

Godwin, Paul H.B. 'The PLA Faces the Twenty-First Century: Reflections on Technology, Doctrine, Strategy, and Operations', in Lilley, James R. and David Shambaugh (ed.) *China's Military Faces the Future* (Washington, D.C.: East Gate, 1999)

Gompert, David C., Astrid Stuth Cevallos, Cristina L. Garafola, *War with China: Thinking Through the Unthinkable* (Washington, DC: RAND, 2016)

Gorshkov, Sergei G. *The Sea Power of the State* (Oxford: Pergamon Press, 1979)

Handberg, Roger, *Seeking New World Vistas: The Militarization of Space* (Westport, CT: Praeger, 2000)

Handberg, Roger and Zhen Li, *Chinese Space Policy: A Study in Domestic and International Politics* (Abingdon: Routledge, 2007)

Handel, Michael I. *Masters of War: Classical Strategic Thought* (Abingdon: Frank Cass, 2001)

Harding, Robert C. *Space Policy in Developing Countries* (Abingdon: Routledge, 2013)

Harvey, Brian *Emerging Space Powers* (Chichester: Springer, 2000)

Havercroft Jonathan, and Raymond Duvall, 'Critical Astropolitics: the geopolitics of space control and the transformation of state sovereignty' in Natalie Bormann and Michael Sheehan, ed. *Securing Outer Space* (Routledge, 2009)

Hays, Peter L. *United States Military Space: Into the Twenty-First Century* (Montgomery, AL: Air University Press, 2002)

Heginbotham, Eric, Michael Nixon, Forrest E. Morgan, Jacob L. Heim, Jeff Hagen, Sheng Li, Jeffrey Engstrom, Martin C. Libicki, Paul DeLuca, David A. Shlapak, David R. Frelinger, Burgess Laird, Kyle Brady and Lyle J. Morris. *The U.S.-China Military Scorecard: Forces, Geography, and the Evolving Balance of Power 1996–2017* (Washington, DC: RAND, 2015)

Hertzfeld, Henry, 'Commercial Space and Spacepower', in Lutes, Charles D. and Peter L. Hays with Vincent A. Manzo, Lisa M. Yambrick and M. Elaine Bunn, eds, *Toward a Theory of Spacepower: Selected Essays* (Washington, DC: NDU Press, 2011)

Heuser, Beatrice, *The Evolution of Strategy: Thinking War from Antiquity to the Present* (Cambridge: Cambridge University Press, 2010)

Hill, John R. *Maritime Strategy for Medium Powers* (London: Croom Helm, 1986)

Holmes, James R., Andrew C. Winner and Toshi Yoshihara, *Indian Naval Strategy in the Twenty-First Century* (Abingdon: Routledge, 2009)

Jasani, Bhupendra, ed., *Space Weapons and International Security* (Oxford: Oxford University Press, 1987)

Johnson-Freese, Joan, *Space as a Strategic Asset* (New York: Columbia University Press, 2007)

Johnson-Freese, Joan, *Space Warfare in the 21st Century: Arming the Heavens* (Abingdon: Routledge, 2017)

Johnston, Alastair Iain, *Cultural Realism: Strategic Culture and Grand Strategy in Chinese History* (Princeton: Princeton University Press, 1995)

Jomini, Antoine-Henri, *The Art of War*, G. H. Mendell and W. P. Craighill, trans. (Westport, CT: Greenwood Press, 1971)

Kagan, Frederick W. *Finding the Target: The Transformation of American Military Policy* (London: Encounter Books, 2006)

Katzenstein, Peter J. 'Introduction', in Katzenstein, Peter J., ed., *The Culture of National Security: Norms and Identity in World Politics* (New York: Columbia University Press, 1996)

Kennedy, Paul, 'Grand Strategy in War and Peace: Toward a Broader Definition', in Kennedy, Paul, ed., *Grand Strategies in War and Peace* (London: Yale University Press, 1991)

Kier, Elizabeth, 'Culture and French Military Doctrine before World War II', in Katzenstein, Peter J., ed., *The Culture of National Security: Norms and Identity in World Politics* (New York: Columbia University Press, 1996)

Kiesling. Eugenia C. 'Introduction', in Castex, Raoul, *Strategic Theories*, Eugenia C. Kiesling, trans., ed. (Annapolis, MD: Naval Institute Press, 1994)

Kilgore, De Witt Douglas, *Astrofuturism: Science, Race, and Visions of Utopia in Space*, (Philadelphia, PA: University of Pennsylvania Press, 2003)

Klein, John J. *Space Warfare: Strategy, Principles, and Policy* (Abingdon: Routledge, 2006)

Kosmodemyansky, A. *Konstantin Tsiolkovsky: His Life and Work*, X. Danko, trans. (Hawai'i, HI: University Press of the Pacific, 2000)

Lai, David and Marc Miller, 'Introduction', in Kamphausen, Roy, David Lai and Andrew Scobell, eds, *Beyond the Strait: PLA Missions Other Than Taiwan* (Washington, DC: US Army War College, 2009)

Lambakis, Stephen, *On the Edge of Earth: The Future of American Space Power* (Lexington: University of Kentucky Press, 2001)

Lambeth, Benjamin S. *Mastering the Ultimate Highground* (Washington, DC: RAND, 2003)

Launius, Roger D. *Reaching for the Moon: A Short History of the Space Race* (London: Yale University Press, 2019)

Logsdon, John M. *John F. Kennedy and the Race to the Moon* (Basingstoke: Palgrave, 2010)

Long, Franklin A., Donald Hafner and Jeffrey Boutwell, eds, *Weapons in Space* (New York: W. W. Norton, 1986)

Lostumbo, Michael J., David R. Frelinger, James Williams and Barry Wilson, *Air Defense Options for Taiwan: An Assessment of Relative Costs and Operational Benefits* (Washington, DC: RAND, 2016)

Lupton, David E. *On Space Warfare* (Montgomery, AL: Air University Press, 1988)

Lutes, Charles D. and Peter L. Hays with Vincent A. Manzo, Lisa M. Yambrick and M. Elaine Bunn, eds, *Toward a Theory of Spacepower: Selected Essays* (Washington, DC: NDU Press, 2011)

Lutes, Charles D. and Peter L. Hays with Vincent A. Manzo, Lisa M. Yambrick and M. Elaine Bunn, 'Introduction', in Lutes, Charles D. and Peter L. Hays with Vincent A. Manzo, Lisa M. Yambrick and M. Elaine Bunn, eds, *Toward a Theory of Spacepower: Selected Essays* (Washington, DC: NDU Press, 2011)

Luttwak, Edward N. *Strategy: The Logic of War and Peace* (Cambridge, MA: Harvard University Press, 1987)

Macdonald, Scot, *Rolling the Iron Dice: Historical Analogies and Decisions to Use Military Force in Regional Contingencies* (London: Greenwood Press, 2000)

McDougall, Walter, . . .*The Heavens and the Earth: A Political History of the Space Age* (Baltimore, MD: Johns Hopkins University Press, 1985)

McKinley, Cynthia A. S. 'When the Enemy Has Our Eyes', in DeBlois, Bruce M., ed., *Beyond the Paths of Heaven: The Emergence of Space Power Thought* (Montgomery, AL: Air University Press, 1999)

McVadon, Eric A. 'China's Navy Today: Looking toward Blue Water', in Erickson, Andrew S., Lyle J. Goldstein and Carnes Lord, eds, *China Goes to Sea: Maritime Transformation in Comparative Historical Perspective* (Annapolis, MD: Naval Institute Press, 2009)

Mahan, Alfred Thayer, *The Gulf and Inland Waters: The Navy in the Civil War* (New York, NY: Charles Scribner's Sons, 1883),

Mahan, Alfred Thayer, *The Influence of Sea Power upon History 1660–1783* (London: Marston & Co., 1890)

Mahan, Alfred Thayer, *The Influence of Sea Power upon the French Revolution and Empire 1793–1812: Volume II* (Sampson Low, Marston & Co.: London, 1892)

Mahan, Alfred Thayer, *Sea Power in its Relation to the War of 1812: Volume I* (Boston, MA: Little & Brown, 1905)

Mahnken, Thomas G. 'US Strategic and Organizational Subcultures', in Johnson, Jeannie L., Kerry M. Kartchner and Jeffrey A. Larsen, eds., *Strategic Culture and Weapons of Mass Destruction: Culturally Based Insights into Comparative National Security Policymaking* (London: Palgrave Macmillan, 2009)

Mearsheimer, John J. *The Tragedy of Great Power Politics* (London: Norton, 2001)

Mei Lianju, *Space Operations Teaching Materials* (Beijing: AMS Publishing House, 2013)

Menon, Raja, *Maritime Strategy and Continental Wars* (London: Frank Cass, 1998)

Moltz, James Clay, *The Politics of Space Security* (Stanford, CA: Stanford University Press, 2011)

Moltz, James Clay, *Crowded Orbits: Conflict and Cooperation in Space* (New York: Columbia University Press, 2014)

Mowthorpe, Matthew, *The Militarization and Weaponization of Space* (Lanham: Lexington Books, 2004)

Musashi, Miyamoto, *The Book of Five Rings*, Thomas Cleary trans., ed. (London: Shambala, 2003)

Niven, Larry and Jerry Pournelle, *Footfall* (London: Sphere Books, 1985)

Nye, Joseph S. *The Future of Power* (New York: Public Affairs, 2011)

O'Hanlon, Michael, *Neither Star Wars nor Sanctuary: Constraining the Military Uses of Space* (Washington, DC: Brookings Institution, 2004)

Ó Tuathail, Gearóid, *Critical Geopolitics* (London: Routledge, 1996)

Oberg, James, *Space Power Theory* (Montgomery, AL: Air University Press, 1999)

Pace, Scott, Gerald Frost, Irving Lachow, David Frelinger, Donna Fossum, Donald K. Wassem and Monica Pinto, *The Global Positioning System: Assessing National Politics* (Washington, DC: RAND, 1995)

Paikowsky, Deganit, *The Power of the Space Club* (Cambridge: Cambridge University Press, 2017)

Panikkar, Kavalam Madhava, *India and the Indian Ocean: An Essay on the influence of Sea Power on Indian History* (London: George Allen & Unwin, 1945)

Pape, Robert A. *Bombing to Win: Air Power and Coercion in War* (London: Cornell University Press, 1996)

Pekkanen Saadia M. and Paul Kallender-Umezu, *In Defense of Japan: From the Market to the Military in Space Policy* (Stanford, CA: Stanford University Press, 2010)

Pfaltzgraff, Robert L. Jr. 'International Relations Theory and Space-power', in Lutes, Charles D. and Peter L. Hays with Vincent A. Manzo, Lisa M. Yambrick and M. Elaine Bunn, eds, *Toward a Theory of Spacepower: Selected Essays* (Washington, DC: NDU Press, 2011)

Porter, Patrick, *Military Orientalism: Eastern War Through Western Eyes* (New York: Columbia University Press, 2009)

Posen, Barry R. *Restraint: A New Foundation for U.S. Grand Strategy* (London: Cornell University Press, 2014)

Preston, Bob, *Plowshares and Power: The Military Use of Civil Space* (Washington, DC: National Defense University Press, 1994)

Richelson, Jeffrey T. *America's Space Sentinels: DSP Satellites and National Security* (Lawrence, KA: Kansas University Press, 1999)

Ropp, Theodore, 'Continental Doctrines of Sea Power', in Earle, Edward Mead, ed., *Makers of Modern Strategy: Military Thought from Machiavelli to Hitler* (Princeton: Princeton University Press, 1943)

Sadeh, Eligar, ed., *Space Strategy in the 21st Century* (Abingdon: Routledge, 2012)

Schuler, Mark A. 'It Isn't Space, It's Warfare! Joint Warfighting Space and the Command and Control of Deployable Space Forces', in Brown, Kendall K., ed., *Space Power Integration: Perspectives from Space Weapons Officers* (Montgomery, AL: Air University Press, 2006)

Sheehan, Michael, *The International Politics of Space* (Abingdon: Routledge, 2007)

Sheldon, John B. and Colin S. Gray, 'Theory Ascendant? Spacepower and the Challenge of Strategic Theory', in Lutes, Charles D. and Peter L. Hays with Vincent A. Manzo, Lisa M. Yambrick and M. Elaine Bunn, eds, *Toward a Theory of Spacepower: Selected Essays* (Washington, DC: NDU Press, 2011)

Sheng-Chi Wang, *Transatlantic Space Politics: Competition and Cooperation above the Clouds* (Abingdon: Routledge, 2013)

Shimko, Keith L. *The Iraq Wars and America's Military Revolution* (New York: Cambridge University Press, 2010)

Shultz, Richard, and Robert Pfaltzgraff, eds, *The Future of Air Power in the Aftermath of the Gulf War* (Montgomery, AL: Air University Press, 1992)

Smith, M. L. and Matthew Uttley, 'The Changing Face of Maritime Power', in Dorman, Andrew, M. L. Smith and Matthew Uttley, eds, *The Changing Face of Maritime Power* (Basingstoke: Palgrave Macmillan, 1999)

Smith, Michael V. *Ten Propositions Regarding Spacepower* (Montgomery, AL: Air University Press, 2002)

Spires, David N. *Beyond Horizons: A Half Century of Air Force Space Leadership* (Montgomery, AL: Air University Press, 1998)

Stares, Paul B. *Space and National Security* (Washington, DC: Brookings Institution, 1987)

Sumida, Jon T. *Inventing Grand Strategy and Teaching Command: The Classic Works of Alfred Thayer Mahan Reconsidered* (Washington, DC: Woodrow Wilson Center Press, 1997)

Sumida, Jon T. *Decoding Clausewitz: A New Approach to On War* (Lawrence, KA: Kansas University Press, 2008)

Sun Tzu, *The Art of Warfare*, Roger T. Ames, trans. In Carr, Caleb, ed., *The Book of War* (New York: The Modern Library, 2000)

Sun Tzu, *The Art of War*, Thomas Cleary, trans. (London: Shambala, 1988)

Till, Geoffrey, *Seapower: A Guide for the Twenty-First Century* (Abingdon: Routledge, 2004, 2nd edition)

Till, Geoffrey, *Seapower: A Guide for the Twenty-First Century* (Abingdon: Routledge, 2013, 3rd edition)

Waldman, Thomas, *War, Clausewitz and the Trinity* (Farnham: Ashgate, 2013)

Waltz, Kenneth N. *Man, the State, and War: A Theoretical Analysis* (New York: Columbia University Press, 1959)

Wawro, Geoffrey, *Warfare and Society in Europe 1792–1914* (Abingdon: Routledge, 2000)

Weigley, Russell, *The American Way of War* (Bloomington, IN: Indiana University Press, 1973)

Wendt, Alexander, *Social Theory of International Politics* (Cambridge: Cambridge University Press, 1999)

Westad, Odd Arne, *The Cold War: A World History* (London: Penguin, 2017)

White, Rowland, *Into the Black* (London: Penguin, 2016)

Wohlforth, William C. 'Hegemonic Decline and Hegemonic War Revisited', in Ikenberry, G. John, ed., *Power, Order, and Change in World Politics* (Cambridge: Cambridge University Press, 2014)

Wong, Wilson W. S. and James Fergusson, *Military Space Power: A Guide to the Issues* (Oxford: Praeger, 2010)

Worden, Simon P. 'Space Control for the 21st Century: A Space "Navy" Protecting the Commercial Basis of America's Wealth', in Hays, Peter L., James M. Smith, Alan R. Van Tassel and Guy M. Walsh, eds, *Spacepower for a New Millennium* (London: McGraw-Hill, 2000)

Wortzel, Larry M. *The Dragon Extends its Reach: Chinese Military Power Goes Global* (Washington, DC: Potomac Books, 2013)

York, Herbert F. 'Nuclear Deterrence and the Military Uses of Space', in Long, Franklin A., Donald Hafner and Jeffrey Boutwell, eds, *Weapons in Space* (New York: W. W. Norton, 1986)

Yuen Foong Khong, *Analogies at War: Korea, Munich, Dien Bien Phu, and the Vietnam Decisions of 1965* (Princeton: Princeton University Press, 1992)

Ziarnick, Brent, *Developing National Power in Space: A Theoretical Model* (Jefferson, NC: McFarland, 2015)

Articles

Acton, James, 'Escalation through Entanglement: How the Vulnerability of Command-and-Control Systems Raises the Risks of an Inadvertent Nuclear War', *International Security*, 43:1, 2018, pp. 56–99

Anson, Peter and Dennis Cummings, 'The First Space War: The Contribution of Satellites to the Gulf War', *RUSI Journal*, 136:4, 1991, pp. 45–53

Armstrong, Dale, 'American National Security and the Death of Space Sanctuary', *Astropolitics*, 12:1, 2014, pp. 69–81

Beidleman, Scott W. 'GPS versus Galileo: Balancing for Position in Space', *Cadre Paper*, no. 28, May 2006

Beyerchen, Alan, 'Clausewitz, Nonlinearity, and the Unpredictability of War', *International Security*, 17:3, 1992–3, pp. 59–90

Biddle, Stephen, 'Afghanistan and the Future of Warfare', *Foreign Affairs*, 82:2, 2003, pp. 31–46

Biddle, Stephen and Ivan Oelrich, 'Future Warfare in the Western Pacific: Chinese Antiaccess/Area Denial, US AirSea Battle, and Command of the Commons in East Asia', *International Security*, 41:1, 2016, pp. 7–48

Bloomfield, Alan, 'Time to Move On: Reconceptualizing the Strategic Culture Debate', *Contemporary Security Policy*, 33:3, 2012, pp. 437–61

Boot, Max, 'The New American Way of War', *Foreign Affairs*, 82:4, 2003, pp. 41–58

Bowen, Bleddyn E. 'British Strategy and Outer Space: A Missing Link?', *British Journal of Politics and International Relations*, 20:2, 2018, pp. 323–40

Bowen, Bleddyn E. 'The RAF and British Space Doctrine: A Second Century, a Second Space Age', *RUSI Journal*, 163:3, 2018, pp. 58–65

Bowen, Bleddyn E. 'From the Sea to Outer Space: The Command of Space as the Foundation of Spacepower Theory', *Journal of Strategic Studies*, 42:3–4, 2019, pp. 532–56

Brachet, Gerard, 'From Initial Ideas to a European Plan: GMES as an Exemplar of European Space Strategy', *Space Policy*, 20:1, 2004, pp. 7–15

Brooks, Stephen G. and William C. Wohlforth, 'The Rise and Fall of Great Powers in the Twenty-First Century' *International Security*, 40:3, 2015, pp. 7–53

Brown, Trevor, 'Space and the Sea: Strategic Considerations for the Commons' *Astropolitics*, 10:3, 2012, pp. 234–47

Brun, Itai, 'While You're Busy Making Other Plans – The "Other RMA"', *Journal of Strategic Studies*, 33:4, 2010 pp. 535–65

Burris, Matthew, 'Astroimpolitic: Organizing Outer Space by the Sword', *Strategic Studies Quarterly*, Autumn, 2013, pp. 108–29

Chaterjee, Promit, 'Legality of Anti-Satellites under the Space Law Regime', *Astropolitics* 12:1, 2014, pp. 27–45

Cheng, Dean, 'China's Military Role in Space' *Strategic Studies Quarterly*, Spring, 2012, pp. 53–77

Craig, Campbell, 'Power Preponderance and the Nuclear Revolution', *Review of International Studies*, 35:1, 2009, pp. 27–44

Danchev, Alex, 'Liddell Hart's Big Idea', *Review of International Studies*, 25:1, 1999, pp. 29–48

Deudney, Daniel, 'Turbo Change: Accelerating Technological Disruption, Planetary Geopolitics, and Architectonic Metaphors', *International Studies Review*, 20:2, 2018, pp. 223–31

Dudley-Flores, Marilyn and Thomas Gangale, 'Forecasting the Political Economy of the Inner Solar System', *Astropolitics,* 10:3, 2012, pp. 183–233

Duvall, Raymond and Jonathan Havercroft, 'Taking Sovereignty Out of This World: Space Weapons and the Empire of the Future', *Review of International Studies*, 34:4, 2008, pp. 755–75

Fox, John G. 'Some Principles of Space Strategy (or "Corbett in Orbit")', *Space Policy*, 17:1, 2001, pp. 7–11

Futter, Andrew, '"Cyber" Semantics: Why We Should Retire the Latest Buzzword in Security Studies', *Journal of Cyber Policy*, 3:2, 2018, pp. 201–16

Gaskarth, Jamie, 'Strategizing Britain's Role in the World', *International Affairs*, 90:3, 2014, pp. 559–81

Gray, Colin S. 'The Influence of Space Power upon History', *Comparative Strategy*, 15:4, 1996, pp. 293–308

Gray, Colin S. 'Clausewitz Rules, OK? The Future is the Past: With GPS', *Review of International Studies*, 25:4, 1999, pp. 161–82

Gray, Colin S. 'Inescapable Geography', *Journal of Strategic Studies*, 22:2–3, 1999, pp. 161–77

Gray, Colin S. and John B. Sheldon, 'Space Power and the Revolution in Military Affairs: A Glass Half Full?', *Airpower Journal*, 13:3, 1999, pp. 23–38

Hagt, Eric and Matthew Durnin, 'Space, China's Tactical Frontier', *Journal of Strategic Studies*, 34:5, 2011, pp. 733–61

Handberg, Roger, 'Is Space War Imminent? Exploring the Possibility', *Comparative Strategy*, 36:5, 2017, pp. 413–25

Hays Peter L. and Charles D. Lutes, 'Toward a Theory of Spacepower', *Space Policy*, 23:4, 2007, pp. 206–9

Hebert, Karl D. 'Regulation of Space Weapons: Ensuring Stability and Continued Use of Outer Space', *Astropolitics*, 12:1, 2014, pp. 1–26

Hilborne, Mark, 'China's Rise in Space and US Policy Responses: A Collision Course?' *Space Policy*, 29:2, 2013, pp. 121–7

Hitchens, Theresa and David Chen, 'Forging a Sino-US "Grand Bargain" in Space', *Space Policy*, 24:3, 2008, pp. 128–31

Hitchens, Theresa and Victoria Samson, 'Space-Based Interceptors: Still Not a Good Idea', *Georgetown Journal of International Affairs*, 5:2, 2004, pp. 21–9

Hunter, Cameron, 'The Forgotten First Iteration of the "Chinese Space Threat" to US National Security', *Space Policy*, 47, 2019 pp. 158–65

Hunter, Cameron and Bleddyn E. Bowen, 'Donald Trump's Space Force Isn't As New Or As Dangerous As It Seems', *Journal of Space Safety Engineering*, 5:3–4, 2018, p. 131

Klein, John J. 'Space Warfare: A Maritime-Inspired Space Strategy', *Astropolitics*, 2:1, 2004, pp. 33–61

Kleinberg, Howard, 'On War in Space', *Astropolitics*, 5:1, 2007, pp. 1–27

Krepon, Michael, Eric Hagt, Shen Dingli, Bao Shixiu, Michael Pillsbury and Ashley Tellis, 'China's Military Space Strategy: An Exchange', *Survival*, 50:1, 2008, pp. 157–98

Lambakis, Steven, 'Space Control in Desert Storm and Beyond', *Orbis*, Summer, 1995, pp. 417–33

Lambeth, Benjamin S. 'Airpower in India's 1999 Kargil War', *Journal of Strategic Studies*, 35:3, 2012, pp. 289–316

Lawson, George, 'The Eternal Divide? History and International Relations', *European Journal of International Relations*, 18:2, 2010, pp. 203–26

Liemer, Ross and Christopher F. Chyba, 'A Verifiable Limited Test Ban for Anti-Satellite Weapons', *Washington Quarterly*, 33:3, 2010, pp. 149–63

Lopez, Laura Delgado, 'Predicting and Arms Race in Space: Problematic Assumptions for Space Arms Control', *Astropolitics*, 10:1, 2012, pp. 49–67

Mahnken, Thomas G. 'Weapons: The Growth and Spread of the Precision-Strike Regime', *Deadalus*, 140:3, 2011, pp. 45–57

Mendenhall, Elizabeth, 'Treating Outer Space Like a Place: A Case for Rejecting Other Domain Analogies', *Astropolitics*, 16:2, 2018, pp. 97–118

Moltz, James Clay, 'The Changing Dynamics of Twenty-First-Century Space Power', *Strategic Studies Quarterly*, 13:1, 2019, pp. 66–94

Mueller, Karl P. 'Totem and Taboo: Depolarizing the Space Weaponization Debate', *Astropolitics*, 1:1, 2003, pp. 4–28

Murray, William S. 'Revisiting Taiwan's Defense Strategy', *Naval War College Review*, 61:3, 2018, pp. 13–44

Peoples, Columba, 'Assuming the Inevitable? Overcoming the Inevitability of Outer Space Weaponization and Conflict', *Contemporary Security Policy*, 29:3, 2008, pp. 502–20

Peoples, Columba, 'The Securitization of Outer Space: Challenges for Arms Control', *Contemporary Security Policy*, 32:1, 2011, pp. 76–89

Pollpeter, Kevin, 'Upward and Onward: Technological Innovation and Organizational Change in China's Space Industry', *Journal of Strategic Studies*, 34:3, 2011, pp. 405–23

Pollpeter, Kevin, 'Space, the New Domain: Space Operations and Chinese Military Reforms', *Journal of Strategic Studies*, 39:5–6, 2016, p. 709–27.

Porter, Patrick, 'Geography, Strategy, and the National Interest: The Maps are Too Small', *The World Today*, 66:5, 2010, pp. 4–6

Posen, Barry R. 'Command of the Commons: The Military Foundation of U.S. Hegemony', *International Security*, 28:1, 2003, pp. 5–46

Rendleman, James D. 'A Strategy for Space Assurance', *Astropolitics*, 8:2–3, 2010, pp. 220–55

Shabbir, Zaeem, 'Counterspace Operations and Nascent Space Powers', *Astropolitics*, 16:2, 2017, pp. 119–40

Sheehan, Michael, 'Counterspace Operations and the Evolution of US Military Space Doctrine', *Air Power Review*, 12:2, 2009, pp. 96–113

Sheehan, Michael, 'The Crucial Role of European Space Popularisation', *Space Policy*, 41, 2017, pp. 68–9

Shimabukuro, Alessandro, 'No Deal in Space: A Bargaining Model Analysis of U.S. Resistance to Space Arms Control', *Space Policy*, 30:1, 2014, pp. 13–22

Solomon, Jonathan F. 'Maritime Deception and Concealment: Concepts for Defeating Wide-Area Oceanic Surveillance-Reconnaissance-Strike Networks', *Naval War College Review*, 66:4, 2013, pp. 91–120

Straub, Jeremy, 'Application of a Maritime Framework to Space: Deep Space Conflict and Warfare Scenario', *Astropolitics*, 13:1, 2015, pp. 65–77

Wilgenbusch, Ronald C. and Alan Heisig, 'Command and Control Vulnerabilities to Communications Jamming', *Joint Forces Quarterly*, 69:2, 2013, pp. 56–63

Wortzel, Larry M. 'The Chinese People's Liberation Army and Space Warfare', *Astropolitics*, 6:2, 2007, pp. 112–37.

Reports, papers and documents

Air Command and Staff College Space Research Electives Seminars, *AU-18: Space Primer* (Montgomery, AL: Air University Press, 2009)

BryceTech, 'State of the Satellite Industry Report', May 2019

Coats, Daniel R. 'Worldwide Threat Assessment of the US Intelligence Community', 13 February 2018, Washington, DC, <https://www.dni.gov/files/documents/Newsroom/Testimonies/2018-ATA---Unclassified-SSCI.pdf> (last accessed 19 March 2018)

Committee on Armed Services for the U.S. House of Representatives, 'Commission to Assess United States National Security Space Management and Organization', 11 January 2001, Washington, DC

Easton, Ian, 'The Great Game in Space: China's Evolving ASAT Weapons Programs and their Implications for Future U.S. Strategy' (Washington, DC: Project 2049 Institute, 2009)

Easton, Ian, 'Able Archers: Taiwan Defense Strategy in an Age of Precision Strike' (Arlington, VA: Project 2049 Institute, 2014)

Easton, Ian, 'China's Evolving Reconnaissance-Strike Capabilities: Implications for the U.S.-Japan Alliance' (Arlington, VA: Project 2049 Institute, 2014)

Easton, Ian and Mark Stokes, 'China's Electronic Intelligence (ELINT) Satellite Developments: Implications for U.S. Air and Naval Operations' (Washington, DC: Project 2049, February 2011)

Gunzinger, Mark and Bryan Clark, *Winning the Salvo Competition: Rebalancing America's Air and Missile Defenses* (Washington, DC: CBSA, 2016)

Krepinevich, Andrew F. *Maritime Competition in a Mature Precision-Strike Regime* (Washington, DC: Center for Strategic and Budgetary Assessments, 2014)

McLaughlin, Kevin, 'Military Space Culture', paper for the Commission to Assess United States National Security Space Management and Organization, Washington DC, 2001, <http://fas.org/spp/eprint/article02.html> (last accessed 29 June 2018)

Organisation for Economic Co-operation and Development, 'The Space Economy at a Glance 2014'

Stokes, Mark A. and Dean Cheng, 'China's Evolving Space Capabilities: Implications for U.S. Interests' (Washington, DC: Project 2049 Institute, 2012)

UK Ministry of Defence (MoD), *The UK Military Space Primer* (Shrivenham: Defence Concepts and Doctrine Centre, 2010)

UK Ministry of Defence (MoD) 'UK Air and Space Doctrine', Joint Doctrine Publication 0–30, 2013

United States Air Force (USAF), 'Annex 3–14 Space Operations', Curtis E. LeMay Center for Doctrine Development and Education, 27 August 2018, <https://www.doctrine.af.mil/Doctrine-Annexes/Annex-3-14-Counterspace-Ops/> (last accessed 7 September 2019)

United States Defense Intelligence Agency, 'Challenges to Security in Space', Washington, DC, 2019

United States Department of Defense (DOD), 'Annual Report to Congress: Military and Security Developments in the People's Republic of China 2016', Washington, DC, 2016

United States Department of Defense (DOD), 'Summary of the National Defense Strategy of the United States of America, Washington, DC, 2018

United States Joint Chiefs of Staff, *Joint Publication 3–14: Space Operations*, 2018

Watts, Barry D. *The Military Uses of Space: A Diagnostic Assessment* (Washington, DC: Center for Strategic and Budgetary Assessments, 2001)

Weeden, Brian, 'Radio Frequency Spectrum, Interference and Satellites Fact Sheet' (Washington, DC: Secure World Foundation, 2013)

Weeden, Brian, 'Through a Glass, Darkly: Chinese, American, and Russian Anti-Satellite Testing in Space' (Washington, DC: Secure World Foundation, 2014)

Weeden, Brian and Victoria Samson, eds, *Global Counterspace Capabilities: An Open Source Assessment* (Washington, DC: Secure World Foundation, 2019)

Woolf, Amy F. 'Conventional Prompt Global Strike and Long-Range Ballistic Missiles: Background and Issues', Congressional Research Service Report, 24 February 2016, Washington, DC.

Theses, manuscripts and presentations

Deudney, Daniel, 'Dark Skies: Space Weapons, Planetary Geopolitics and Whole Earth Security' as presented at the International Studies Association Conference 2017, Baltimore, MD (forthcoming, Oxford University Press)

Hays, Peter L. *Struggling towards Space Doctrine: U.S. Military Space Plans, Programs, and Perspectives during the Cold War* (PhD thesis, Tufts University, 1994)

Piotrowski, John L. *Space Warfare and the Principles of War* (Peterson Air Force Base, CO: U.S. Space Command, 1989) unpublished manuscript

Sheldon, John B. *Reasoning by Strategic Analogy: Classical Strategic Thought and the Foundations of a Theory of Space Power* (PhD thesis, University of Reading, 2005)

Stroikos, Dimitrios, *China, India in Space and the Orbit of International Society: Power, Status, and Order on the High Frontier* (PhD thesis, London School of Economics, 2016)

Internet sources

Bodner, Matthew, 'As Trump pushes for separate space force, Russia moves fast the other way', *Defense News*, 21 June 2018, <https://www.defensenews.com/global/europe/2018/06/21/as-trump-pushes-for-separate-space-force-russia-moves-fast-the-other-way/> (last accessed 29 June 2018)

Bowen, Bleddyn E. 'Better the devil you know? Galileo, Brexit, and British defence space strategy', *Defence-in-Depth*, 23 May 2018, <https://defenceindepth.co/2018/05/23/better-the-devil-you-know-galileo-brexit-and-british-defence-space-strategy/> (last accessed 8 June 2018)

Burr, William, 'U.S. detected Indian nuclear test preparations in 1995, but photo evidence was "clear as mud"', 22 February 2013, <http://www2.gwu.edu/~nsarchiv/nukevault/ebb412/> (last accessed 17 September 2019)

Center for Strategic and International Studies, 'Space-based missile defence: How much is enough?' <https://aerospace.csis.org/data/space-based-missile-interceptors/> (last accessed 15 April 2019)

Costello, John, 'The Strategic Support Force: update and overview', Jamestown Foundation, 21 December 2016, <https://jamestown.org/program/strategic-support-force-update-overview/> (last accessed 8 June 2018)

Federation of American Scientists, 'India blasts take U.S. intelligence by surprise', *Washington Times*, May 1998, <http://fas.org/irp/news/1998/05/980512-wt.htm> (last accessed 17 September 2019)

Grego, Laura, 'A history of anti-satellite programs', Union of Concerned Scientists, January 2012, <http://www.ucsusa.org/sites/default/files/legacy/assets/documents/nwgs/a-history-of-ASAT-programs_lo-res.pdf> (last accessed 17 September 2019)

Hertzfeld, Henry R., Brian Weeden and Christopher D. Johnson, 'How simple terms mislead us: the pitfalls of thinking about outer space as a common', IAC-15-E7.5.2, presented at the 66th International Astronautical Congress, Jerusalem, Israel, 2015, <https://swfound.org/media/205285/how-simple-terms-mislead-us-hertzfeld-

johnson-weeden-iac-2015.pdf?utm_content=buffer32406&utm_medium=social&utm_source=twitter.com&utm_campaign=buffer> (last accessed 17 September 2019)

Hirsch, Steve, 'Departing Head of Space Ops Center cites importance of cooperation with allies', *Air Force Magazine*, 4 June 2018, <http://www.airforcemag.com/Features/Pages/2018/June%202018/Departing-Head-of-Space-Ops-Center-Cites-Importance-of-Cooperation-with-Allies> (last accessed 8 June 2018)

Indian Space Research Organisation, 'Dr. Vikram Ambalal Sarabhai (1963–1971)', <https://www.isro.gov.in/about-isro/dr-vikram-ambalal-sarabhai-1963-1971> (last accessed 29 June 2018)

Kania, Elsa, 'PLA Strategic Support Force: The "information umbrella" for China's military', *The Diplomat*, 1 April 2017, <https://thediplomat.com/2017/04/pla-strategic-support-force-the-information-umbrella-for-chinas-military/> (last accessed 8 June 2018)

Los Angeles Times, 'Indian test deception reported', 20 May 1998, <http://articles.latimes.com/1998/may/20/news/mn-51736> (last accessed 17 September 2019)

Mallet, Victor, 'France follows US to set up military space command', *Financial Times*, 14 July 2019, <https://www.ft.com/content/a479bcb6-a628-11e9-984c-fac8325aaa04> (last accessed 17 January 2019)

Messier, Doug, 'IMF: Ukraine space sector possibly suffered 80 percent revenue loss', *Parabolic Arc*, 16 February 2016, <http://www.parabolicarc.com/2016/02/16/ukraine-space-sector/> (last accessed 15 April 2019)

North Atlantic Treaty Organization (NATO) Allied Command Operations, 'New satellite imagery exposes Russian combat troops inside Ukraine', 28 August 2014, <http://aco.nato.int/new-satellite-imagery-exposes-russian-combat-troops-inside-ukraine.aspx> (last accessed 3 March 2015)

Oberhaus, Daniel, 'India's anti-satellite test wasn't really about satellites', *Wired*, 27 March 2019, <https://www.wired.com/story/india-anti-satellite-test-space-debris/> (accessed 9 April 2019)

Richelson, Jeffrey T. 'U.S. Intelligence and the Soviet Space Program', *National Security Archive Electronic Briefing Book* (no. 501), 4 February 2015, <http://www2.gwu.edu/~nsarchiv/NSAEBB/NSAEBB501/> (last accessed 17 September 2019)

Russian Ministry of Defence, 'Space forces', <http://eng.mil.ru/en/structure/forces/cosmic.htm> (last accessed 8 June 2018)

Sheetz, Michael, 'The space industry will be worth nearly $3 trillion in 30 years, Bank of America predicts', *CNBC*, 31 October 2017,

<https://www.cnbc.com/2017/10/31/the-space-industry-will-be-worth-nearly-3-trillion-in-30-years-bank-of-america-predicts.html> (last accessed 6 November 2017)

Smith, Michael V. 'America needs a space corps', *The Space Review*, 17 March 2017, <http://www.thespacereview.com/article/3193/1> (last accessed 9 June 2018)

Swarts, Phillip, 'Air Force lays out its case for keeping space operations', *Space News*, 19 May 2017, <http://spacenews.com/air-force-lays-out-its-case-for-keeping-space-operations/> (last accessed 4 July 2018)

Weeden, Brian, 'Dancing in the dark: The orbital rendezvous of SJ-12 and SJ-06F', *The Space Review*, 30 June 2010, <http://thespacereview.com/article/1689/1> (last accessed 17 September 2019)

Weeden, Brian, 'Through a glass darkly: Chinese, Russian, and American anti-satellite testing in space: Page 1', *The Space Review*, 17 March 2014, <http://www.thespacereview.com/article/2473/1> (last accessed 17 September 2019)

Weeden, Brian, 'Dancing in the dark redux: Recent Russian rendezvous and proximity operations in space', *The Space Review*, 5 October 2015, <http://thespacereview.com/article/2839/1> (last accessed 17 September 2019)

Zak, Anatoly, 'Proton successfully returns to flight delivering a secret Olymp satellite', *Russian Space Web*, updated 19 October 2015, <http://www.russianspaceweb.com/olymp.html#mission> (last accessed 17 September 2019)

Index

A2/AD strategies, 143, 238, 241,
   242, 251, 259
adaptation
   by actors without spacepower
      support, 218–19
   to the dispersing effect of
      spacepower, 215
   during the Gulf War (2003),
      221–2
Afghanistan, 85, 180–1, 202, 219,
   222
airpower theory, 41, 63–4, 83
analogical reasoning, 45–7
analogies
   of bluewater seapower theory with
      spacepower theory, 5, 33, 34,
      54, 61–3, 94–6, 129
   of Clausewitzian military thought
      to outer space, 43–4
   coastal analogy for Earth orbit, 4,
      78, 94, 105, 107–9, 271
   false analogies, 47
   historical analogies, 45, 46–7
   strategic analogies, 45–6, 48, 67
   terrestrial analogies, 2, 24
anti-satellite (ASAT) systems
   anti-satellite weapons test, 27–8,
      29
   China's capabilities, 27, 28
   dispersal of satellite systems, 201

Earth-based weapons systems, 62,
   78, 116, 140
   during the Gulf War (1991), 119,
      199
   India's capabilities, 27–8,
      29
   range of, 118, 120
   Russia's capabilities, 27, 28
   in the Taiwan war scenario, 237–9
astroculture
   cultural motivations for
      spacepower, 164–6, 278–9
   defined, 159
   differing national approaches to,
      176–7
   formation of national space forces,
      174–7
   geocentrism of, 158, 171,
      183–5
   human capital and, 172–3
   military astroculture, 161–2,
      186–7
   space strategy and, 159–61
astrodeterminism, 4–5, 76, 83,
   109
astroeconomic warfare,
   124–30, 138–9, 260; *see also*
   economics
astrofuturism, 33
astropolitics, 22